Harry Waugh

12th November 1987.

Diary of a Winetaster

Recent Tastings of French and California Wines

Other Books by Harry Waugh

Bacchus on the Wing
The Changing Face of Wine
Pick of the Bunch

published by Wine and Spirit Publications Ltd.

Diary

of a Winetaster

Recent Tastings
of French and California Wines

by Harry Waugh

NYT Quadrangle Books
A New York Times Company

Library of Congress Card Number: 71–190483

Design by Anita Duncan

Grateful acknowledgement is made to Arthur Gough for the use of his photographs on wine tasting, to John Chillingworth for his photograph of Jean Paul Gardère, to Michael Broadbent for his charming line drawing

Acknowledgement is also made for permission to reprint "Dining in London Clubs," copyright © 1972 by *Vintage Magazine.*

Contents

Foreword by Michael Broadbent   ix

Preface   xi
    Collecting Wine   xii
    The Art of Decanting   xiv

VISIT TO AMERICA, 1970   1

    Tastings of French and California Wines   1
        An Englishman's View of the American Wine Scene   3
        Washington, D. C.   7
        The Beaulieu Vineyard: A Bastion of Quality   21
        A Whiff of Gastronomy   28
        The Heitz Wine Cellars   32
        Tastings of 1966 White Burgundy   35
        Dinner at the Rhodes   36
        A Tasting from the Domaine de la Romanée-Conti   37
        A Visit to Sacramento   39
        A Lucullan Fantasy   41
        A Tasting of 1959 Vintage of the Hospices de Beaune   46
        California Jug Wines   48

FRANCE, 1970 VISIT   57

        Burgundy, The Côte d'Or   59
        Santenay   62
        Henri de Villamont, Savigny-les-Beaune   66
        The 1961 Vintage: Saint-Emilions and Pomerols   69

The Médocs of 1967   74
The Red Graves   81
The Bordeaux Market   88
The Year of the Century   91

VISIT TO AMERICA, 1971   95

Tastings of French and California Wines   95
    A Week with Les Amis du Vin   97
    The Napa Valley   107
    The Day to Day Wines of California   113
    Montrachet, the Great White Burgundy   118
    Four Exceptional White Wines   121
    The Grand Cru Club: A Tasting of 1964 Claret   122
    A Galaxy of 1945's   125
    A Visit to Freemark Abbey   128
    Ridge Vineyards   131
    Dinner with the Petersons   133
    Mayacamas   134
    Mirassou   138
    Chappelet   144
    With Les Amis du Vin in San Francisco   146
    Dinner with the Rhodes   149
    At Yountville   151
    With the Wine and Food Society in New York   155

FRANCE, 1971 Visit   157

    Dining in London Clubs   159
    A Claret Tasting: Château Malescot   165
    Three Great Vintages for Red Bordeaux   167
    A Great Vintage: 1970 Saint-Emilions and Pomerols   173
    The 1967 Vintage, Once Again   179
    The Fronsadais   182
    Côtes de Bourg   188
    A Visit to Mouton-Rothschild   189
    Les Forts de Latour   193
    A Cru Bourgeois: Château Cissac   196
    The Côte Chalonnaise and Southern Burgundy   199

Contents

207

The Beaujolais   201
Vintage Port   209

WHAT TO DRINK IN 1972   212

A Dissertation on What to Drink in 1972   214

Index   219

Foreword

It will take the reader only a few paragraphs to discover for himself the charm and infectious enthusiasm which are so characteristic of Harry Waugh.

He has long been influential in English wine circles. His written words, familiar to so many through the pages of *Wine Magazine*, are read avidly for their refreshing openness and frankness, particularly when he is discoursing on his favorite subject, claret. He is an authority, but mercifully lacks pompous trappings; he is transparently honest without the slightest risk of giving offence; he is generous to a fault, particularly to the younger wine buff.

At a period in time when most wine writers seem to be professional journalists, Harry speaks with the authority of an experienced wine merchant, and one, moreover, who is not afraid to express an opinion about the merit of any specific wine or vintage. Indeed, there are many important buyers in England and America who act solely upon his candidly expressed and honestly held judgments.

I have known Harry Waugh for about seventeen years and his enthusiasm is undiminished. In 1955, when I joined Harveys, I came almost immediately under Harry's wing in the old King Street premises, not a stone's throw from where I now work. Harry was a senior director on the Harvey Group Board and it was entirely due to his influence that the firm gained a phenomenal reputation in the table wine field at a time when all the odds seemed to favor only Bristol Cream and the highly successful sherry market.

When I left Harveys to recommence wine auctions at Christie's, it was of course Harry who gave me strong moral support when I needed it. My other friends in the trade reacted with dismay when, without auction experience, I gave up a seat on the board of one of England's leading wine merchants to revitalize and manage Christie's auction department.

Harry knew the Christie Board well and, when he retired from Harveys to concentrate on consulting work and writing, he did me the honor of becoming an associate of Christie's Wine Department. This happy association has resulted in the great sale of Barolet burgundies (no one had heard of the now legendary Dr. Barolet until Harry discovered the cellar and Christie's organised the first sale). The sale of wines of the Fronsac area was inspired by Harry's article on the Fronsadais in *Wine Magazine,* and Christie's recent excursion into Burgundy with our first wine sale in France was likewise due to Harry. I mention all this not to puff myself or Christie's but to demonstrate how Harry's influence and enthusiasm can lead to all sorts of exciting things in the world of wine.

His appearance in print on the American scene is, in my opinion, timely. A new style of effusive wine writing is cropping up west of the Atlantic which, if not brought down to earth, will nip some embryo wine lovers in the bud. A group of literary wine pundits are creating a new cult, a new mystique to surround wine with its own rules and esoteric language. Harry's approach may not be dry enough for the new intellectuals. Indeed, it is just possible that he may not match up to the insatiable desires of this in-depth and hyper-serious brigade. In which case I can only add— thank God for that.

Wine is a gift of civilisation, and we will only cloud our joy in it if we smother it with our pontificating. Harry Waugh has an engaging enthusiasm, a few healthy prejudices, and a mass of formidable information. As quite the most unprepossessing man on the current wine scene, his ideas are full of the exuberance and perspective we need.

Michael Broadbent
Christie's, London
February, 1972

Sketch by Mr. Broadbent, drawn from the terrace of the Hostellerie de la Plaisance in Saint-Emilion.

Preface

There are two ways of writing about wine. The first, the usual one, is to narrate the history, the facts and figures of the various districts, which after all do not change much and, in a general sense, describe the wine. Far too many books have already been written in this category, especially on the wines of France, for this really means dressing up old material in a fresh guise. The second is to endeavour to write about the wines themselves, with the express object of assisting would-be purchasers as much as possible to make their selection.

The first can be achieved in a reasonable space of time, because the data is always at hand, but the second takes longer, for it is founded primarily on wine tastings and the vagaries of vintages and, so far as this writer is concerned, it takes about two years of traveling to gather together all the necessary information. Admittedly, news concerning a vintage can be got out fairly fast through articles, say, in *Wine Magazine*, but even there, because it is a bimonthly, inevitably there must be a time lag.

All this, then, is to explain why the details of two entirely separate visits to California, in 1970 and 1971, as well as visits to France over the same period, are included in one and the same book. It is also, therefore, to crave the reader's indulgence.

I would like to express my gratitude to Dr. and Mrs. Bernard L. Rhodes and many other friends in California, for it is thanks entirely to them that my recent visits there have been so instructive and enjoyable. Although not actively engaged in the wine business themselves, Barney and Belle, as they are known throughout northern California, have, in their quiet delightful way, probably done more good than anyone else in furthering the interests of the wine growers, great and small. Also to my wife, who so patiently helped me sort out my scattered notes and put them in some sort of order.

Collecting Wine

Perhaps a few words on collecting and buying wine may be helpful to the young, or not so young, amateur who is just starting a cellar (though, in these days, the actual word "cellar" is not always applicable). Collecting together a small cellar is by no means as alarming an enterprise as it sounds, and by concentrating on red wine your field of operations is halved at the start. White wine is not normally for long keeping, so, by and large, you buy it more or less from hand to mouth.

To begin with, the average person cannot afford a cellar, or at least so he thinks, and then, on top of that, he is almost sure to lack a proper place in which to store his precious bottles. Here the wine lover in America has an advantage over us in England: it is not so difficult to set aside a small part of an air-conditioned home for this purpose. The last time I was in the States I was intrigued to find that from the point of view of prestige, an air-conditioned wine cellar has become almost as important as a swimming pool! It is certainly less expensive. Although from time to time it would be a pleasure to gloat over beloved bottles in your own cellar, it may not be always possible to house your own collection. But a good wine merchant will always take care of his customer's bottles for a small annual charge, really a trifling sum when you consider that a small well-selected stock can easily turn into something quite valuable in the course of only a few years.

Every collector has to start somewhere, whatever his interest may be—china, books, wine or pictures. He usually finds one or two things that take his fancy; from time to time he sees something else he cannot resist, and then suddenly, without any real intention, he finds he has a small collection already in being.

Naturally, being in the business has been a great advantage to me in collecting interesting wines, but that was of little help when I had no spare cash, as certainly was my case for a number of years after the war. Afford it or not, and I couldn't, I began to put a very few bottles aside each year, not great or expensive wines, but bottles that I felt might turn out well in the course of time.

To my way of thinking, over and above everything else, the first and easily the most important step is to find for yourself a really good merchant. Like doctors, accountants, solicitors and so on, wine merchants can be good or bad, with all the varying shades in between. It is worth taking considerable trouble to see that your selection (about which you may not know much yourself in the beginning) lies in the hands of some of the reliable firms. These, alas, are the days of mass production and the wine trade, too, has been hit: fortunately, a number of good firms still exist in England, and I have certainly met many keen and knowledgeable enthusiasts in the liquor stores of America.

You will soon find an individual who will take you under his wing and advise you to the best of his ability. There still remain, believe it or not, a few merchants who love the wine they sell for its own sake as well as for the commerce it brings; such people will take a special interest in the beginner, guide his faltering footsteps and set him off along the right lines.

Now let us look at things from the point of view of the wine merchant himself, and at an important moment—say, when he has just completed his purchase of a good vintage of claret,* such as 1970. The merchant knows pretty well which are his best wines and also which ones are the best value for the money. Among these he is bound to have some special favourites (I know I have always had mine). The merchant advises his friends as to which, in his opinion, are winners, in all grades of that vintage, and, being only human, sells all his favourites off first. This is the best moment for the collector to buy, because a few years later, when the vintage is becoming ready to drink, most of the real plums have disappeared from the lists and those that remain, not necessarily the left-overs, will have become appreciably more expensive.

As soon as he hears of a good vintage such as 1970, the collector should get in touch with his wine merchant and ask him to put something aside for him. As claret is rarely agreeable to drink until some years after the vintage, this is especially important for the young married man who usually has little or no spare money for indulging in luxuries and certainly no space for storage. What does he do? He asks his merchant to put aside for him a case, or even a few bottles of whatever he recommends, and repeats the performance after each subsequent good vintage. Then, hey presto! by the time the first bottles he laid down are ready to drink, he finds he is the proud possessor of a modest but well-selected collection of wines in varying stages of maturity, a collection that will suit his needs during the years to come. This means he should have far better wine than any of his friends could lay their hands on at that particular moment without the outlay of a considerable sum of money.

* "Claret" is a term used by the English for the red wine of Bordeaux.

Inevitably, too, people seek advice, not only on what to buy, but also as to when certain wines, or vintages, will be ready to drink. With the best will in the world, it is not always possible to give a definite answer, particularly to the latter question. Just imagine looking around a room full of people and somebody saying to you: "Tell me at what date each of these individuals is going to meet his death." Such requests regarding wines are readily understandable, however, for if you possess three bottles of a good 1961 claret, or even a 1966, naturally you do not wish to open them one by one, experimentally; you would like to know when they are ready to drink and so enjoy them at their peak. In the following pages, I shall endeavour to clarify this problem.

There is a point that I would like to make to American readers: from personal experience, I have found that a claret is inclined to develop more rapidly in the United States than in Europe. Very roughly, this wine will perhaps be one year advanced on the Eastern Seaboard, and two years ahead in California. Why it is, I cannot say—it may be the journey. The journey must make some difference, for the friend in Vancouver, B.C., tells me that after the long voyage his finer wines take a good year and sometimes longer to settle down. Surely it cannot be the storage, which is usually air-conditioned. In any case, I imagine that the 1966 and 1967 clarets will be more ready to drink in America during 1972 than in England.

In the body of this book, then, I hope to advise the wine lover on what he might be buying judiciously and storing away at the moment, and when these might be ready to drink as well as to report on various recent vintages.

The Art of Decanting

With the tremendous upsurge of interest in table wine spreading so rapidly throughout the United States, the future of the wine trade would appear to be unlimited, but somehow the legions of "budding wine lovers" and more particularly the American *sommeliers* must be led firmly to understand that, as a beverage, wine is neither beer nor Coca-Cola; most importantly, the natural sediment to be found in a wine is to be expected, and is a sign of maturity. After a few years in bottle, it is both right and proper for a fine red wine to throw a sediment, and this is easily handled at the time of consumption, either by standing the bottle upright for a while, or better still by decanting (depending upon the school of thought to which you subscribe).

The wine cradle, in which restaurateurs delight, is anathema to me, because all it does is swish the wine and its sediment back and forth until they are both hopelessly intermingled; thus the remainder becomes cloudy and spoiled. I, personally, am a "decanter," not literally of course, but I belong to that school and for at least three reasons. First, you serve your wine "star bright," secondly, you can regulate the time it needs to breathe, and thirdly, an attractive decanter of red wine (preferably two!) adds immeasurably to the furnishing and beauty of your dinner table. It can afford as much pleasure to search for and collect one or two elegant wine decanters (and they do not necessarily have to be antiques) as any other embellishment of your home.

The drill of decanting is perfectly simple. You stand the bottle up, preferably overnight, to let the sediment fall to the bottom. (Since the drinking of a wine should be a joy rather than a drudge, even when guests arrive at the last minute I often stand a bottle up, if only for half an hour!) Without shaking the bottle too much, remove the capsule, extract the cork, wipe the neck of the bottle with a clean cloth, and insert a glass funnel into the top of your decanter. If you have no decanter, another clean bottle will do. Hold the neck of the bottle over an electric light bulb, or an upright torch (the lighted candle is a thing of the past except when there is a power strike!) and pour slowly and steadily until the sediment begins to appear at the shoulder. What is left in the bottle will not amount to much and can always be used for cooking.

There is no hard and fast rule as to when a wine should be decanted before it is consumed, and normally I would decant, say, a 1964 or a 1962 about an hour before serving it (it depends very much upon when my wife will let me into our tiny kitchen!). Older wines, such as a pre-war Burgundy from the Barolet collection or a 1928 claret, are decanted at the very last minute, i.e., in between courses, because often such venerable rarities will only survive for about half an hour and then go quickly downhill. Though in general I do not agree with drinking the 1961 clarets yet (there are some exceptions, of course), if I had to open one of my precious bottles I might decant it a little earlier than I would a 1962, owing to the vintage being rather backward in its development. This would allow it more time to breathe. You simply have to find these things out for yourself and it is all part of the fun of this absorbing subject.

It is regrettable that, at the request of some American restaurants, Burgundian negociants are at times asked to decant their older wines prior to shipment. This may make the task of the *sommelier* easier, but except in the case of an old wine specially ordered for a particular banquet this practice should be discouraged as much as possible. Elimination of the sediment ensures only a brief span of life for the wine and after a few months it will tend to deteriorate rather than improve. In other words, the practice of eliminating the possibility of sediment from a fine red wine just to suit an untutored public results in lowering the standards for the future. "Instant red wine" is all right for run-of-the-mill *vin ordinaire*, but certainly not for wines of fine quality.

No mention would have been made of this matter, had I not overheard this elimination of the sediment being seriously discussed at a winery of considerable renown. At the risk of being considered "square," but in the interest of quality, I hope that this "sacrifice to Mammon" will be resisted as vigorously as possible. All that is required is proper education in what is, after all, one of the finer points of the art of good living.

Visit to America, 1970

Tastings of French and California Wines

An Englishman's View
of the American Wine Scene

I am not absolutely sure, but I believe my first visits to America date back to about 1958 or 1959, certainly before the first rumbles of the wine explosion were heard.

At that time I was export director of Harvey's, and my task was to encourage sales of their sherry; since our agents were Heublein Inc., distribution could hardly have been bettered. My visits were more or less annual, and after conferences either in Hartford or New York, I used to sally forth on trips—not "trips" in the newest sense of the word—but in the company of the import sales director. Together we covered quite a large part of the country, except, of course, for those sombre areas, the Controlled States.

When the imports director felt he had had all he could stand of me, I was let loose with local representatives, and like that I pounded the streets, sometimes visiting a dozen or so stores in the morning, and more after lunch. It was hard work but interesting nevertheless, for in this manner I must have visited hundreds of liquor stores in many parts of the country. They were indeed liquor stores in those days, because at that time the wine bug had not yet begun to bite at the American public. They were full to the brim with Scotch and every kind of strong liquor, also some fortified wines, but precious little imported table wine was in evidence.

Then slowly and imperceptibly one could watch the change beginning to take place; from a mere shelf or so, a whole corner would be developed, and I well remember the pride with which one or two proprietors began to show a newly constituted annex expressly for the sale of imported wine, about which, though, they appeared to know remarkably little.

In view of this trend in the early sixties, Harvey's persuaded Heublein's to handle a Harvey's selection of table wine, but once launched, it was quite a job to get it moving. It seemed to me at that time that the task of both the representative and the store proprietor was to sell "boxes," and since the profit mark-up in

3

America is much better than in England, it was naturally easier to handle a well-known brand rather than something with an awkward-sounding French name. In any case, how on earth could the poor representative, or storekeeper for that matter, be expected to know anything about the finer points of claret and Burgundy?

During these innumerable calls on shops, the representative's opening gambit, and a successful one too, was Smirnoff, then Scotch followed by cocktails and Bristol Cream. By that time, he had more or less shot his bolt, and I had to take over with my little piece, seldom successfully though, because not only had the shop owner had enough of the sales pressure, but he was scarcely aware of much more than the famous names, the wines easy to sell— boxes again! In those days, it seemed to me that only about one percent of the storekeepers ever tasted the wine they sold; they were merely moving merchandise.

In the early sixties considerable stress was laid on the wines of the Domaine de la Romanée Conti and the first growth clarets from Bordeaux. No doubt these formed admirable ambassadors for the wines of France, but now after some years of experience the wine lovers are no longer looking only for the most famous and the most expensive, but have learned to pick and choose. Naturally, there have always been a number of real wine merchants in the United States, but they were relatively few and far between in comparison with the liquor store dealers.

What has brought about this great change in American drinking habits—for a great change it is? From being a hard-liquor nation, the Americans are fast becoming a race of wine lovers, and what is really important, the young people appear to be much more interested in table wine than they are in hard spirits. The evil days of Prohibition have been left far behind!

Most probably the new trend was triggered off by U.S. troops returning from Europe, then slowly the conversion gathered momentum as more and more Americans spent their holidays in the European wine-growing countries. Another factor, and an important one too, is the remarkable value offered by the big wineries of California. To my mind, the American consumer is much better off with these wines than the French with their *"vin ordinaire"* or the English with the branded table wines sold in the supermarkets. All this has been helped too by the many books and articles written about wine and gastronomy in general.

Originally the Wine & Food Society did much of the pioneering work among the well-to-do, but this has now been extended to a far broader field covered by Les Amis du Vin, with 10,000 members spread across the length and breadth of the land, a splendid development which has emerged during the past four or five years. At the beginning, the centres of table-wine consumption were concentrated in areas like New York, Chicago, Washington, D.C., and California, but now the enthusiasm is spreading like a forest fire, but with far less damage, because the drinking of wine, if properly applied, can be a very civilised affair.

Since the interest has spread to wider sections of the public, not everyone can afford the great wines, and through my lecturing I find there is a growing demand for the lesser ones, such as I like to drink myself at home, the crus bourgeois of the Médoc and those from the Côtes-de-Fronsac, Bourg, and Blaye. Here, of course, more skill is required of the storekeeper, because it is not so easy to find quality among the smaller fry. When I visited a store in California in 1968, I was surprised to be told by the proprietor that after reading a chapter on the 1966 clarets in one of my books, he had ordered no less than 6,000 cases of the wines I had mentioned. He is still in business, so presumably the recommendations proved to be sound!

There can be few better ways of ascertaining the general feeling than by lecturing, and one cannot fail to witness the rapid advance in knowledge of all concerned both with tradesmen and their customers. It is good, too, to meet the new generation of young men coming up in the trade. Completely dedicated, they are full of enthusiasm, have surprising knowledge, and are doing a first-rate job. These must be exciting times for them, because the tidal wave of wine lovers has by no means abated; there are fresh fields to conquer, and always more to learn.

While on the subject of commerce, the only handicap I can see is that the American wine merchant lives so far away from the European vineyards, and thus it is not easy to maintain contact. To give an example of this, recently I have noticed a number of the suspect 1964 Médocs in some of the stores, wines with well-known names but which should never have been bought. When I asked why a particular one had been purchased, the answer was that it had been highly recommended by a sales representative! Living so far away, how is one to know?

So far, all this has been concerned with imported wine, but what about the domestic scene, which to a European has become as such a revelation? Things were very different when I first visited California some ten years ago.

In the early days I did not travel so far as the West Coast, but being naturally curious about the wines of California, a good friend arranged some tastings for me, samples of what was available in the liquor stores of Hartford, Connecticut, and, with but few exceptions, the result was sadly disappointing; thus I was able to appreciate why, for preference, people chose imported wine that was hardly more expensive. At that time most California wine was still sold under generic names and without a vintage. It was common practice to say that in California the climate was so consistently good that all vintages were the same. So far as I could see, this was a myth built up by some producers to enable them to sell sound but rather common or garden wine, and only recently has this been broken down.

My eyes were first opened to the possibilities of California sometime around 1962 when I visited the Beaulieu vineyard and André Tchelistcheff opened for me three or four vintages of the Cabernet Sauvignon wines he had made in the 1940's. The quality was so exceptional that at once I realised there was much more potential in these vineyards than I had ever imagined.

One of the great advances has been the gradual discontinuation of generic names and the substitution of varietal ones in their place. A California Chardonnay sounds much more genuine than California white burgundy. Let us hope then that this correct nomenclature will spread one day to California champagne, in spite of the fact that the latter can be very good.

Until recently I have found that serious amateurs have been inclined to dismiss the wines of California, saying that not only are European wines better but also less expensive. In many cases this may still be so, but at times I have been interested to watch their reaction when they have tasted the really fine wine from California. As for the rest, the general standard of quality is rising so rapidly, it will be fascinating to watch the progress over the next twenty-five years.

Washington, D. C.

Recovering partially from the flight over the Atlantic, and with the spare time I had purposely allowed, I was able to enjoy a long-delayed treat. Ever since my last visit to Washington, a city of such interest, some five or six years ago, I had wanted to see again those fascinating rooms displaying early Americana in the Smithsonion Museum, and also indulge in the pleasures to be beheld in the National Gallery of Art. The study of how these early settlers lived intrigues me greatly and is made all the more instructive since the rooms are so admirably laid out. Exciting as it was, life must have been hard enough in those days, and especially so for the American pioneers. No wonder this era of early American life holds such a fascination.

The purpose behind this enticing and unexpected visit to Washington was meeting Les Cent Chevaliers du Vin, a newly formed group who had invited me to be the guest of honour at their inaugural meeting on the 4th February, 1970. It is needless to say that I accepted with alacrity!

Les Cent Chevaliers du Vin is not, as I had first imagined, a dining club, but consists of a number of enthusiasts who are anxious to further their knowledge of the finer wines. This is to be achieved by means of talks and tastings, and if this initial gathering is anything to go by, there are few heights they will leave unexplored, for on this occasion there were no less than thirteen different vintages of Château Latour to be both assessed and enjoyed.

At lunchtime, two members of the committee, Marvin Stirman and Henry Greenwald, introduced me to an unusually good restaurant called Le Provençal, directed by Jacques Blanc, who was born and bred in that sunny part of France. It is perfectly obvious why the standard of cuisine is so high, for Jacques Blanc, like so many of the great restaurateurs, spends the major part of his time in the kitchen. This meal will also be remembered for the wines; to begin with, and really just for tasting, Château d'Angludet 1967, Cantenac, and Margaux, which of course is still in its infancy. The

7

"bonne bouche" was a bottle of Château Lafon-Rochet, 1945, fourth growth, Saint-Estèphe: a lovely dark colour, a mature fruity nose, a big full-bodied affair. It is not every day that one has the opportunity to drink such ambrosia.

There was an invitation to dine with Marvin's dynamic young partner, Alfio Moriconi, but Alfio was snow-bound in Rochester, and so bad were the conditions that it was touch and go whether he would appear at all. Eventually he arrived, but hours late, and his poor wife, Jocelyne, a Belgian girl, had her dinner pretty well ruined. I should like to return, though, to try again her cassoulet, for clearly it was out of the ordinary. To accompany this, Alfio produced a simply superb bottle of 1947 Corton which had been presented to him by the growers, Rapet Père et Fils of Pernand Vergelesses. It is seldom that one drinks so fine a Burgundy. If one may judge by this bottle, the fine red Burgundies of 1947 have fared better than some of their counterparts in the Médoc of the same year.

Wednesday, 4th February, 1970

My long-awaited visit to the National Gallery of Art had to be curtailed because too long a time was spent in the Pan Am office. Instead of going direct to California on the sixth as planned, I had been invited to go to Hartford, Connecticut, to see my old friends at Heublein's of Smirnoff Vodka fame.

As it was, there was scarcely time to see even the paintings by the early American artists John Singleton Copley and Gilbert Stuart, amongst others, It is not often that one has the chance to see their work in Europe, so this was an opportunity not to be missed. It grieves me, though, to think of the other treasures I failed to see.

The tasting that evening took place in a private room at the Embers restaurant in Washington, but beforehand a small group of us dined together elsewhere in the restaurant, where we enjoyed a magnum of 1961 Les Carruades de Château Lafite. It's a shame of course to drink it now, but it will be wonderful in a few years' time, though no doubt it is probably more developed in bottles. It has that deliciously rich nose and full flavour characteristic of the successful 1961's.

The committee of Les Cent Chevaliers du Vin, which consists

of Sidney Goldman, Harry Greenwald, and Marvin Stirman, had arranged the tasting extremely well. There were six tables at which the Chevaliers were seated (a captive audience is vital on such an occasion) around a large platter of excellent French cheeses. One Chevalier was appointed at each table to be responsible for the de-canting of the older wines. The corks of the younger vintages had been drawn sometime previously so as to let the wines breathe. A spare seat was left so that I could move from table to table as I spoke briefly about the history of Château Latour and discussed the wines in turn.

At Château Latour, we pride ourselves on producing a better wine than most in the off-vintages, and as I had not tasted a number of these older vintages for some time, it provided a good oppor-tunity to do so again. As there are limits to all good things, I could not help feeling a little apprehensive beforehand as to how the 1931 and the 1940 vintages would present themselves on the other side of the Atlantic. Both of these were poor years, and with regard to the 1931 in particular, it is expecting rather a lot of a wine already thirty-eight years old. As they were likely to be overwhelmed by some of their younger and more successful brethren, rightly or wrongly, the order of serving was switched around. Hopefully, then, the 1931 and 1940 were decanted first so as to form the open-ing wines, and as things turned out, the plan proved successful.

One of the points which struck me, and a gratifying one at that, was how well all these old vintages were showing in America. In general, I believe that wines age more quickly in America than they do in Europe. However, while I do not know how long any of these wines have been on the western side of the Atlantic, I could see little difference between them this evening than the same vintages tasted at the château. It would seem they had been carefully nur-tured, or else had arrived fairly recently.

These are the notes taken at that time, but listed for con-venience in reverse chronology rather than in the order of tasting:

Château Latour, Grand Vin, Pauillac

> 1962: A lovely dark colour, a fine fruity bouquet, heaps of fruit, quite powerful in fact, but still very backward. There is a good future ahead. (In its early youth, the vintage was not regarded with much excitement, and it was only a year or so later that its charms began to be recognised.

Now 1962 is looked upon as a very good year and many of the wines are drinking delightfully. By and large, it is a vintage which was more successful for the Médocs than for the Saint-Emilions and Pomerols.)

1961: A deep, deep colour, almost raven, with a huge majestic nose! This is a tremendously complex wine of really great quality. Totally unfit to drink now, but one day it will make pure nectar for the gods. (A miraculous vintage and a successful one in all districts. It is only rarely that one comes across quality such as this; 1961 is certainly the best year since the outstanding vintage of 1945, and before that one has to go all the way back to 1928 and 1929. This is not to say that you should acquire any 1961's "regardless," because there are always one or two less successful wines in every great vintage; in fact, I have come across one quite recently. As the 1961's are now so expensive, it is well to seek sound advice before purchasing.)

1959: A good deep colour and a bouquet far more developed than the 1961. Mouton-Rothschild is usually noted for its fine "cedar" smell, but at times this also happens with Latour, as was apparent on this occasion; the sweetness of the bouquet too emerged nicely. As to the taste, there is heaps of fruit and flavour, with the natural sugar coming through attractively. This vintage of Latour is developing splendidly; it can be enjoyed now, but it will surely improve in the long life that lies before it. (Notable as the year when the Americans made their first serious impact on the Bordeaux market and it was hailed by the press as "the year of the century." That made the prices shoot up to the skies, although in retrospect, if one judges by present-day vintages, they do not appear unduly exorbitant! This was the first expensive vintage, and since then the prices have never reverted, and probably never will, to what we once considered as reasonable. As to quality, although they do not reach the heights of 1961, the 1959's are fine wines and are becoming ready to drink. This was another vintage which was successful in all districts.)

1957: The colour is intensely dark, the bouquet pleasantly perfumed, and the taste is developing surprisingly well. (A good vintage, but what hard wines the 1957's have turned out to be! Strangely enough, Latour, which is usually such a slow developer, is less rigid than many a wine of its year.)

1952: Good deep colour, a full attractive bouquet, and plenty of fruit. After all these years, seventeen of them, the 1952 Latour is at last beginning to taste well. Even so, there are better examples of 1952. This one is rather dry and could have more flesh! (This has always been a fine vintage, but, owing to its tannin, the 1952's were over-shadowed for some years by their immediately more at-tractive younger brothers, the 1953's. Now while the 1953's have displayed most of their charms, with many indeed on the downward slope, their more robust and originally less pleasing elder brethren, the best 1952's from St. Emilion and Pomerol, are coming into their own.)

1949: Beautiful colour, a mature "bouquet garni" of all sorts of delicious smells. A glorious full flavour, though there is still a little tannin to ensure a good length of life.

   A vintage which was heralded by a fanfare of trum-pets but then for years remained numb and rather un-exciting. Now, at last, some of the finer 1949's are blossoming out to fulfill early predictions.

1947: A remarkable colour, considering its age, and as I had rather expected, just a little sharp on the nose, a little thin when you come to taste it, and there's a touch of acidity at the finish. (Such an attractive vintage in its youth, but many of the Médocs, including the "greats," did not fulfill their promise and have not lasted the course as well as they might have done; indeed, some of them now have a trace of volatile acidity. This is one of the vintages where the Médocs were far surpassed in quality by the Saint-Emilions and the Pomerols, for if one was lucky enough to come across any of the finer Saint-Emilions and Pomerols, they had a richness of bou-quet and a depth of flavour which was almost past belief!)

1946: This was another bad year, with nothing like the in-built advantages of 1944, yet somehow the wine was sounder. Both the colour and the bouquet were good, as was the taste—but the finish was disappointing, a touch of bitterness. Ah well! You can't make a silk purse out of a sow's ear, and it is asking rather a lot to expect a fine wine from an indifferent vintage when it has reached the equivalent of its three score and ten.

1945: A splendid deep colour, a bouquet so fragrant and so powerful that it comes up to meet you, and a flavour which is perfection. This is a great, great wine, and it stole the day. (One of the great vintages of the century, and remarkable still for the amazingly dark colour of its wines. A few of the 1945's have not lasted the course, but the successful ones, and there are many, are still running strongly up to the finishing post! On account of the abnormal amount of tannin, they have taken all this time to get here!)

1944: While the colour was satisfactory, this wine had a disappointing bouquet, there was little or no charm, and the taste was no better. Perhaps mine was a bad bottle? (An off-vintage. While never anything great, the 1944's provided an admirable stopgap in the early years after the war, and they were quite attractive while they were young. The trouble with them was that they did not age gracefully.)

1940: A wartime vintage, and a poor one at that; yet this Latour 1940 had a good nose, good fruit, and—unbelievably— there was still plenty of tannin. Another surprise!

1931: One always expects a good deep colour from Château Latour, but this 1931 was definitely medium to pale. The bouquet, though old, was completely sound, and the taste surprisingly good. Certainly an unexpected success. Once a bottle of an old wine such as this is opened, it is sometimes wiser to drink it up, for as happened with this 1931, it can fade fairly quickly in the glass. In general, whether you like it or not, 1931 was a poor vintage, and it's as simple as that—although I must confess that quite lately I have been astonished by the quality of the Domaine de Chevalier of the same year.

Thursday, 5th February

The progamme was too crowded to accomplish any more sight-seeing, but we did manage to enjoy another excellent meal at Le Provençal. This time the other guest was Julius Wile from New York, an interesting man to meet and one who bears a great name in American wine circles.

After dinner I was to address Les Amis du Vin (a number of whom I was to meet in the evening), a group—in fact, almost an army of wine enthusiasts—which is spreading rapidly throughout the United States. Founded only three or four years ago, Les Amis du Vin has already 7,000 members, and it is confidently expected that the number will exceed the 10,000 mark by early 1972.

The latent interest in table wine in the huge country of America is most stimulating to watch, and the consumption is swelling almost in torrents. To take the red wines of Bordeaux as an example, this interest is not confined entirely to the famous names but also lies very much with the smaller châteaux, such as those of Côtes de Bourg and Blaye. One cannot help wondering what will happen to the supply situation when the inhabitants of the present vast "deserts" of America become aware of the enjoyment of wine drinking and join the enthusiastic throng. As things stand at the moment, it is not possible to increase further the production of the well-established European vineyards, and the expanding domestic ones of California and New York State may not be able to compete with the wine explosion when it really bursts.

Partly in an endeavour to satisfy this growing thirst for knowledge, Les Amis du Vin was formed and has grown so fast as to have become almost an embarrassment for its founders, Marvin Stirman and Alfio Moriconi, the enterprising young directors of the Calvert Wine and Spirits Shop of Georgetown, Washington, D.C. Briefly, Les Amis du Vin is primarily a "wine-of-the-month" club in which each member receives a series of informative newsletters as well as a free subscription to the well-known and popular *Wine Magazine*. All this is reinforced by regular lectures, accompanied by wine tastings wherever a branch has been formed.

On this occasion it was my duty to address the mother chapter of Les Amis du Vin, and I had been warned to be prepared to face about 400 people, a large enough assembly in all conscience. However, such is the keenness of this Washington chapter, that the

number rapidly swelled to well over 500! This caused a slight embarrassment and a shortage of wine, but it was easily overcome, as
will be seen later, by adding two extra châteaux for consumption.

Once again everyone was seated at a table (from the rostrum it
looked like a sea of faces), and the wines were tasted, one by one,
in an orderly fashion. Such a large concourse was by no means easy
to control, for after tasting one or two wines tongues became
pleasantly loosened! From a speaker's point of view, it was a most
agreeable experience.

On arrival, each Ami and his guests were presented with a vin
blanc au Cassis in the form of an aperitif, and then it took some time
to get this multitude safely seated at their tables. The theme of the
talk, and indeed of the tasting, was a review of the vintages of
the sixties. In general this has been a good decade for the wines of
Bordeaux, although we would all have been happier if it had ended
on a higher note.

Now that we have the sixties in perspective, the score is three
poor vintages, 1963, 1965, and 1968, and two average ones, 1960
and 1969 (hopefully). Climbing up the scale, we have four fine years,
1962, 1964, 1966, and 1967, which range from good to very good;
and then, to crown it all, one corking good year, the best in fact
since 1945, and that, needless to say, is 1961.

In the following notes the vintages of 1963 and 1965 have been
omitted, for with a few exceptions there is nothing much to say
about them; 1968 has been included, although briefly, because it is
of more current interest.

1960: When the 1960's were first made, sandwiched as they
were between the great years of 1959 and 1961, they
were regarded rather as poor relations! In a way the vintage is similar in quality to that other ugly duckling,
1958. The 1960's vary, of course, but some have turned
out rather well, and they, together with the 1958's, have
proved an excellent stopgap until the 1959's and 1957's or
even the 1962's have become ready. Since they were not
fashionable, the 1960's had the added advantage of being
pleasantly inexpensive and soon became what is commonly known as a good "wine merchants' vintage."

This was a better year for the Médocs than the Saint-
Emilions and Pomerols. In general the 1960's have nice
bouquet and fruit, and although perhaps on the light
side, they are attractive. Good examples of the Médocs

are: Grand-Puy-Lacoste, Palmer, Léoville-Las-Cases, Cos d'Estournel, Montrose, Latour and Mouton-Rothschild.

1961: A great, great vintage—one which will be talked about for many years to come. The wines have an intensely dark colour, a rich bouquet, and a wonderful flavour. The 1961 are notable for their richness, a quality they have to a marked degree. Most of them will take some time to come round, and it is really a shame to drink them now.

Among the many outstanding wines are:

Saint-Estèphe	(Lafon-Rochet)
Pauillac	(Lafite, Latour, Mouton-Rothschild, Pontet-Canet, the Pichons, and Batailley)
Saint-Julien	(Ducru-Beaucaillou and Gruaud-Larose)
Margaux	(Palmer)
Saint-Emilion	(Cheval Blanc, Ausone, Magdelaine, Trottevieille, and Figeac)
Pomerol	(Pétrus, Trotanoy, and Latour-Pomerol)
Red Graves	(Haut-Brion, La Mission-Haut-Brion, and Pape-Clément)

Although naturally there are one or two disappointments, even the little wines, the cru bourgeois, are exceptional in this spectacular vintage.

1962: This is a highly successful vintage and one which surprised the negociants of Bordeaux, for happily, it turned out to be better than expected. The 1962's are very good to drink now, but they will still go on improving. Whilst not very big wines, they have considerable charm. In general, the Saint-Emilions and the Pomerols are less successful than the Médocs. They seem to lack the warmth and stuffing that one expects from these districts.

Among the better Médocs are: Ducru-Beaucaillou, Montrose, Cos d'Estournel, Léoville-Barton, Palmer, Léoville-Las-Cases, Haut-Brion, La Mission-Haut-Brion, Lafite, Latour, Mouton-Rothschild, and Lynch-Bages.

1964: A successful vintage, particularly for the Saint-Emilions and the Pomerols. There were great hopes for the 1964's in the Médoc too, but it began to rain on 7th October and continued steadily for two weeks. Those châteaux which had gathered all their grapes in before the seventh made fine wine, but the others, who were waiting for just that little extra sunshine, were badly caught and had to vintage under the rain, with a result manifest for all to see. It is therefore important to be selective when buying your 1964's, though in general, you are fairly safe with the Saint-Juliens.

It is a sad reflection on some merchants, including those who should know better, when on their lists one sees the 1964's which are known to have been vintaged under the rain. This is just the occasion when one should be able to rely on the sound judgment of one's merchant.

Nineteen-sixty-four was one of those years when the Cabernet Franc, the Malbec, the Merlot, etc.—i.e., the vines planted in Saint-Emilion, Pomerol, and the districts of Côtes de Blaye, Bourg and Fronsac—had a distinct advantage over those of the Médoc, which are chiefly Cabernet Sauvignon with but a proportion of Merlot, for they tend to ripen about a week earlier than the Cabernet Sauvignon. Thus, the vintage in Saint-Emilion and Pomerol and so on, was harvested under ideal conditions, that is, well before the rain began to fall.

Much as one would like to have things both ways, it should not be overlooked that the varietal grapes predominant on the right bank of the river Dordogne are, at the same time, more susceptible to wet weather. Thus they fare worse during a rainy September, as in 1969. To sum up, then, it does not appear to be widely understood that good vintages for the Médoc are not necessarily always equally good for the districts of Saint-Emilion and Pomerol, and of course, vice versa. On the other hand, in 1958, 1960, and 1962 the Médocs have the upper hand.

Among the red Graves of 1964, Haut-Brion and La Mission-Haut-Brion are outstanding; in fact, so highly do I regard the latter that I have presented a case of it to the Saintsbury Club, founded in memory of the late Professor George Saintsbury, which, although it meets but twice a year, is surely one of the most interesting dining clubs to which one could wish to belong.

1966: A most successful vintage for all districts. Not really big wines like the 1961's, but beautifully balanced and full of charm. They should not take too long to mature. This is an important vintage to consider for laying down.

Léoville-Las-Cases is excellent, but Gruaud-Larose, also from Saint-Julien, is even better.

Other successes are: Montrose, Cos d'Estournel, the two Pichons, Batailley, Lafon-Rochet and Lynch-Bages; Palmer, too, is particularly good.

In such a vintage, it would be a mistake to over-look the districts of the red Graves, Saint-Emilion, and Pomerol, for Haut-Brion, La Mission-Haut-Brion, Haut-Bailly, Pape-Clément, Pétrus, Trotanoy, Latour-Pomerol, Cheval Blanc . . . will all repay investment.

1967: As with 1966, a prolific vintage, and it had the added advantage of being less expensive! Not quite so regular in the Médoc perhaps as 1966, but very good all the same. It is still too early to say much, but on balance, the 1966's may be slightly better; this happens to be one of those rare occasions when two vintages in succession are rather similar.

Among the Médocs, the following are worthy of attention: Ducru-Beaucaillou, Montrose, Cos d'Estournel, Pichon-Lalande, and of course Palmer, which once more is remarkable.

Also to be considered, though perhaps not on so high a plane, are Grand-Puy-Lacoste, Lafon-Rochet, and Gloria.

As for the red Graves, Haut-Brion, La Mission-Haut-Brion, and Haut-Bailly are all excellent.

As with 1966, this is a year in which to pay special attention to the Pomerols and Saint-Emilions; for instance: Pétrus seems even better than in 1966, and that is certainly saying something.

Nineteen-sixty-eight being virtually a failure, 1969, with such a diminished crop, will be very expensive, so the best counsel is to invest now in the 1966's and 1967's.

1968: Nobody can call this a good vintage. The wines are very light in colour, some of them alarmingly so, the bouquet is not up to much either. Only a very few châteaux made even a reasonably good wine; amongst them are Haut-Brion, La Mission-Haut-Brion, and Latour.

1969: In February 1970 at the time of writing, and even before the spring rackings have taken place, it is still too early to prognosticate. There had been such heavy rainfall during September 1969 that the outlook was gloomy when I arrived in Bordeaux towards the end of that month, but fortunately the situation was retrieved by the wonderful weather which came in with October; 1969 should be better than the poor years 1963, 1965, and 1968, and perhaps up to the standard of 1960, but certainly not so good as 1966 or 1967.

Adding to the debit side, the 1969 clarets are already very expensive. This is because only about half a normal crop was gathered in and consequently there is a shortage of good wine on the market.

Here are notes on the wines which we tasted in Washington on this occasion, as well as some comments on the communes they represent:

1967 *Château d'Angludet.* Cru Exceptionnel. (Cantenac-Margaux). Although sometimes slightly lighter in colour than the other communes in the Médoc, the wines of Margaux have a most distinctive and fragrant bouquet. They are light and elegant and are noted especially for their breeding. Among the best known châteaux for quality are Margaux and Palmer, and now that the wines of Château d'Issan are "coming of age," this may also be a château to watch.

Likewise the vineyard of Château d'Angludet has been mostly resuscitated and replanted since the second war, and its vines are showing more and more promise.

The 1967 vintage has a good colour, an attractive bouquet; though not a big wine, it has a good flavour. It is still undeveloped, but it should not be too long before it makes quite a good bottle.

1966 *Château Batailley.* Fifth Growth. (Pauillac). This commune produces some of the greatest wines in the world, Château Lafite, Latour, and Mouton-Rothschild, to mention but a few. The Pauillacs can be distinguished by their beautifully deep colour and an incomparable bouquet; they are full-bodied and of superb quality.

The 1966 Château Batailley has a powerful bouquet which is pleasantly sweet; it is a lovely big, fruity wine of fine quality—here is one to lay aside for the future.

1964 *Château Léoville-Las-Cases.* Second Growth. (Saint-Julien). Not quite so big as the Pauillacs, but usually darker in colour and fuller than the Margaux, the Saint-Juliens are justly noted for their style and breeding and are much appreciated by connoisseurs. In fact, apart from the first growths, some of the finest vineyards of all lie in Saint-Julien.

As well as Léoville-Las-Cases there are Léoville-Barton, Léoville-Poyferré, Ducru-Beaucaillou, Gruaud-Larose, and Beychevelle.

This 1964 Léoville-Las-Cases is a good ambassador for its commune, with a good colour, a pretty bouquet; it is refined and elegant and has an attractive flavour. Fine quality.

1962 *Château Lafon-Rochet.* Fourth Growth. (Saint Estèphe). Adjoining Pauillac, Saint-Estèphe is the most northerly commune of all. The wines are distinguished by their very dark colour and sturdy, full fruity flavour. They may not have the subtle breeding of some of their southern competitors, but they make up for it in other ways.

The most noted châteaux are Montrose, Cos d'Estournel, and Calon-Ségur, but this Lafon-Rochet, formerly rather neglected and comparatively unknown, is to be reckoned with in the future. In 1959 it was purchased by Monsieur Guy Tesseron, who has moved heaven and earth to re-establish it as the fine vineyard it is now proving to be.

As is to be expected, the 1962 Lafon-Rochet has a good, deep colour and a powerful bouquet; being a fine full-bodied wine, it needs a year or so yet to be at its best.

1962 *Château Montrose.* Second Growth. (Saint-Estèphe). With a deep colour, a fine strong bouquet, this is a splendid big wine, but it also needs time to mature properly.

1961 *Château Trottevieille.* First Growth. (Saint-Emilion). The Saint-Emilions, as with the Pomerols, are full, round, and rich. These are big, generous wines which are often easier for the amateur to appreciate than the more austere and perhaps rather haughty aristocrats of the Médoc. In 1961, these two districts were most successful.

The 1961 Château Trottevieille has a good deep colour and a rich bouquet; it is nicely rounded with a lovely flavour.

1961 *Château Tertre-Daugay.* First Growth. (Saint-Emilion). Medium colour, but a very pretty nose, this is a fine big fruity wine, in fact a typical 1961.

1960 *Domaine de Chevalier.* (Red Graves). Some of the earliest vineyards of all the Bordeaux region were planted in the Graves district, which lies immediately to the south of the city; unfortunately, many of them have already been engulfed by the spreading suburbs. The red Graves have a decided character all of their own, and this special bouquet and flavour are directly attributable to the gravelly soil on which the vines are grown. One has the feeling that the red wines of the Graves, apart of course from Haut-Brion, are not as well-known as they deserve to be.

The 1960 Domaine de Chevalier was not perhaps the best example either of its château or for its district, so much so that it was tasted first of all in order that it would not be overwhelmed by the fuller wines which were to precede it.

The colour was not too strong, and although there was a good distinctive Graves smell, it seemed a little thin when compared with the others; 1960, after all, was not a great vintage, so one really must not expect too much. (An excellent white wine also comes from this property.)

15th February, 1970

The Beaulieu Vineyard: A Bastion of Quality

It must be some ten years since I was first taken to Rutherford in the Napa Valley, and I was introduced under unusually good auspices, for my guide and mentor was none other than the delightful Professor Harold Berg, chairman of the Department of Enology (the study of wines and winemaking) at the University of California at Davis. It was he who directed my steps to Beaulieu Vineyard and organised what turned out to be one of the most significant tastings of my life—certainly one I shall never forget. Rutherford may not be well known outside California, but as the commune of Vosne-Romanée is revered by devotees for being the Burgundian navel of Bacchus, likewise the district around Rutherford can surely claim an equal distinction among the wine-growing areas of America.

Little did I appreciate beforehand the importance of that first tasting, for the range of Cabernet Sauvignons we tried that morning, dating back to the early 1940's, showed such astonishing quality that they left an indelible mark on my memory, and especially the rest of that splendid bottle which Harold tucked under his arm for our lunch! It was so rich that it reminded one somehow of the gorgeous 1947 Pomerols when they were in their prime —I forget the actual vintage, but know it was of a similar date.

The genius who received us and had made these wines was none other than the great André Tchelistcheff. Though, maybe, medium in height, when it comes to achievement he is certainly great of stature, for it is he who ever since the last war has been responsible for the outstanding quality produced at B.V., and it is also he who has done so much to establish the renown of California wine. We hear, almost ad infinitum, of Colonel Agoston Haraszthy, the "father" of California wine, who, if one reads between the lines, does not now appear to have been quite so reliable as one somehow would expect, but surely for a long time to come we shall hear of Andre Tchelistcheff as the man who has done so much to build up its reputation. In the company of just a few others, he can claim responsibility for bringing a wine district, which foreigners and indeed many native Americans used to shrug off as being of no importance, to a matter for very serious attention.

Even so short a time ago as that visit, although widely distributed throughout the United States, the wines of California appeared to be little accepted insofar as quality was concerned. Wherever one went outside the state, it was the imported wine which was drunk and respected, the native variety being deprecated, especially as, often as not, it was equally, and frequently more, expensive. Steeped as I was in French wine, I could not, nevertheless, help being interested in the produce of California, and so whenever the opportunity arose, I purposely used to order a bottle in a restaurant, but unfortunately it usually proved a disappointing experience. After discussing this one day with Sandy McNally (originally trained by Alexis Lichine in Bordeaux), who had recently joined Heublein, Inc. as their "wine man," he undertook to scour the liquor stores in Hartford, Connecticut, and finally came up with about a dozen or so different wines—or should I say indifferent wines—all from California. These were tasted most carefully, and prejudice apart, I found little reason to change my opinion. Always, however, in the back of my mind, lurked the memory of those fine old vintages once tasted at Beaulieu, shining still brightly like stars in the firmament, ever encouraging me to search yet further afield. It was not until I returned to the West Coast in 1965 that I really discovered for myself the true potential of this important wine-growing district. Great strides had been taken to improve quality, strides which since then have been developing into six-league leaps.

During the past decade or so, a number of outstanding but smaller growers have appeared on the vinous scene, commencing with Lee Stewart of Souverain and Fred McCrea of Stony Hill, and these have been followed by such doughty competitors as the late Mr. Zellerbach of Hanzell, and Joe Heitz of the Heitz Cellars. All these have underlined for me the great potential of the Napa Valley.

In spite of this general upsurge of achievement, towering above them over the years, as did the Coit Tower over San Francisco or the Empire State Building over New York, there has always been Beaulieu—Beaulieu Vineyard, a household name for quality for the past three decades.

All this success can be laid at the door of the founder of the estate, Georges de Latour, and above all, to the unusual ability of André Tchelistcheff, who has guided its destiny since 1938.

Founded in 1900, rather late in the day in comparison with some of the other great wineries, Beaulieu Vineyard has made up for lost time, and if one were at all superstitious, the name of the founder, Georges de Latour, strikes the right note, when one thinks of the great Burgundian firm of Louis Latour or even of Château Latour of Bordeaux. (The name "Beaulieu" has proved difficult for many Americans to pronounce, so, almost affectionately it seems, it is usually referred to as B.V.)

Comparisons are odious, but B.V. could well be described at the Latour or Lafite of the Napa Valley, for its reputation may be attributed to the situation of the vineyard and the ideal composition of the soil for the growing of vines. Given the site and the soil, however, it is still the human factor which counts for so much. This is a lesson for many to learn in Bordeaux, where vineyards, blessed by nature and often bearing famous names, yet do not always produce the high standard of which they are capable, while others hitherto less well known are more and more in demand. The excellence of this human factor has been most evident at B.V., where André Tchelistcheff has been at the helm since before the last war.

The situation, the soil, and the climate in the small area surrounding Rutherford are all three ideal for the cultivation of the Cabernet Sauvignon vine, indeed, so far as is known, the best of all in the United States, and it is the red wine from this grape which is generally recognised as being the finest the country produces. Although this is the one for which the property is best known, a number of other varietals are also produced at B.V., namely Pinot Noir, Pinot Chardonnay, Johannisberg Riesling, Gamay Beaujolais, and so on. Whilst on the subject of Pinot Noir, although quite a lot of it is produced in California, its quality in general does not normally (in the writer's opinion, at any rate) compare favourably with that of Cabernet Sauvignon, but interestingly this is often refuted at B.V.

In order to distinguish the produce of the estate from that of competitors, the word "Beau" has been incorporated into the labelling, thus we have the proprietary names of Beaufort Pinot Chardonnay, Beaumont Pinot Noir, Beauclair Johannisberg Riesling, and Beaurosé, which, of course, needs no explanation. Incidentally, a certain quantity of the better vintages of Cabernet Sauvignon is always held in reserve in order to acquire bottle age, and this is sold later on under the Private Reserve label. In consequence, this designation has become a hallmark for quality, and some of these Private Reserve vintages age remarkably well in bottle; indeed, among them are some of the finest red wines America has ever produced.

A few people such as Dr. George Linton, living in El Cerrito, recognised early the importance of good California wine. Dr. Linton is reputed to have the finest collection of native wine in existence. Having what could well be described as a very perceptive palate, he quickly appreciated the quality of the greater wines of the Napa Valley and so had begun to collect them in the early 1950's.

At that time, there was little or no demand from the American public, so the great wineries were prepared to let their best wines, their Private Reserves and so on, go for prices which would nowadays appear to be ludicrous. George used to buy two or three hundred cases at a time and distribute them among discerning friends. Nowadays the average person has almost to go down on his bended knees to get a case or so, and sometimes even then only a few bottles will be available!

The managers of this estate have always prided themselves on the quality of their white wine, especially the Pinot Chardonnay, but sometimes, as with the 1968 vintage, they have really hit the jackpot, an exceptional wine if ever there was one. It is through this varietal that once again Andre Tchelistcheff has demonstrated his brilliance because for years he has been casting around to find the ideal locality for its planting. Finally, he chose Carneros, which, as it turns out, has the perfect microclimate for this particular vine. Carneros is an area which lies to the south of the Napa Valley, where, in fact, the valley has spread out and is open to the maritime climate of the bay area. Admittedly, the idea of Carneros is not really original, because Colonel Haraszthy first grew Zinfandel vines there during the 1860's and 1870's, but no doubt they failed on account of lack of water, and no vines have been planted there since those days. The unsurmountable obstacle was the meagre rainfall, a mere twelve inches a year, and virtually none between March and November; consequently, no one had considered the area seriously ever since.

It is thanks then to the pioneering efforts of this gifted wine-maker, as also Louis Martini, that vines are growing there at all, for it was they who conceived the idea of constructing a dam, thus ensuring adequate irrigation throughout the year. Consequently, in 1963 B.V. was able to plant out seventy acres of Pinot Chardonnay and eighty of Pinot Noir, for the locality has proved equally suitable for the latter varietal, so much so that Carneros is becoming known

as the Burgundian district of the neighbourhood. So successful indeed has it been that the other great wineries are laying out their
vineyards alongside.

Inevitably the years pass, and as time passes, changes must take
place. After thirty years at the helm, André, though still devoting
all his days to B.V., is gradually relinquishing his command to Dr.
Richard Peterson, a brilliant young wine chemist, already endowed
with invaluable experience of winemaking elsewhere. As the
trusted captain slowly loosens his grasp on the tiller, it is a pleasure
to behold the great accord between these two exceptional makers
of wine, men of differing generations, but each so clearly imbued
with the utmost respect for the other.

The other change, and it could well have been a desperate one,
not only for B.V. itself, but also for the dedicated and well-informed
body of connoisseurs who live in California, was a change of ownership, for the latter have always regarded B.V. as well as the vineyard across the way, Inglenook, as objects of their personal pride.
Only about a year ago B.V. suddenly changed hands, from those of
Mrs. Dagmar Sullivan, the granddaughter of Georges de Latour, and
her associates, to the powerful firm of Heublein, Inc. Local people
shuddered at the thought of the hard-liquor image descending upon
their beloved Napa Valley, and into the bargain, onto the most precious part of it!

Happily, from the beginning, I had quickly realised from the
first sips, as it were, of those concerned with the table-wine divi-
sion, their enthusiasm and sincerity of purpose, and with wine such
an attitude is of vital importance. It was not at all surprising therefore to hear from Dr. Peterson how smooth the takeover had been
and how eager everyone in Heublein was to help and, wherever
possible, to make improvements.

There comes a time in every business when an infusion of new
capital is needed, and this was precisely the case at B.V., so, knowing the insistence upon quality of the new president, Chris Carriuolo (the senior vice-president of Heublein), and his personal love
for fine wines, one may rest assured that the estate will now continue to go from strength to ever greater strength. My advice,
therefore, to the myriads of Smirnoff buffs is from time to time, to
indulge in just that extra noggin so that the good work may carry
on at B.V.!

Under normal circumstances, it is not customary to let visitors
taste the very young wine, the reason being that the uninitiated
would neither understand nor appreciate it. Very young wine tastes

pretty nasty anyway! Therefore it was a privilege during my visit in April 1969 to be allowed to taste a range of the "scions of the family" and to see for myself what was in store for the future. The moment was singularly appropriate, because, contrary to the situation in Europe, 1968 was one of the finest vintages on record for California. From the very outset, it was abundantly clear that the 1968's were going to be of great quality.

White Wines

> *Pinot Chardonnay 1966* (Founder's Wine).
> Good colour, excellent bouquet, not dissimilar from that of a Meursault. A fine, full-bodied wine with a very good flavour. I could easily have mistaken this for a good white Burgundy.

> *Pinot Chardonnay 1967* (Founder's Wine).
> Good colour, lovely fragrant nose. As clean and dry as a good Chablis. Has a splendid fruit acidity which should make it keep well.

These two were both quite different from one another in style, yet each was of fine quality.

Red Wines

> *Pinot Noir 1966* (Estate–Bottled).
> Medium colour, attractive bouquet, good fruit and flavour, and finishes nicely.

> *Pinot Noir 1967* (Still in wood).
> Big, full bouquet, good fruity flavour.

> *Pinot Noir 1968* (Still in wood).
> Great robust bouquet, a huge rich wine, well-balanced, and clearly with a great future. When the time comes, I would like to lay my hands on a case of this!

André Tchelistcheff is quoted as saying that in thirty-two years' experience, he has made two really great vintages of Pinot Noir—1946 and 1968. At the time of this visit I had not yet tasted the 1946 (with Dr. Linton), but this 1968 will certainly be a winner.

Cabernet Sauvignon 1966.
> Good colour, a nice, what the French call *'roti'* smell. Good quality and considerable character. (One comes across *'roti,'* "roasted," wines following a hot, dry summer.)

Cabernet Sauvignon 1967.
> Deep colour, an attractively aromatic fragrance, and the body is pleasantly rounded.

Cabernet Sauvignon 1968.
> A powerful, yet distinguished bouquet. Full-flavoured and fruity, this will undoubetdly make a great bottle.

It is obvious that 1968 is an exceptionally fine vintage for California, as fine for red wine as, say, 1961 was for Bordeaux. What more can one say than that! The whites, too, appear to be unusually successful. If I had the good fortune to live in this pleasant land, like a bird dog after game I would soon be sniffing around to flush some of these fine 1968's from covert!

Here also are the notes made during my last visit to the property in February 1970:

Gamay Beaujolais 1968 (made from the Gamay Precoce grape).
> A fresh, fruity bouquet and a similarly delightful flavour. The first vintage B.V. has produced from this particular grape.

Cabernet Sauvignon Private Reserve 1965 (newly released on the market).
> A good complex bouquet, round, full-bodied, and beautifully balanced. It leaves a nice taste in the mouth. Should reach its best in about five years' time.

Beaufort Pinot Chardonnay 1968 (from the Carneros vineyard).
> An outstanding bouquet, which André Tchelistcheff described as being reminiscent of white sage. Fine flavour with good fruit acidity and of considerable elegance. If this is a sample of what the very young vines from the Carneros vineyard can produce, then what can we expect when they reach full maturity?

From the results of these recent tastings of the wines coming along and those just on the market, it is quite evident that, as the years go by, we shall be hearing more and more of Beaulieu Vineyard and its produce.

A Whiff of Gastronomy

Since they have the reputation of being some of the finest in the United States, I am often asked my opinion of the San Francisco restaurants. The truth is that I hardly ever visit them, for I am entertained famously in the homes of my many friends.

Where good wine is made, there is usually good cooking to be found, and San Francisco is no exception to this rule. I would go even further and state that the cooking, at least in the home of my own friends, is of an extraordinarily high average. For example, within my own particular group of friends, the husbands as well as the wives have attended cookery classes, and the Pupu Pupu Club is but one of the ways in which married couples improve their gastronomic skills. My wife, who qualifies as a Cordon Bleu cook, accompanied me on my visit in the spring of 1971, and it is safe to say that she was deeply impressed by the high standard, and returned with many delicious recipes.

Without wishing to bore the reader with descriptions of endless meals, there is one so outstanding that it would be a shame to ignore, so here is an account of a dinner given for ten people by Dr. George Linton in February 1970 at his home in El Cerrito, in the bay area of San Francisco.

Our host, educated in England, is a noted veterinarian, as well as an importer of high-class wine, and he came to California soon after the war. As was mentioned earlier, he was among the very few connoisseurs who were early to appreciate the quality of the finer California wines.

The American custom of serving the first course before one sits down to dinner is always agreeable. On this occasion we had a selection of the Olympia oysters from Washington State, local smoked salmon and soft cream cheese on spiced bread, a terrine and, new to me, duck livers on toast. Not unlike the fresh goose livers one eats in and around Bordeaux in the fall season, these are a special Chinese delicacy and were obtained from the Chinese quarter of San Francisco.

With these goodies we drank a delightful low-strength light sherry, about 15 percent, which our host had made himself. This is a truly fascinating part of the world to visit, for I find most of my hosts, one way or another, own parts of vineyards and/or make their own wine. One day I hope to have a special tasting of these home-made wines, for many of them are infinitely better than the name might imply, and what is more, often better than some of the commercial varieties.

With the next course, cracked crab, we tasted no less than three champagnes, two from California and one from New York State. Then, with roast ribs of beef, the serious part of the evening began, a tasting of what must surely be some of the finest Cabernet Sauvignons existing in America.

This was a blind tasting, of course, and it is as well to point out that the vintages of 1946 and 1947 were both outstanding for California. What absolutely astounded me was the exceedingly dark colour of them all.

I imagine that only a very few if any people in America can have many of these gems in their cellars, but a record such as this may be useful, if only to show what quality can be achieved in California. It is unfortunate that few of the recent vintages seem to come up to this standard. This, no doubt, can be put down to what we are pleased to term "modernity"! Maybe the 1968's will prove I am wrong. (Such progress has been made lately that one or two of the 1970's may come up to this standard.)

In the early fifties when George Linton was buying these wines, he only paid from twelve to forty dollars a case for them! Clearly, in those days the American public had not taken to table wine; in fact, so little interest was evinced by the general public that he was able to bargain and buy up to 300 cases at a time, of what are now priceless wines. Nowadays, in spite of his record of faithfulness as a large buyer, he says all he can get, at most, are 50 cases, then as a favour, and paying, of course, the top price! This is just another example of how the demand has increased here in America during the past decade.

With our cheese course, we turned to Pinot Noir. Though perhaps it is my fault, I must confess that normally I cannot get on well with the average Pinot Noir as made in California, but the two wines that followed were a complete revelation and, without exaggeration, confounded me!

Cabernet Sauvignons

Vintage	Characteristics	My Placing	Points Against	Group Placing
1946 Charles Krug				
Vintage Select (special bottling) Cabernet Sauvignon	A real "cedar nose," such as one finds sometimes with the great wines of Bordeaux. (I am always at odds over this, because what I call a "cedar" nose is described here as a "eucalyptus" nose on account of the many trees of that variety which grow locally. There is some similarity in the smell; anyway, everyone knows what is meant.) Heaps of fruit, and it follows all through. Still very hard.	5	61	6
1947 Charles Krug				
Vintage Select (special bottling) Cabernet Sauvignon and some Merlot	Full, fruity bouquet, a huge wine, with a delightful finish.	4	41	5

1946 Beaulieu Vineyard Pinot Noir.
   A huge, immensely rich nose and a most powerful rich full-bodied masterpiece. It was a great experience to taste.

1947 Beaulieu Vineyard Pinot Noir.
   A nice big fruity bouquet and a deliciously rounded wine with an excellent finish.

These two alone were enough to restore anyone's confidence!

Cabernet Sauvignons (continued)

Vintage	Characteristics	My Placing	Points Against	Group Placing
1946 Beaulieu Vineyard				
Private Reserve 100% Cabernet Sauvignon	A splendid, rich bouquet which some-how was different from the others. A big wine with a very good flavour.	3	26	2
1947 Beaulieu Vineyard				
Private Reserve 100% Cabernet Sauvignon	A really splendid rich bouquet, a huge luscious wine too, with many years ahead of it. A masterpiece!	1	11	1
1946 Inglenook				
100% Cabernet Sauvignon	A beautiful full nose, huge and powerful, still lots of tannin.	2	28	3
1947 Louis M. Martini				
Private Reserve	Fine elegant bouquet, heaps of fruit yet beautifully smooth. I only put this down a bit because I thought it was slightly oxidised, though only two other people agreed with me.	6	35	4

The Heitz Wine Cellars

For two years now I have been privileged to attend a private tasting of this small but outstanding California winery, one which in so short a space of time has acquired for itself so great a reputation.

In April 1969 I tasted Joe Heitz's recent vintages of Pinot Chardonnay, Pinot Noir, and the remarkable Cabernet Sauvignon, and on this occasion in 1970 I was once more in the company of Barney and Belle Rhodes, as well as Martin Bamford, who directs the International Distillers and Vintners operations at Château Loudenne in Bordeaux.

Let us note here that the Zinfandel Associates Vineyard belongs to a group of enthusiasts, amongst whom are the Rhodeses and Dr. and Mrs. Robert Adamson. When their grapes are ripe, the policy is to sell them to winemakers such as Joe Heitz, who from then onwards handle the fermentation, bottling, and subsequent marketing.

Before we began our work, Joe, a man of great sincerity and integrity, enjoined us not to pull our punches, but to state our opinions with complete honesty. He has been known to say that although sometimes the truth may hurt, such criticism can be invaluable when it concerns the making of wine! The tasting, of course, was a blind one.

Joe started off the proceedings by setting out for us two examples each of Pinot Chardonnay of the 1968 and 1969 vintages. One represented the produce of the Zinfandel Associates Vineyard, the other what Joe Heitz terms his regular wine.

Pinot Chardonnay

> 1969 *Pinot Chardonnay* (Zinfandel Associates).
> A fruity, rather full nose, lots of fruit and flavour, very nice finish.

> 1969 *Pinot Chardonnay* (Regular).
> Pleasantly fresh bouquet, not quite so pronounced as the Zinfandel Associates, good flavour and well made.

I preferred the bouquet of the "regular" wine and the taste of the Zinfandel Associates; the latter had a more exciting flavour, caused probably by its good fruit acidity.

1968 *Pinot Chardonnay* (Zinfandel Associates).
Good full bouquet, this is most attractive, also with good fruit acidity.

1968 *Pinot Chardonnay* (Regular).
Good nose, with more finesse perhaps than the Zinfandel Associates. Most attractive flavour and well-balanced.

Again, though, the Zinfandel Associates wine had a slightly better finish. These two 1968's are now in bottle, and each is kept separate. The name of the vineyard appears on the label, a pleasing piece of authenticity for the connoisseur. Also printed on the label is the number of bottles made, i.e., the total quantity of Zinfandel Associates is 4,200 and of the other, only 1,990. No wonder there is not enough to go round!

If a merchant wishes to obtain any stock at all of these rare birds, it is necessary for him to join what I call the Joe Heitz Club! In fact, as with any good club, one has to get on to what is virtually a waiting list! A fortnight before, when I was in Washington, D.C., Marvin Stirman, of the Calvert Wine Shop, told me that he had just received his "membership" allocation, which, in his case, amounted to only five dozen! There is not much a successful business can do with a mere five cases, but no doubt there are some deserving throats around!

1967 *Pinot Chardonnay.*
Well-developed, rather elegant bouquet, plenty of flavour, but there was a trace of something slightly metallic on the taste, and the finish was not quite so good as some of the others.

1966 *Pinot Chardonnay.*
A nice bouquet, with finesse. This 1966 was extremely attractive, the taste delicious.

It may be too early to say much, but it looks as though where the Heitz Cellars are concerned, the 1969 vintage for white wine is going to be as successful as the 1968.)

Now came the turn of the Cabernet Sauvignons. With the memory fresh in my mind of the splendid wines I had tasted here in April 1969, particularly those coming from Martha's Vineyard, I had been looking forward very much to this moment. It is sad that there are only twelve acres of this outstanding vineyard. Incidentally, it was originally planted out by the Rhodes, much of it with Barney's own hands.

Cabernet Sauvignon

1969 (Martha's Vineyard).
A superb colour, bouquet, beautifully fragrant, reminiscent of black currants. A fine, long, well-made wine, which carried through with it a similar taste. Very, very good.

The (Regular).
Good colour and nose, medium body, slightly sharp finish.

1968 (Martha's Vineyard).
Very deep colour, a lovely complex nose, a great big affair this, with heaps of fruit. Very, very good.

The (Regular).
Good colour and bouquet. A nice wine of medium body, and it is hardly fair to compare this against the overwhelming quality of Martha's Vineyard.

1967 (Martha's Vineyard).
Deep colour, again this delightful black currant nose, splendid fruit and flavour, quite excellent! This is to be bottled at any time before the summer of 1970.

1966 The (Regular).
Nice bouquet, full-bodied, rich, and well-balanced, good quality.

19th February, 1970

Tastings of 1966 White Burgundy

This tasting was held by the Berkeley Wine & Food Society at the home of Mr. and Mrs. Larry Seibel.

1966 Vintage Burgundy

The Wine	Characteristics	My Placing	Points Against	Group Placing
Corton-Charlemagne Domaine Bonneau du Martray Josephs $5.50	Attractive nose, sweet and attractive, nice finish	3	34	2
Château de Meursault Comte de Moucheron Josephs $5.95	Full and rather powerful nose, full-flavoured, fair finish, rather dull	4	113	5
Meursault, Dave E. Robert (Coron) Esquins $3.68	Slightly hard nose (sulphur), thin, and not too attractive	5	116	6
Chassagne-Montrachet Ruchottes, Domaine Ramonet-Prudhon Esquins $5.98	Lovely nose, fine full-bodied but could have more fruit acidity	2	48	3
Bâtard-Montrachet Averys Esquins $7.19	Fair nose, nice fruit and flavour, good, some acidity	6	44	4
Chassagne-Montrachet Domaine Jacques Gagnard Josephs $3.50	Beautiful nose, delightfully fresh, round, rich, and good quality	1	17	1

23rd February, 1970

Dinner with the Rhodes

This was a most memorable dinner party given by Dr. and Mrs. Bernard L. Rhodes for Mr. Alfio Moriconi, from Washington, D.C. With the caviar beforehand (pounds of it!) we drank Louis Roederer 1962, and Louis Roederer Cristal 1964. Both were excellent, particularly the latter. Here are my notes:

The Wines

Batard-Montrachet 1961 (Ramonet-Prudhon).
A nice pale colour; fresh, clean, and dry.

Château Nenin 1949 (Château-Bottled).
Good colour, a big fruity bouquet, full-bodied, but it still needs time.

Château Nenin 1947 (Château-Bottled).
Good colour, lovely bouquet, that delicious 1947 Pomerol taste, but just beginning to edge off at the end.

Bonnes-Mares 1945 (Domaine Belorgey).
Good colour, delightful bouquet, fine powerful flavour.

Wackenheimer Gerumpel Trockenbeerenauslese 1947 (Dr. Burklin Wolf, *Fass* 055).
Golden colour, delicious bouquet with a special perfume of raisins, and the taste was similar. A splendid wine.

Taylor 1920.
Deep colour, a fine full-bodied wine, much deeper than one would have expected for its age.

A Tasting from the Domaine de la Romanée-Conti

It is not often that many of us have the opportunity to taste the whole range of a single vintage from this famous domaine, but what struck us all most forcibly at this tasting was the fantastic cost of these wines. It must be highly satisfactory from the point of view of the Domaine de la Romanée-Conti that there should be such a ready sale at these prices here in the United States.

One cannot help wondering, however, what on earth would happen and who would buy the wine at this price, if anything were to go wrong with the American market. As it is, over the next ten years, it is not difficult to envisage even greater demand, as more and more well-to-do Americans take to the gentle art of drinking fine wine.

These tastings were arranged by Larry Seibel at the offices of Esquin Imports, San Francisco.

(See page 38)

1967 Montrachet $24.95	Nose still undeveloped, but already full and fragrant. A fine full-bodied wine, still hidden in its cloak of acidity. Should make a very good bottle.

1966 Vintage, Wines of the Domaine de la Romanée Conti

The Wines	Characteristics	My Placing	Points Against	Group Placing
Echézeaux $14.95	Medium colour, good firm nose, but too dry and thin	5	75	6
Romanée-Conti $33.00	Good dark colour, lovely fragrant bouquet, attractive flavour, a fine wine	2	42	2
Romanée-St.-Vivant $21.50	Rather light colour, quite a nice nose, but on the thin side, with some acidity	6	69	5
Richebourg $21.50	Dark colour, fine firm bouquet, but not too much of it yet, good fruit and a better finish	3	61	4
La Tâche $21.50	Medium colour, lovely fragrant nose, still a little hard, good fruit, and very well-balanced	1	55	3
Grands Echézeaux $17.50	Light colour, a nice fragrant bouquet, quite a lot of fruit	4	35	1

(It must be remembered that this was a tasting of "aristocrats" and that the notes on them are comparative. They apply only within this table.)

A Visit to Sacramento

Belle Rhodes drove me ninety miles down the highway to Sacramento to spend the day with Darrell Corti and his family.

The gardens around the Capitol are unexpectedly beautiful, superb trees, as well as avenues of stately palm trees. They were ablaze with flowers, magnolias and more camellias than I have ever seen at one time before. No wonder it is known as the town of camellias.

Corti Brothers have two splendid stores in Sacramento, of which Darrell is in charge of the wine departments. These, from virtually nothing, he has brought up to a most flourishing side of the business, which is beginning to be recognised as far away as Los Angeles. This is a very remarkable young man who clearly will go a long way.

Lunching at home with his father, Frank Corti, and other guests, it was Darrell who cooked the meal, and with great skill too. Sand dabs, poached, and a casserole of very tender squabs. With this we drank a Kiedricher Nussbrunnen Riesling feine auslese 1962 Eiswein and three off-vintages of the Domaine de la Romanée-Conti, 1960, 1963, and 1951. All bore the breeding of this great vineyard, but it was only the 1951 that I should have liked to have in my cellar. These are the notes:

La Tâche 1960.
> Colour turning brown, fragrant bouquet, not at all a big wine, and it didn't last well in the glass.

La Tâche 1963.
> Brownish colour, lovely bouquet, very little depth though, and a little sharp.

La Tâche 1951.
> Brownish colour, full rich bouquet, very good flavour, has kept well for such an unfashionable year.

At eight o'clock that evening I gave a talk on claret to about seventy people whom Corti Brothers had invited, and it took place in most agreeable surroundings at the Sutter Club in Sacramento.

It is always an interesting experience to taste a range of wines from a good vintage so far from their native heath. The first thing that impresses one is the fine dark colour of them all. There can be no doubt the 1966's are going to be very good. A table follows.

1966 Bordeaux Tasting Notes[a]

The Wines	Characteristics	My Placing	Group Placing
Château Chasse-Spleen (Moulis) $3.60	An exceptional growth. Its colour and nose both are good. Flavour reflects good fruit; it is still immature, but of good quality.	7	6/7
Château Giscours (Margaux) Third Growth $4.33	Deep colour and attractive nose. The flavour is attractive like the nose.	6	5
Château Fonroque (Saint-Emilion) $3.15	Great growth. The colour is good and the flavour big, round and fruity. A full, round nose.	5	4
Château Moulinet (Pomerol) $3.47	Good colour; rich, round and lovely nose. The flavour is rich, round, special and delicious.	4	6/7
Château Haut-Batailley (Pauillac) $4.33	Good colour, and the nose is that distinctive Pauillac bouquet of eucalyptus. It has an excellent fruit flavour.	3	3
Château Léoville Barton (Saint-Julien) Second Growth $4.62	Good colour and a delightful, fruity nose. The flavour denotes good fruit and great quality.	2	2
Château La Mission-Haut-Brion (Graves) Classified Growth $8.16	Very deep colour, fine, powerful nose. The flavour is full-bodied, of splendid quality.	1	1

[a] With comparative 1970 prices

27th February, 1970

A Lucullan Fantasy

One of the most notable events which has taken place in the last
few years since Christie's, the famous London auctioneers, re-
started their wine sales was when their director, Michael Broadbent, on Wednesday, the 31st May 1967, presented a range of
remarkable old bottles; these had lain all their lives in the cellars
of Dalmeny House and Hopetoun House, the Scottish seats of the
Roseberry and Linlithgow families.

The wines, many of them quite fabulous, had remained in their
original bins ever since the time they had been put into bottle. I remember the sale well, for I had been commissioned to buy a dozen
bottles of Château Latour 1874 at almost any price on behalf of
Keith Showering, whose family business (Harveys of Bristol) are
part-owners of that well-known château. With a number of lots of
similar calibre on offer, no wonder the sale made such a stir in the
world of wine!

As was only to be expected, the sale room was crowded with a
most distinguished gathering, and among them were my Californian
friends Dr. Bernard L. Rhodes and Dr. Robert Kay Adamson, together with their wives. They were over for their annual visit to
the European vineyards, and as the sale coincided with their visit,
they had crossed to London with a view to acquiring some fine
vintage port from the early years of the twentieth century; also, if
possible, some of the pre-phylloxera claret, preferably in magnums
or even larger sizes still.* Amongst their purchases, and egged on
by both Ronald Avery and myself, they bid for and obtained a
triple magnum of 1865 Château Lafite, a wine made by Sir Samuel
Scott, an Englishman, three years before he sold the Lafite property
to the Rothschild family.

I had no compunction whatsoever in persuading Barney Rhodes
to go on bidding up to what was really a rather high figure, because
in the private cellar at Latour, we still have a small bin of our own
1865 vintage. Although it is in bottles, the wine is still so extraordi-

* Phylloxera, a plant louse which attacks the roots of vines, destroyed
most European grape vines between 1860 and 1880. New vines were
grafted to resistant American roots.

narily virile and splendid that it seemed to me that a container six
times the size, and of the same vintage, had an even greater chance
of survival, particularly in view of its "case history," which is as
follows:

This huge bottle was purchased by the first Earl of Roseberry
from Cockburn's of Leith (Scotland), an old established firm of
wine merchants, and in 1869 it was laid down in its original bin at
Dalmeny House. Since then it has been moved only twice, the first
time for the cork to be resealed with wax, done in 1930 by that
distinguished firm of wine merchants, Berry Brothers of St. James's
Street, London, and the second, of course, when it was shipped to
California.

The vital factor for the good preservation of this 1865 Lafite
was the very cold cellar in which it was stored. It is a well-known
fact that when wine is kept at a cool, constant temperature such as
this (around 50 degrees Fahrenheit) it takes longer to mature, but
it does so under ideal conditions. Added to that, a triple magnum
will take much longer to develop than a bottle, and thus should
keep for a correspondingly longer time.

Having given the wine a year or so in which to settle down
after its lengthy journey, tiring enough in any case for a young
wine, but surely even more so for a centenarian, Barney Rhodes,
Bob Adamson, and Ben Ichinose, the third partner in this Lucullan
fantasy, decided to plan a gastronomic feast around this august and
aristocratic bottle.

It was indeed fortunate for me that such *un grand diner* should
coincide with one of my periodic visits to California, and a great
honour indeed to be included among the group of distinguished
guests, for once the word got out, there was a rush for attendance,
and in spite of the high cost of each plate, quite a large number of
people had to be disappointed. As it was, many of *les convives*
came specially for the occasion, from as far away as Sacramento,
Los Angeles, and one even from Aspen, Colorado.

As may be imagined, great were the preparations which went
on beforehand. Apart from choosing a suitable menu to embellish
the proceedings and other wines considered worthy to accompany
this noble bottle, the transport and the decanting of such old treasures required the utmost attention. It was well, perhaps, that the
three owners of the triple-magnum were all doctors, so that they
could bring to bear all their technical skill to the decanting of the
runner-up, a jeroboam of 1929 Château Bel Air (Saint-Emilion) and
the triple-magnum which were so proudly set out for all to admire.

So instead of tipping up the bottles in the usual manner, with the utmost expertise they syphoned off the contents into a number of decanters. Thanks to the unbroken wax which covered the tip of the neck of this outsize prima donna, the cork itself was in perfect condition, no mean feat after some forty years in contact with the wine within.

The fourth member of the committee, James F. Smith, an old friend of André Simon, had kindly arranged our presence at the Cercle de l'Union in San Francisco, together with the services of its excellent chef. As Monsieur Pompidou, the President of France, was in San Francisco on that very day, one cannot help feeling he would have preferred to spend his evening at the French Club, instead of at the state function which he had to attend!

When a wine reaches a venerable age, there is usually some evaporation, and the air-gap, or what is commonly called ullage, if excessive, can cause the contents of the bottle to become oxidised and thus spoiled. This is why the old vintages lying in Bordelais cellars are examined, refilled, and recorked approximately every twenty-five years, but when stood up, the extraordinary thing about this triple-magnum was that after over a hundred years and only one recorking, there was an air gap of less than an inch between the wine and the cork!

To describe the splendid food would take too long, but some remarks on the wines may not come amiss. The magnums of champagne were all excellent, and having been so recently disgorged, the Moet & Chandon 1952 was beautifully fresh and delightful. What was so unusual, however, were the magnums of Bollinger (1937 and 1934), for these had both been disgorged and corked in the regular manner, and under normal circumstances Champagne of such an age would undoubtedly have taken on colour and generally be showing some grey hairs! Not a bit of it, though; each of these two wines had a very pale colour, and both were as fresh as a daisy. This must surely be due to the excellent conditions prevailing in Madame Bollinger's own cellar, where it had been housed for so long.

The 1870 Sercial, which accompanied the soup, had a superb bouquet and flavour, and the 1949 Montrachet, which followed, was equally well preserved. Just by looking at its pale colour, one could tell there would be no fear of oxidation there, something which at that age could easily have set in.

Nineteen-twenty-nine has always been my favourite vintage for claret. In the late forties and early fifties the 1929's were quite unique. Their individual, almost unbelievable bouquet and flavour made them stand out amongst all others, but for a number of years now, time has set its seal upon them, and in most cases the glory has departed. Alas, good things do not go on forever! All the same, the 1929 Bel Air, decanted at the last minute from its jeroboam, had an excellent colour, a fine bouquet (though admittedly aged), and a lovely flavour as well. Sadly, though, it began to thin out towards the end of the taste. Even a few of the grey hairs had fallen, leaving that tell-tale patch of baldness!

There is no need to enlarge upon the apprehension surrounding the welfare of the triple-magnum, the *pièce de résistance* of the whole evening. In case the 1929 Bel Air had not come up to scratch, there was a jeroboam of 1923 Bel Air standing by, but what on earth can one have as a substitute for such *une grande bouteille* as 1865 Lafite?

There was considerable interest and much flashing of light bulbs attending the extraction of the cork, and one had to admire Doctors Adamson, Ichinose, and Rhodes for their ingenuity over the operation. Once the wax was chipped off, the top quarter of the cork was cut out. This was done just in case such an old cork should be pushed down into the bottle and the soiled top part of it come into contact with the wine. As mentioned before, the contents were then expertly siphoned out, leaving the sediment at the bottom of the bottle.

To say the least, the result was staggering. Such a beautiful deep colour was really unexpected in such a very old wine; the bouquet, too, was a delight—far, far younger than that of the 1929 Bel Air! The flavour was almost miraculous, so much fruit and such a lovely finish. There is something about these great pre-phylloxera clarets that no modern successor can equal, certainly not for longevity anyway.

The unfortunate 1928 Romanée-Saint-Vivant which followed, so overshadowed by its immediate predecessor, stood up wonderfully well under almost impossible circumstances, dark of colour, fine of bouquet, sturdy and full-bodied, and it even had some tannin still to brag about! A splendid bottle!

It was quite a task, too, for a very ancient vintage port to follow hard on the heels of anything so luscious and delectable as the double-magnum of 1953 Château d'Yquem, but what a glass of port that 1860 was! Bottled at Chard in Somerset by Mitchell Toms, its colour was unusually dark for a centenarian, and into the bargain it both tasted and smelled like fine vintage port. Except, perhaps, for the fact that it had lost most of its sugar, there was no need whatever to make polite noises in its defence. This was one of the finest really old bottles of vintage port I have ever tasted, and that together with the excellent cigars so kindly provided by Mr. Charles Woodruff of Dunhill's, rounded off this Lucullan feast in a most fitting manner.

4th March, 1970

*A Tasting of 1959 Vintage
of the Hospices de Beaune*

At the home of Dr. and Mrs. W. Dickerson in San Anselmo, California, the following tasting took place:

(See opposite page)

1959: The Hospices de Beaune

The Wines	Characteristics	My Placing	Points Against	Group Placing
Beaune Toussaints Remoissenet $6.65	Medium colour, fairly full nose, good fruit, agreeable nice finish, and some tannin. Very good	4	80	4
Corton Paul Chanson $6.50	Very pale colour, lovely, but tiny trace acetic; has fruit but is drying off. Fair finish	6	101	8
Corton Clos du Roi Comte d'Orthez $8.95	Medium colour, fine nose, very good fruit and flavour, still some tannin, good quality	2	84	6
Beaune Clos des Mouches Coron $6.44	Very pale colour, odd nose, thin, not very attractive, sharpish. Finish bitter?	8	94	7
Hospices Clos des Avaux Comte d'Orthez $8.95	Medium to pale colour, old but full nose, good fruit and flavour. Could have more charm. Some tannin	5	65	3
Hospices de Beaune Cuvée Guigone de Salins Patriarche $9.95	Medium colour, *nice* toffee nose, great big wine, *coarser* than the rest	7	63	2
Corton Dr. Peste Hospices de Beaune Avery's $11.58	Medium colour, rich nose, well made, finishes nicely	3	83	5
Hospices Clos des Avaux Avery's $10.70	Pale colour, good rich nose, great big wine full of fruit, lots of natural sugar	1	51	1
Hospices de Beaune Volnay Blondeau Avery's $9.22	Medium colour, query nose ageing? Has volatile acidity	9	116	9

March, 1970

California Jug Wines

Tested both by time and experience, the vineyards of France and Germany still produce the finest wines of the world, but apart from the vagaries of the seasons, the quality remains more or less the same, or, if there are changes, they are almost imperceptible. By contrast, in California, where the vineyards are only now growing to man's estate, changes are taking place all the time; consequently, the atmosphere there is charged with a different kind of electricity, a different kind of enthusiasm.

Before Prohibition, the greater part of the wine produced in California was fortified, and there was little demand for the table variety. The repeal of Prohibition was swiftly followed by the war, so it is really only since the 1940's that the domestic table wines have begun to assume importance. In fact, it is only during the last ten years or so that generic names have been discarded and varietals have received the respect they deserve.

Enormous progress has been made in the methods of vinification, and though everyone may not agree, the changeover from the ageing of fine wine in huge wooden casks to small Limousin or Nevers oak casks has made a considerable difference to the quality.

Although there has been a wine industry in California for well over a hundred years, there are still fascinating and, as yet, untried possibilities to be explored. For instance, even in that holy of holies, the Napa Valley, growers are not yet absolutely certain which soil best suits which varietal. So much is to be learned, so much to be discovered, and it is refreshing to find this so openly admitted. No wonder then there is an exhilaration in the air, no wonder a wine man like myself is drawn back, as if by a magnet, year after year.

In the wine regions of Europe, the outlook is, quite naturally, somewhat "chauvinistic"; for instance, in Bordeaux, one drinks only Bordeaux, in Burgundy, Burgundy, on the Moselle, Moselle. I have often found that the average Frenchman, because he is French, thinks he knows all about wine, whereas, in fact, usually he has spent most of his life drinking *vin ordinaire* bought according to alcoholic degree. One has only to study the wine lists in

48

French restaurants to understand that because the good vintages are too expensive, the average restaurateur, although prepared to buy the better-known names, often concentrates on the off-vintages.

In England, we too think we know all about wine, certainly at least more than the Americans; this may well have been true in the past, but it is no longer the case. Admittedly the English have always bought the good vintages, and they are still to be seen on our restaurant lists. The bulk of the great wines used to come to England, and, indeed, a great deal of good château-bottled claret still does, but less and less nowadays of the first growths. Also, because of rising prices and greatly increased duty, many English wine lovers are literally forced off the classified growths and have to content themselves with supermarket wine. (The current British duty on table wine is £3.48 per dozen bottles.)

My friends in London are quite astonished when I describe to them the enthusiasm and the expertise of many Californians, of whom the members of the San Francisco Wine Sampling Club are but an example. There are English wine-tasting clubs, to be sure, but relatively few of them, and they do not meet very often.

In the San Francisco club, a wine is selected by a competent committee and is distributed each month for consumption and discussion. Although there are occasional dinners, the members meet every Wednesday throughout the year for a blind tasting organised by their committee in members' homes, and each guest brings his own set of glasses. All the host has to provide is some bread and cheese and perhaps something very simple to accompany the *vin d'honneur* at the end. The fair sex has proved to be every bit as interested and as competent as the men. The success and development of this most interesting group is entirely owing to the unbounded enthusiasm and organising ability of its founder, Walter Peterson.

So far in my writing I have concentrated more on the wines from the small growers of California, just as in Bordeaux I find it more exciting and more challenging to discover—not that "discover" is really the correct word—and write about the comparatively unknown wines of striking quality in their own category, rather than to discuss the classified growths.

At the same time, I have been fully aware that this information is rather academic to residents in the United States (other than those living in California) for the very good reason that the production of these vineyards is so minute that the wine is virtually unobtainable elsewhere. Here, then, is a brave attempt to touch on some of the inexpensive wines in general distribution, especially the "Jug" ones, which are to be found in every store. Where a price is mentioned, though, it will be relevant only to California, and at the time of tasting. Although, on account of the weather, there must be some difference from one year to another, wines in this category are blended so skillfully that they remain virtually the same from year to year.

In order to be on exactly the same level as the consumer, the wines had to come straight from liquor stores, so I assembled a huge collection of them, but then the problem arose as to how to taste them. This is where I was able to call upon the knowledge and expertise of the members of the San Francisco Wine Sampling Club.

Although, as may be seen, one or two of the undermentioned wines were somewhat indifferent, the majority were really most agreeable and quite remarkable value for the money. It will be remembered sadly by English readers that a good bottle of table wine, obtainable at around 50 pence a bottle, has become almost a matter of history.

It should be remembered though that the duty on table wine in California seems to be only about six cents a bottle. Even so, the actual quality of these "Jug" wines seems to be much better than that of the branded table wines which are sold in England.

(See pages 51-56)

Red "Jug" Wines
Selling at the rate of $1.00 and under for a usual bottle.

The Wines	Characteristics	My Placing	Points Against	Group Placing
Petri Burgundy	Nose rather rough, oxidised, poor quality	11	125	10
Gallo Chianti	Very "winey" nose, big and blatant	10	147	12
C. K. Mondavi Chianti	Ordinary nose, slightly fierce flavour, could have more breeding	6	104	6
Guild, Vino da Tavola Extra Mellowed Table Wine	Fair nose, plenty of fruit, quite a good flavour	4	96	3
Italian Swiss Colony Burgundy	Strident, rather oxidised nose, rough stuff, poor quality	12	137	11
Italian Swiss Colony Claret	Good bouquet, quite well-balanced, very good quality	1	101	4/5
Italian Swiss Colony Zinfandel	Good nose, quite nice, but a little acidity, plus some tannin	5	91	2
Gallo Paisano Pure Country Red Table Wine	Rather full nose, full-bodied, some sweetness	3	117	9
Gallo Hearty Burgundy	Deep colour, good nose, strong flavour, but good	2	81	1
C. K. Mondavi Claret	Unusual bouquet, tastes as it smells	9	114	8
C. K. Mondavi Zinfandel	Rough nose, very winey flavour, but on the thin side	7	111	7
Italian Swiss Colony Napa, Sonoma, Mendocino Premium Burgundy	Quite a nice bouquet, has fruit but some acidity	8	101	4/5

Similar Wines
Selling at $1.15 and over

The Wines	Characteristics	My Placing	Points Against	Group Placing
Sebastiani Mountain Red, Light Burgundy	Quite a nice bouquet, but a little sharp, lacks charm	5	49	3
Almadén Mountain Red Burgundy	Coarse bouquet, rather rough, poor finish	6	80	6
Almadén Mountain Red Claret	Nice nose, quite good, but could have more charm	3	70	4
Louis M. Martini Mountain Red Light Burgundy	Powerful bouquet, a big strong wine. Good quality	2	41	1
Christian Brothers Burgundy	Fruity bouquet, trace of acidity, but quite a good flavour. Good quality	1	45	2
Paul Masson Burgundy	Plenty of fruit, but this was slightly corked, so this disadvantage had to be discounted as far as possible	4	76	5

In spite of the fact that this second group were more expensive, the lesser wines, i.e., those selling at under one dollar, appeared to be relatively better value.

Generic California Burgundy

The Wines	Characteristics	My Placing	Points Against	Group Placing
Live Oaks Premium California Burgundy $0.92	Medium colour, fruity nose, fruit and character. Very good value	1	31	1
Beringer Private Stock Napa Valley Burgundy $1.59	Medium colour, rather poor nose, thin and sour	11	98	10
Uvas Bonesio Winery California Burgundy $0.93	Weak colour, acetic nose, volatile acidity	12	126	12
Buena Vista Sonoma Burgundy $1.69	Medium colour, odd nose, sharp, thin, and acid	10	112	11
Inglenook 1966 North Coast Counties Vintage Burgundy $1.79	Medium colour, fair nose, dry, has fruit but tails off a bit	7	55	4
Samuele Sebastiani Premium Quality Bin 216 California Burgundy $1.50	Good colour, smells pleasantly of what— is it raspberry?— dry, and lacks finesse	6	62	6/7
D'Agostini Reserve California Burgundy $0.93	Good colour, good nose, has fruit and flavour, very good value in fact	2	54	3
Weibel California Burgundy $1.59	Good colour, only fair nose, trace of acidity, thin, dry, some tannin, unattractive	9	77	8/9
D'Agostini California Burgundy $0.78	Good colour, strange nose, sweet, round, the sugar covers lack of quality. Good value for the money	8	56	5

Generic California Burgundy (continued)

The Wines	Characteristics	My Placing	Points Against	Group Placing

Paul Masson
  Pure California
    Burgundy
        $1.59
	Good colour, quite
	a nice nose, dry
	but pleasant flavour
		4	77	8/9

Christian Brothers
  Select California
    Burgundy
        $1.59
	Medium colour,
	nice nose, plenty of
	fruit, dry finish
		5	62	6/7

Souverain
  Napa Valley Burgundy
        $2.00
	Medium colour,
	scented nose, light,
	and rather dry, but
	better quality
		3	44	2

All of the wines above have national distribution, with the exception of Uvas, D'Agostini, and Live Oaks, all small local wineries. Upon reflection, I think I was a little severe on the Inglenook and also on the D'Agostini, which the group placed fifth. Although three of them were "plain bad" and others not madly attractive, on the whole, they appeared to be considerably more agreeable than the cheap wine to which the British public is subjected. It must be admitted that few, if any of them, bore much resemblance to the name "Burgundy"!

These "jug" wines, as they are called here, are quoted at the rate per bottle, although they are obtainable in half-gallon and gallon containers.

White Wines, Group 1
From $0.89 to $1.00 a bottle

The Wines	Characteristics	My Placing	Points Against	Group Placing
Italian Swiss Colony Chablis $0.89	Slightly clumsy bouquet. Can this be the *Labrusca* grape? Tastes as it smells, with a tiny tang of bitterness at the finish	4	38	3/4
C. K. Mondavi Chablis $0.89	Fresh fruity nose, though slightly metallic, fruity, and quite pleasant	3	22	2
Gallo Chablis $0.99	Quite a pleasant bouquet, flavour not bad, but there is some acidity, or is it bitterness at the finish?	2	38	3/4
Italian Swiss Colony Napa, Sonoma, Mendocino $1.00	Pleasant fresh bouquet, good fruit and flavour	1	20	1

At first, I thought there must be something wrong with my own tasting, but everyone agreed there was a decidedly bitter finish to most of these wines. Can it be that for economic reasons they are squeezed through the press once too often, in order to extract the last "bitter drop"? It seemed, too, that the first group was really of better value than the second. Could it be that Group 2* came from the lesser wines of the finer grape varieties, and Group 1 from better grapes from the lesser varieties? Adverse as some of these comments may be, it must be remembered that these are all inexpensive, and one must not expect too much from cheap wines; in fact, most of them represent very good value.

* See page 56.

Similar Wines, Group 2
From $1.00 upwards a bottle

The Wines	Characteristics	My Placing	Points Against	Group Placing
Sebastiani Mountain White Dry Chablis $1.15	Nice bouquet, but dull and rather neutral. Slightly bitter finish	2	28	2
Louis M. Martini Chablis $1.39	Earthy nose, but good fruit, tastes better than it smells, tiny trace of bitterness	1	25	1
Almadén Mountain White Chablis $1.39	Fresh nose, but is there a touch of *Labrusca* here? Tastes as it smells, with touch of bitterness at the finish	4	31	3
Paul Masson Chablis $1.69	Nice fresh bouquet, quite a nice flavour, but once again that bitter finish	3	35	4

There were two other tastings, but since the results were unsatisfactory, the details are not recorded.

Rosé Wines. Most of these had an unattractive finish, a bitterness at the end of the taste.

California Champagne. With the exception of Hans Kornell and Christian Brothers, the wines were disappointing. However, this tasting could hardly be considered complete, because samples of Almadén Blanc de Blanc, Schramsberg, and Korbel were not present.

France,
1970 Visit

Burgundy, The Côte d'Or

Although there have been some good vintages during the past decade, 1961, 1962, 1964, 1966 and 1969—somehow, it does not appear that the Burgundians have been so affected by this tiresome "year-of-the-century" tag, and of these vintages, 1961 and 1969 have been outstanding.

Present-day Burgundy tends to develop early, so, except for those wise virgins who have kept some stock in their cellars, the 1961's have by now mostly been consumed, but the good ones which remain will doubtless continue to improve. The 1964's, many of which are ready to drink, are already stepping high and showing their paces, and soon it will be the turn of the 1966's, a fine all-round vintage which will afford a great amount of pleasure; 1967, a success for white wine, was nothing much to write home about for red, and 1968 (as in Bordeaux) was much worse. These relatively poor years in succession left the Burgundians, and everyone else, for that matter, deprived of stock of fine red wine, so when the 1969's appeared on the scene, there was widespread excitement. Digressing for a moment, it is interesting to note that 1967 was more successful for claret than red Burgundy, whereas the reverse appears to be the case in 1969.

As so often happens in a very good year, only a small amount of wine was produced, but the fine quality more than made up for this, so depending, of course, upon the source of supply, one can safely say that the 1969's, both red and white, are good, in fact, very good.

The season started off badly, the spring was cold and rainy, causing the vines to be some three weeks behind in their development. The continuing bad weather created havoc during the flowering season, one of the results being *coulure*, i.e., the dropping off of many of the tiny nascent grapes, indeed, one of the reasons for the small crop. Thus it was a godsend when in July the sun burst through and shone so strongly, belatedly retrieving a difficult situation.

The confidence which had been restored was dampened by a cold spell in August, but from the end of that month, continuing through September and October, splendid weather ensued, lasting until the harvest was gathered in. This engendered a quality which was beyond everyone's hopes.

This 1969 vintage, then, without perhaps the distinction of a "year-of-the-century" rating, is extremely good. The red wines have a deeper colour than usual, they are round and plump, and should, in time, develop a delightful bouquet. In a way, they may be similar to the good 1964's, which have turned out so well. The white wines too are successful, and may even be compared with the fine 1961's, which after nine years are still keeping well; they are fruity, with a very good flavour, and will provide some delights for the connoisseurs. (How lucky the Burgundians are with these two strings to their bow, for their white wines are the best in the world, and apart from 1963 and 1965, they have had a very good decade for white Burgundy.)

On account of the small crop, the prices were extremely high, but apparently this made little difference, for the merchants, both French and foreign, with very little stock of fine wine left in their cellars, rushed in to buy. My broker friends tell me that never before have they been so busy struggling with the horde of buyers, all scrambling madly for the new wine, and never before have they sold out a vintage so quickly. No wonder, then, that now in September of 1970 one is faced with the unprecedented situation of there not being any good 1969's either red or white left for sale in the growers' cellars—the cupboard is bare! Such, in fact, was the scramble to buy immediately after the vintage, that the growers who usually set aside some stock for domaine bottling and eventual sale at higher prices, at once disposed of everything they had. On this particular occasion, they found it proved easier to sell all their wine in wood (at the enhanced price they would eventually have sold it in bottle), thus avoiding all the responsibility of storage, bottling, and so on. They were then able to sit back and enjoy *la chasse* until the end of the season, for as football is to the Englishman, so is *la chasse* to the Frenchman!

Although merchants paid what they considered very high prices immediately after the vintage, it only cost them about half of what they would have had to pay had they waited until Christmas 1969; for example, wines such as Nuits, originally 1,800 francs had, by Christmas, reached over 3,000! Of course, this did not affect the great wines, because, in spite of their astronomical price at the outset, later on there were none left for sale!

This year the vineyards again suffered from a cold late spring, after which the weather slowly improved throughout the summer, finishing dry and sunny during the vital months of September and October. Thus the vintage was gathered in under good conditions, with the grapes in a state of perfect maturity.

As so often happens, however, on the 6th August parts of the Côte de Beaune were stricken by a violent hailstorm which devastated a large proportion of the vineyards, as much as from 30 percent to 70 percent; the most affected area being in the neighbourhood of Chassagne-Montrachet.

Grapes which have been lashed by hailstones do not make satisfactory wine, but in this case those affected dried up and fell off of their own accord, leaving incomplete but healthy bunches. There is thus no fear of the taste of hail in the resultant wine. (I would be loath to have to define this special taste, and must leave it to the reader's imagination!)

From the point of view of quantity, 1970 should prove to be an abundant vintage, especially for the red wines, the average quantity of 35 hectolitres per hectare being exceeded to reach about 45. (A hectare is roughly 2 ¼ acres.) This large production may mean that the red 1970's may cost less than the 1969's, though it is difficult to say much at this period just prior to the sale at the Hospices de Beaune.

Some of the cuves from the vines which overproduced are less good than others, so, once again, very careful selection will be necessary; all the same, the quality from the vines which produced more than the average, although less good perhaps, may well prove to be at least honest and straightforward.

On account of the smaller production, the quality of the white wines of 1970 should be superior to that of the red, and the price may be on the same level as for the 1969's.

Without attaining the deep hue of a great year, the red 1970's already have a pretty colour, which will no doubt improve still further with time. The vintage, as a whole, is a good healthy one, and probably will cause the vignerons less worry than usual during its early life.

Santenay

This delightful, typical Burgundian district lies at the very south-ernmost tip of the Côte de Beaune, not far, in fact, from the vine-yards of Chassagne-Montrachet. Though about 5 percent of its production is white wine, a wine incidentally one seldom comes across, it is chiefly known for the quality of the red, and, as else-where, this is made from the noble Pinot grape.

The vines cover gently sloping hillsides which are well exposed to the sun, and the wines, firm and velvety, acquire an attractive bouquet as they mature and develop in bottle. Locally, they are bottled some 15 to 18 months after the vintage, and one of their assets is that they can be drunk while comparatively young, but of course, they age splendidly in bottle and thus gain an increasingly attractive bouquet.

For some reason difficult to understand, Santenay is relatively little known insofar as classic Burgundy is concerned; it is therefore still comparatively reasonable in price and thus is much sought after by connoisseurs. The best-known vineyard, Les Gravières, dates back to the beginning of the seventeenth century; the other *premier crus* are La Comme, Clos de Tavannes, Beauregard, Le Passetemps, Beaurepaire, La Maladière, and Clos Rousseau.

Apart from the rigours and hardships of agriculture—and it can be extremely cold in Burgundy in wintertime—the trend of life is peaceful in these vineyards, where the proprietors hand down their land from generation to generation. All the growers I have met seem to own bits and pieces of vines scattered over the district, not that the plots owned by each one are necessarily large. Consequently, as you descend with them into the deep cellars with their walls glistening from moisture, your eye will take in not only the bins of bottles covered with thick Burgundian cobwebs, but also a wide variety of Santenay all maturing in cask, a few barrels, say, of the ordinary Santenay, some of Les Gravières, Clos de Tavannes, and so on. Tasting them in turn, you will quickly discover there is a decided difference between the ordinary Santenay and Les Gra-vières, also that each *premier cru* has its own special style and in-dividuality. These too vary from grower to grower on account of the soil, the vinification, post-natal care, and so on; thus, to seek out the best wine available can become quite a fine art.

I look forward so much to my annual visit to this unspoilt country village of Santenay, for somehow it is different from the others; here one is among the growers and accepted by them as a friend rather than as a customer. The day is arranged by my broker friend, Robert Paillard, in conjunction with Monsieur Louis Clair, in whose twelfth-century cellar the tastings take place. On this occasion, apart from Monsieur Lucien Muzard, who at the last minute was unable to come, three others were present, all of whom had kindly brought bottles of their own wine for the tasting: Louis' brother, Francois Clair, André Monot together with his son, and Monsieur Jean Moreau.

There had been some overnight rain, and the weather was still unsettled, rather unwelcome only a week or so before the vintage was due to begin. All the same, conditions could have been much worse, and given three weeks of sunshine, some useful wine could still be made in 1970. Insofar as the finest quality of Santenay is concerned, there will not be an abundance of *grand vin* this year, because from 80 to 100 percent of the best vineyards—Les Gravières, Clos de Tavannes, La Comme, etc.—had been seriously damaged by hail earlier in the summer. (Although complained of bitterly at the time, these hailstorms, by reducing the crop, turned out to be beneficial in the long run for the white wines of 1970, and on the whole they are more successful than the red. There was overproduction among the red wines, and this is never very good where quality is concerned.)

Beginning with 1969, there were three vintages to taste, 1966 and 1964, all successful years for red Burgundy. Good as a few of them may be, the 1967's generally are somewhat irregular.

The 1969's were especially noticeable on account of their splendid dark colour.

In spite of the slight tingle of fermentation present in one or two of these wines, they are all clearly of very good quality.

The names of the growers have been included, but at the time of the tasting, I did not know which wine was which.

Santenay 1969 (all from the cask)

Santenay, Clos de Tavannes. (Louis Clair).
Although this had recently been fined, it was possible to

discern the high underlying quality. Good bouquet, fruity, full-bodied, and well-balanced.

Santenay. (Louis Clair).
Still fermenting a little, and also recently fined. Very good fruit and flavour. At 14 percent, this is fairly strong in alcohol!

Santenay, Croix Sorine. (Francois Clair).
Lovely bouquet, a fine big, round, full-bodied wine.

Côte de Beaune-Villages, Clos de la Boutière. (André Monot).
M. Monot's vines grow just over the border of Santenay, but in style the wine is very similar. Interesting bouquet, a wine full of charm and very well-balanced.

Santenay, Clos des Mouches. (Jean Moreau).
Distinguished bouquet, this has a delicious taste combined with great elegance.

Santenay 1966 (all in bottle)

Santenay. (Louis Clair).
Deep colour, good nose, delightful flavour, round and attractive, and it finishes well. More forward than the other 1966's and ready to drink.

Santenay, Clos de Tavannes. (Louis Clair).
Good colour, fine deep bouquet, lots of fruit, but still has some tannin. An excellent bottle for the future.

Côte de Beaune-Villages, Clos de la Boutière. (André Monot).
Good colour, lovely nose, good fruit, round and full-bodied. Fine quality, needs time.

Santenay. (Jean Moreau).
Good colour, bouquet beginning to develop nicely, big and full-bodied. Good flavour too, but it still needs a year or so in bottle.

Santenay. (Lucien Muzard).
Good colour, nice nose, good fruit.

Santenay 1964

Santenay, Les Gravières. (Louis Clair).
Fine deep colour, a fabulous bouquet, great finesse, and a lovely taste. As far as Santenay is concerned, this bottle seemed near perfection; how I wish I had some in my own cellar!

Santenay, La Comme. (Louis Clair).
Deep colour, delightful bouquet, a huge wine, rich and round. Still some tannin, so will continue to improve, but at a pinch can be drunk now.

Côte de Beaune-Villages, Clos de la Boutière. (André Monot).
Good colour, fine bouquet, rich and round, almost reminiscent of chocolate, though that may be an unfair comparison! Quite delightful anyway, and ready to drink now.

Santenay. (Jean Moreau).
Medium colour, nice deep rich bouquet, a lovely big robust wine, needs two or three years to reach its best.

Santenay. (Lucien Muzard).
Fascinating bouquet, full of facets. Good fruit and body.

As though we had not done sufficient tasting during the morning, M. Moreau invited us all to his house, which is about a hundred yards up the road. There, in his fifteenth-century cellar, which he has decorated attractively to receive his friends, he opened for us not one, but three *vins d'honneur* in the form of his 1962, 1961, and 1959 vintages! Here, if ever, there was ample proof, if any were needed, of the quality and charm of these wines of Santenay and how well they develop in bottle.

14th September, 1970
Henri de Villamont, Savigny-les-Beaune

Our visit to Savigny-les-Beaune took place on a rather stormy morning, following a night of wind and rain. So far, though, the weather had been reasonably good, and apart from hail damage on the Côte de Beaune, the crop should be abundant. It is the same old story, no matter what wine district you may happen to be in, what is needed at this time of the year are several weeks of sunshine to ripen off the grapes.

Henri de Villamont is an old established business whose spick-and-span nineteenth-century premises overlook its own Savigny vineyards. At the time of our visit these vines were almost over-burdened with healthy-looking clusters of purple grapes. A good presage for the forthcoming vintage.

Henri de Villamont was purchased in 1964 by the important Swiss firm of Schenk of Geneva. The managing director is Monsieur S. Haeni, also a Swiss, who for many years was responsible for the purchasing of wine for the vast organisation of Nicolas, an experience which must have been quite invaluable to anyone in the wine world.

Tasting wine in Burgundy can be illuminating—at some establishments you taste a range differing, of course, in style and quality, but with the same theme running through them all. At others, and they are a chosen few, you find the unblended wines. Such things are not to be discerned by reading through a list of tasting notes, but they become abundantly clear to the experienced taster.

Evidently we were in the latter category with Henri de Villamont, whose policy is to sell pure, unblended wines from the growers, and this was to be amply corroborated later on by the brokers who help them with some of their buying. When I commented upon the marked individuality of each wine, M. Haeni told us that these were the growers' unblended ones, no more, no less! In order to illustrate this point, he went on to say that recently he had arranged quite an important tasting for the members of a visiting Italian Chamber of Commerce and included among the tasters naturally was M. Senard, the president of the Chamber of Commerce of Beaune, himself a wine grower. During the course of this blind tasting M. Senard had the excitement of picking out his own wine, a sure proof of the absence of blending. Now this is a pretty remarkable feat, because I have attended many blind tastings in Bordeaux and elsewhere when the proprietors have been present and have been unable to pick out their own ewe lambs! This is not at all surprising, but it is always a great comfort and reassurance for the rest of us who have a lot to do with tasting! Personally, I am always glad when I have got over the hump of deciding whether a wine is Burgundy or Bordeaux!

Since the last good vintage for red Burgundy is 1966, that is to say, apart from 1969, I was interested to know how this particular vintage (i.e., 1966) was developing in bottle, and so had asked M. Haeni if he would be kind enough to let me try some. These, then, are my notes on the wines I tasted, all of which had a good colour:

1966 Vintage Red Burgundy

Vosne-Romanée.
　　　Pleasant bouquet, good fruit, and well-made.

Bonnes Mares.
　　　Fine bouquet, elegant and attractive, though it finishes a little dry.

Gevrey-Chambertin, les Cazetiers.
　　　Fine bouquet and fine quality, well-balanced, not yet fully developed.

Gevrey-Chambertin, Estournelles Saint-Jacques.
　　　A huge bouquet, but not fully developed. A fine wine. full of fruit and flavour, this needs time to mature.

Gevrey-Chambertin Lavaux Saint-Jacques.
　　　Delightful bouquet, here is a fine full-bodied wine.

Charmes-Chambertin.
　　　Unusually deep colour, a great big nose, and the flavour absolutely fills the mouth; this is impressive.

Chambertin Clos de Bèze.
　　　Magnificent bouquet, fine and full-bodied, excellent quality.

Hospices de Beaune, Beaune Clos des Avaux.
> Charming bouquet, light perhaps, but a delightful flavour, and good quality.

Hospices de Beaune, Volnay Général Muteau.
> Good nose, but a little harder than the Clos des Avaux; plenty of fruit, though, and a good flavour. Has more tannin and is the better of the two.

Domaine-bottled wines (Domaine Veuve Modo)

Chambolle Musigny Premier Cru.
> Pretty bouquet, fine quality, and will make a good bottle.

Grands Echézeaux.
> Lovely bouquet, a little fuller than the Chambolle Musigny, and a bigger wine.

Nineteen-sixty-six is clearly fulfilling its promise as a very good vintage, and the quality seems to be well above the average. All the wines tasted appear to be developing nicely, though most of them need a year or so still to reach their best.

Later, on, M. Feurty acted as our host for lunch at a restaurant situated out in the country about six miles away from Savigny. It is called the Hostellerie du Vieux Moulin (Bouilland), and the host there, M. Raymond Heriot, a man of some considerable personality, produces specially good food. You choose the main dish for yourself, but the custom here is to give M. Heriot a free hand with the first courses. We began with *tourteau de caneton*, a hot terrine, enclosed in a pastry crust, spicy, full of flavour, and all the better for having been marinated in the same excellent Meursault Charmes 1966 which accompanied our meal. The light *quenelles de truite* which followed were really delicious, and our main dish was the regional speciality, *poussin de Bresse truffée, à la creme aux morilles.* The sauces served during this lunch were remarkable for their extreme delicacy. This may read as a rather heavy meal, but in fact it was the very reverse, and afterwards it was possible to appreciate that recommendation for any good restaurant, no feeling of having overeaten! The gastronomic temptations in and around Burgundy are so great that, to use an American expression, one has "to watch it!"

The 1961 Vintage:
Saint-Emilions and Pomerols

This vintage still stands supreme—supreme above all others since 1945. Annually our hopes are forever raised that there will be a repetition of similar quality, and if we are to believe the press, something equally good does indeed occur with almost unfailing regularity. Alas, this is a fallacy and like all the unusually good things of life, rather exceptional circumstances are required to produce very great quality. There is no short-cut, it seems; it has to come the hard way, and all too infrequently at that.

Since, by and large, the 1961's are so splendid, and yet so few of them ready to drink, the covetous claret lover, like myself, tends to taste his 1961's at someone else's expense, thus saving his own precious bottles for the time when they will be at their best.

What about the Saint-Emilions and Pomerols of this great vintage? Somehow, writers do not seem to enthuse overmuch over these two districts; it is always the Médocs, *les enfants gâtés*, of Bordeaux which catch the eye.

The pundits write reams about the elegance, the distinction, and the "race" of the Médocs, which they undoubtedly have, but say far less about the wines from across the River Dordogne. They may not be so fashionable, but many of them make really delicious drinking and are especially acceptable to those among us who like a round, full-bodied wine. Unashamedly, I must confess to a decided weakness for them myself, and especially for some of the wines of Pomerol. I will go even further by saying that people are missing golden opportunities in concentrating almost entirely on the Médocs, for to obtain a fully balanced view of red Bordeaux, Saint-Emilion and Pomerol must not be overlooked. For a proof of this, you have only to read the tasting notes further on. All the same, it should be remembered that every year which is good for the Médoc is not necessarily good for Saint-Emilion, and vice versa, and these finer points are worthy of attention by the man who is building up a cellar.

See p. 174

Nowadays, it is admitted that the giants from these two districts, those worthy protagonists, Pétrus and Cheval Blanc, will often give the first growths a good run for their money and at times even be a short neck ahead. Also, it should not be forgotten that some vintages especially favour the Saint-Emilions and Pomerols (1964 and 1967 are a good example of this), and we may find that some of the 1970's from these districts are likely to be even more successful than the Médocs, if only because 1970 was such a splendid year for the Merlot grape.

So far, my notes on the 1961 vintage have covered only the Médocs, but I can now extend the range, for, thanks to M. Jean-Pierre Moueix of Libourne, I was able to taste and assess a number of the leading growths of Saint-Emilion and Pomerol. As will be seen, 1961 was every bit as successful for those districts as for everywhere else in the Bordeaux region. There were three main sections for the tasting: first, seven Saint-Emilions; second, eight Pomerols; and third, the three great, great wines, *les grands seigneurs*, of the two districts—Ausone, Cheval Blanc, and Pétrus. No bottles were visible, merely glasses half-filled with wine, so there was no inkling as to which wine was which. The utmost care was taken not only to make the necessary notes, but also to mark the wines according to quality, on a scale of 1 to 20.

Saint-Emilion

> *La Gaffelière,* (Premier Grand Cru).
> > Very deep colour, full bouquet, heaps of fruit, but a tiny trace of acidity was in evidence. 14+/20

> *La Clotte,* (Grand Cru).
> > Deep colour, good nose, medium body, and well-balanced. 15/20

> *Pavie,* (Premier Grand Cru).
> > Good colour, good nose, a lovely big mouthful of wine, excellent quality. 18/20

> *Curé-Bon-La-Madeleine,* (Grand Cru).
> > Deep colour, lovely bouquet, well-made, well-balanced, still some tannin. Needs some years yet. 16+/20

> *Clos Fourtet,* (Premier Grand Cru).
> > Very deep colour, good nose, but thin, rather sharp, and less attractive than the others. 14/20

Magdelaine, (Premier Grand Cru).
> Deep colour; lovely, rich, deep bouquet; a powerful, round, well-made wine; a real beauty. 18+/20

Figeac, (Premier Grand Cru).
> Almost black colour, lovely bouquet, not quite so big as the Magdelaine, but full of fruit. Well-balanced and has great distinction. Marvellous quality. 18/20

I can remember how good the 1961 Figeac was right from the beginning, and kick myself for not buying some at the time; my only consolation is that, at least, I have a case of Magdelaine! These two wines were so exceptional that I asked for them to be put on one side to take part in a final tasting against Ausone and Cheval Blanc.

Then followed a selection of some of the really great châteaux of Pomerol, and I found these had perhaps an even blacker colour and an even greater density than the Saint-Emilions, and that is indeed saying something.

Pomerol

Vieux-Château-Certan. (Premier Grand Cru).
> Very deep colour, lovely nose, round, buxom, charming, and delicious—how many more adjectives can one think of? 16/20

Lagrange. (Grand Cru).
> Very deep colour, lovely bouquet, a fine powerful wine with a special character of its own, plenty of tannin, beautifully made. 16+/20

La Fleur-Pétrus. (Premier Grand Cru).
> Very deep colour, lovely nose, rich and round, in fact, a great mouthful of delight, fabulous! 18/20

Lafleur. (Premier Grand Cru).
> "Black" colour, fine bouquet, special smell and special taste, the latter strongly reminiscent of black currants. A little lighter than the others, with perhaps less charm and less richness, also a little acidity to lose. 15+/20

Latour-Pomerol. (Premier Grand Cru).
> "Black" colour, full, fragrant bouquet, a great round, rich, full-bodied wine, packed up to the brim with fruit. 19/20.

La Conseillante. (Premier Grand Cru).
>
> Good colour, beautiful nose, good fruit, good quality, but does not finish quite so well, nor has it such charm as some of the others. A lot of tannin. 15/20

Trotanoy. (Premier Grand Cru).
>
> Very deep colour, fabulous bouquet, complete, and very well-made. 17+/20

Evangile. (Premier Grand Cru).
>
> Deep colour, wonderful bouquet, beautifully made, a real aristocrat. 17/20

Such was my enthusiasm after tasting these wines that, at the time, I made the following note: "These are really fabulous; never in my life do I expect to find anything greater!" Thus, fine as the Saint-Emilions were, the Pomerols were even more overwhelming, but much of this enthusiasm may spring, of course, from my own personal predeliction towards Pomerol!

The last group for tasting were the three "greats"—Ausone, Cheval Blanc, and Pétrus—and although there were no bottles around, it was not difficult to tell at once which wine was which. Furthermore, throughout the whole tasting, it was comforting to find I had placed the wines in exactly the same order as Jean-Pierre Moueix and his nephew, Jean-Jacques.

The Great Pomerols

Cheval Blanc. (Premier Grand Cru).
>
> Very deep colour, a great big bouquet, rich and powerful, this is a "knock-out"! 20/20

Ausone. (Premier Grand Cru).
>
> Deep colour, great finesse on nose, well-balanced, and well-made. Distinguished and clearly of fine quality, but not quite so big as the other two. 18/20

Pétrus. (Premier Grand Cru).
>
> Very deep colour, tremendously rich bouquet, round and rich, and a whole cornucopia of flavours—well nigh perfection. Still some tannin to lose. 20+/20

(I have been advised never to give 20/20, always to leave a margin, but these two wines are so great, it was impossible to resist! I had encountered the same problem with the "star performers" of the Médoc!)

Finally, to set my mind straight, we had a last blind tasting of the four best Saint-Emilions, and they came out in this order: Cheval Blanc, Magdelaine, Ausone, and Figeac. This was rather as I had expected.

Realising the exceptional quality of some of the wines tasted on this day makes me regret that when, early in 1962, I laid down my 1961's, I concentrated almost entirely on the Médocs, not that the latter are not of wonderful quality, or that there is anything wrong with buying them, but some 1961 Saint-Emilions and Pomerols would not have come amiss among them. Steps have since been taken to rectify this lapse to a certain extent, but it is not at all easy at this late stage.

To sum up, then, 1961 is an exceptional vintage for the districts of Saint-Emilion and Pomerol, and now, late in 1970, after some seven years in bottle, the wines are beginning to blossom out sufficiently to show what they will be capable of in a few years' time.

1st October, 1970

The Médocs of 1967

Quite naturally the 1967 clarets have engendered considerable interest, and now that the wines have had some twelve months in which to settle down in bottle, it may be a good moment to take a further look at this very useful vintage—useful not only because of its generally high quality but also on account of its being an unusually large crop.

Excellent as they undoubtedly are, the 1966's, when they first came on the market, were considered to be rather expensive, so it was a welcome relief when the attractive and prolific 1967's followed hard on their heels; for reasons too long to go into here, the latter, at the outset, were a good deal cheaper and thus constituted very good value. Unfortunately, these halycon days did not last for very long, because the advent of the indifferent 1968's soon began to push up the prices. All the same, some wise merchants were able to take advantage of the situation and so bought at reasonable rates.

It is unusual for two fine vintages to emerge in quick succession, and even more so that they should be so similar in style. If one compares the two years alongside, wine for wine the 1966's appear to be better than the 1967's and have, generally speaking, more depth, although it does not apply 100 percent. This difference, however, may become more pronounced as time goes by. In any event, the 1967's have a fine deep colour, a delightful bouquet, and a fruity charming flavour; in other words, they are what one could consider as very good claret. They may not take too long to develop, either, so we can look forward to enjoying them before too long a time has elapsed.

Good as they are, though, their imperfections must be faced. As will be seen from these notes, especially concerning the crus bourgeois, some of the grapes in the Médoc could well have been riper when they were picked, and this caused a certain amount of greenness in some of the resultant wine. (Greenness should not be confused with acidity.) As it turns out, 1967 may prove to be an even better vintage for the wines of Saint-Emilion and Pomerol

74

than for the Médoc, because the Merlot grapes which predominate in those two districts were fully ripe and were picked under excellent climatic conditions, whereas about a week later, when it was the turn of the Cabernet Sauvignons in the Médoc, although the weather was not too bad, there were some grey days and occasional showers.

Here I am primarily concerned with the Médocs, but at a blind tasting of a range of the 1967 vintage the top wines of Saint-Emilion and Pomerol, as will be seen, undoubtedly distinguished themselves. The points given are from 1 to 20.

The Great Wines of 1967

Lynch-Bages. (Pauillac).
Medium colour, browning a bit, bouquet fair, good fruit, medium body. 11/20

La Mission-Haut-Brion. (Graves).
Deep colour, nice bouquet, lots of fruit, full-bodied, robust, and finishes well. 16/20

Cos d'Estournel. (Saint-Estèphe).
Medium colour, attractive bouquet, medium body, average quality. 14–15/20

Haut-Brion. (Graves).
Good colour and nose, full-bodied, finishes well, good quality. 17/20

Calon-Ségur. (Saint-Estèphe).
Medium colour, attractive nose, on light side but pleasant. 15/20

Mouton-Rothschild. (Pauillac).
Medium colour, full bouquet, a big wine, plenty of fruit, trace of acidity though. 18/20

Pichon-Longueville-Lalande. (Pauillac).
Good colour, pronounced bouquet, good fruit, but could have more charm. 15+/20

Margaux. (Margaux).
Good colour, fruity bouquet, medium body, a little tannin. but well-balanced. 17–18/20

Pichon-Longueville-Baron. (Pauillac).
Good colour, attractive nose, medium body, a little greenness, which is not too attractive at the moment. 12/20

Cheval Blanc. (Saint-Emilion).
Medium colour, very nice nose, good fruit, attractive, and well made. 19/20

Brane-Cantenac. (Cantenac).
Very good colour, attractive bouquet, medium body, some greenness, but good quality. 17/20

Ausone. (Saint-Emilion).
Good colour and bouquet, on light side, but nicely made and has a good finish. 17/20

Ducru-Beaucaillou. (Saint-Julien).
Good colour, elegant bouquet, a lot of fruit and body, some tannin, so needs time. 17/20

Pétrus. (Pomerol).
Very deep colour, fruity nose, full, round and fruity, most excellent. 19+/20

Latour. (Pauillac).
Very deep colour, full fruity bouquet, good body, but rather backward and somewhat overwhelmed by the potency and seduction of the preceding wine. 17/20

Rausan-Ségla. (Margaux).
Good colour, pleasant bouquet, medium body, special flavour, some acidity. 10/20

Léoville-Poyferré. (Saint-Julien).
Good colour, full bouquet, plenty of body, but has some acidity. 10/20

Léoville-Las Cases. (Saint-Julien).
Deep colour, full bouquet, good fruit and a lot of tannin. 15/20

Lafite. (Pauillac.)
Medium colour, very good nose, medium fruit and body, but has great distinction. 16/20

Beychevelle. (Saint-Julien).
Deep colour, elegant bouquet, not a big wine, but full of fruit and is well-made. 15+/20

Montrose. (Saint-Estèphe).
> Very deep colour, a good full bouquet, a great big wine, some tannin, and there is a little greenness. 16/20

(The points from 1 to 20 apply within each group, but do not serve to compare groups.)

As will be seen, Pétrus came out an easy winner, with Cheval Blanc as a close runner-up. Latour was not showing at its best on this occasion, nor, for that matter, were Haut-Brion and La-Mission-Haut-Brion, two châteaux for which I have a great respect. On the other hand, Lafite was most distinguished, and both Brane-Cantenac and Ducru-Beaucaillou, as it so often does, came out well. Twenty-one wines were more than I like to taste at a time, and I would have preferred to set aside for another occasion the first growths, together with Pètrus, Cheval Blanc, Ausone, and Mouton, as is done so successfully by the tasting groups in California. As a matter of interest, I think La Mission-Haut-Brion could also be included among the celebrities, for I have a shrewd suspicion it would acquit itself well in such distinguished company.

When the time came to taste the *crus bourgeois*, there was such an abundance of samples that they had to be divided into two parts, the better wines being reserved for the second day. As may be expected, there was a sharp rise in quality among the wines tasted during the second phase, so, in accordance with general practice, it should be stressed that the points from 1 to 20 on the first day bear no relation to those on the second.

The Crus Bourgeois and some of the Crus Artisans

La Salle de Pez. (Saint-Estèphe).
> Quite a good colour, pleasant bouquet, plenty of fruit, a touch of greenness, and some tannin. Could have more quality. 12+/20

La Tour de By. (Bégadan).
> Good colour, nice scented nose, plenty of fruit, good quality, still some tannin, a full-bodied wine. (Incidentally, this has been awarded a gold medal.) 16/20

Gallais-Bellevue. (Ordonnac-et-Potensac).
> Medium colour, fragrant bouquet, medium body, on light side. 14/20

Lassalle. (Ordonnac-et-Potensac).
Medium colour, fragrant bouquet, medium body, quite nicely made, well-balanced, with a little tannin. 15/20

Potensac. (Ordonnac-et-Potensac).
Medium colour, light bouquet, on light side, and finishes rather sharp. 12/20

Patache d'Aux. (Bégadan).
Medium colour, fruity bouquet, good fruit, and nicely made. 15/20

Saint-Bonnet. (Saint-Christoly).
Good colour, full bouquet, good fruit, and well-made. 15+/20

Les Ormes Sorbet, A.C. Médoc. (Couqueques).
Medium colour, poor nose, not much body and rather poor quality. 9/20

Des Moulinets. (Saint-Sauveur).
Good colour, full, fruity nose, light to medium body, nothing special. 13+/20

Du Broustéras, A.C. Médoc. (Saint Yzans).
Good colour, attractive bouquet, good fruit with special flavour, lacks breeding. 13/20

Clos la Forest, A.C. Médoc. (Saint-Christoly).
Fair colour, quite a nice nose, but thin with slight bitterness at the finish. 10/20

Crus Bourgeois

Bel-Air Marquis-d'Aligre. (Margaux).
Medium colour, pleasant bouquet, light and attractive, with quite a lot of charm; in fact, easy to taste. 14/20

La Tour-de-Mons. (Margaux).
Good colour, not much nose, but good fruit, bigger than the Bel-Air, but has less charm and is still a little green. 13+/20

Labégorce-Zédé. (Margaux).
Good colour, fairly full bouquet, has fruit and body, but is still hard and rigid. 14/20

Chasse-Spleen. (Moulis).
   Darker colour, attractive bouquet, good fruit, but is rather green. 12/20

Poujeaux. (Moulis).
   Good colour, fruity bouquet, good fruit, but also green and undeveloped. 12+/20

Gressier-Grand-Poujeaux. (Moulis).
   Very good colour, full bouquet, good fruit, well-made, but needs time. Also a touch of greenness. 13/20

Fourcas-Hosten. (Listrac).
   Medium colour, attractive bouquet, good fruit, light to medium body, nice flavour. 15/20

Liversan. (Saint-Sauveur).
   Good colour, quite a full bouquet, but lacks charm, and has a green finish. Needs time. 13/20

Lanessan. (Cussac).
   Deep colour, very nice nose, good fruit and body, well-made. This should make an attractive bottle. 16/20

Terrey-Gros-Caillou. (Saint-Julien).
   Deep colour, good nose, good fruit and body, but still green and undeveloped. 13+/20

Gloria. (Saint-Julien).
   Deep colour, charming bouquet, well-balanced, and has a good flavour. 16/20

Du Glana. (Saint-Julien).
   Good colour, distinguished bouquet, good fruit, good quality, not a big wine, could have more charm. 13/20

Phélan-Ségur. (Saint-Estèphe).
   Rather light colour, attractive nose, medium body, special flavour. 13/20

De Pez. (Saint-Estèphe).
   Good deep colour, fairly full bouquet, a big round, full-bodied wine, still rather overlaid with tannin. 16/20

Beau-Site-Haut-Vignoble. (Saint-Estèphe).
   Good colour, fairly powerful bouquet, good fruit, but lacks charm, still rather green. 11/20

Les-Ormes-de-Pez. (Saint-Estèphe).
Medium colour, attractive bouquet, full-bodied, with a lot of "meat," needs time. 16/20

An interesting point to note is how, at tastings similar to these, vintage after vintage, certain châteaux emerge with a quality which seems, to me at any rate, superior to the others. These are Gloria of Saint-Julien, de Pez of Saint-Estèphe, and Lanessan from Cussac. Château Liversan is often in the running, but on this particular occasion it did not distinguish itself as well as usual.

Since the price of the classified growths has risen to such an "uncomfortable" level, these *crus bourgeois*, as well as the wines from the Côtes-de-Fronsac, Bourg, and Blaye, are assuming an ever-increasing importance for the man of ordinary means. It is hoped, therefore, that the result of these tastings may not only be informative to the well-to-do, but also to the more impecunious collector. The term "collector" is used expressly here, because as yet, the 1967's are by no means ready to drink. When well selected, the *crus bourgeois* can be offered with pride to the most discerning of guests, and for a proper "claret evening," they form an ideal lead-up for the greater wine to follow.

Eight months later, at another blind tasting of this vintage, and again in Bordeaux, there were some minor changes. Although, on this occasion, Lafite was not included, Cheval Blanc came out on top, with Pétrus and Latour equal second. We all know how good the 1967 Pétrus is, so perhaps it was going through an "off period" in bottle.

According to the second tasting, on 28th June 1971, two wines which have made great progress are Brane-Cantenac and Pichon-Longueville-Baron. Paired directly with Château Margaux, the Brane-Cantenac appeared to be the better of the two. Pichon-Baron always takes a long time to get under way, so it is understandable it should only now begin to show its quality.

The Red Graves

What, people ask, is the mystery of the red Graves, and why is so little written about them? Admittedly, the area is very small, but apart from sedate chapters in the textbooks, they are virtually ignored. It appears to be a fact that, except for three or four outstanding châteaux, they are not so fashionable as the Médocs, or even, for that matter, the Saint-Emilions and Pomerols.

Stirred thus to action and knowing I was shortly to spend several days at La Mission-Haut-Brion. I asked my host-to-be if he would be so kind as to arrange some tastings for me, tastings of recent vintages which would be of interest to readers, and, as will be seen, his response was well in accord with his customary generosity. Fortunately, we had two good vintages at our disposal, and my most grateful thanks go to the proprietors who so kindly presented bottles for this occasion; all the same, I only wish I could have been more laudatory with some of my comments!

First of all, though, to put you in the picture, as it were, a little "textbook background" may not come amiss! Although the finest red Graves are produced south of Bordeaux, few people are aware that the district in fact stretches from well to the north of the city from the Jalle de Blanquefort, and then, as is well known, extends southwards as far as Leognan. These vineyards of the Graves district existed in ancient times, long before those of the Médoc were even thought of, and this was the source of the wine which was shipped to England in the Middle Ages. Strange as it may seem these days, the greater part of it was the red and not the white variety. The soil in the northern part of this noted wine district is poor and gravelly and thus more suitable for the production of red wine, but as you travel southwards, the white wines take over, dry at first, from communes like Villenave d'Ornan and Cadaujac, and progressively becoming sweeter on account of the richer soils of Cérons, Barsac, and Sauternes.

The leading light of the district, the only first growth of the Graves in the classification of 1855, is of course, the famous Château Haut-Brion, which property has been proverbial ever since the eighteenth century, one of its many illustrious owners being

Talleyrand, the French foreign minister in the troubled times of Napoleon. Standing nearby is the other bright constellation, Château La Mission-Haut-Brion, documented as having been acquired by the Lazarites in the seventeenth century. Dipping even further into history, the not too distant vineyard of Château Pape-Clément was planted in 1200 by Bertrand de Goth, later Pope Clément V. The most ancient vineyard in the region recorded by name, but now, alas, only half the size it was fifty years ago, the rest having been sold for building land, it still preserves a great reputation for quality. We must be thankful that, unlike oil wells, good vineyards do not dry up. All the same, their produce varies with the seasons, and above all, according to the ability of their respective owners, all of which adds greatly to the interest of red Bordeaux.

There are records from the eighteenth century of "Pontac" or "Pontac claret" being sold in England; this was a red Graves coming from the estates of the Marquis de Pontac (at that time the owner of Haut-Brion), and within only the last two years, one of the properties which once belonged to him, Château Pontac-Monplaisir, a producer of a delightful wine, has been split up and almost destroyed by the new autoroute from Bordeaux to Toulouse. A further vinous disaster is to be perpetrated shortly when yet another autoroute encroaches upon part of the vineyard of La Mission-Haut-Brion, but sufficient unto the day is the evil of that desecration!

True to its name, the soil of this district is gravel, and this gravel was deposited when in prehistoric times the river bed was very much wider. In fact, a band of it follows the line of the river up through the Médoc as far as Pauillac, because this heavily pebbled soil is equally evident in the vineyard of Latour. Vineyards seem to thrive on gravel just as a good car has a better performance on super petrol or gasoline.

The vines grown are more or less the same as in the Médoc, a large proportion of Cabernet Sauvignon with some Merlot and Cabernet Franc. These vines, in conjunction with the stony soil, produce a most splendid and distinctive type of wine which has a bouquet and a flavour all of its own. Slower generally to develop, the fine red wines of this district often outlast the aristocrats of the Médoc.

Curiously enough, the greatest vineyards of the Graves district, and indeed almost of all Bordeaux, are to be found literally in the southern suburbs of the city, namely Châteaux Haut-Brion and La Mission-Haut-Brion. These two estates on either side of the highway to Arcachon lie in the communes of Pessac and Talence respectively, although parts of the Haut-Brion vineyard are also situated across the road, cheek by jowl with La Mission-Haut-Brion.

Château Pape-Clément, in the same area, has also been spared from destruction, but in times not too long ago, other fine vineyards existed in this immediate area, but these, alas, have been strangled and swallowed up by that voracious octopus, the spreading city of Bordeaux. The suburban sprawl now covering their gravelly soil in no way is any compensation for their disappearance.

Year after year, under the able direction of M. Jean Delmas, Château Haut-Brion goes from strength to strength, producing some of the best wine, often rivalling and frequently surpassing the other first growths of the Médoc. In fact, it has had a run of successes recently, i.e., 1966, 1967, 1968, and 1969, four vintages in succession. Combining great elegance with great quality, it matures reasonably early. One does not come across its second wine very often, Château Bahans, but in spite of the fact that it is sold without a vintage, it can still be very agreeable.

Through the skill of its owner, M. Henri Woltner, a veritable wizard among winemakers, Château La Mission-Haut-Brion can now hold its head up with any of the great growths of Bordeaux. Usually darker of colour than Haut-Brion, and perhaps more full-bodied, it takes some time to develop, and one has only to taste its 1965 against any other wine of that vintage to gauge how successful it can be in the off-years. In 1958 too it was a great success, and the 1960 is now coming along nicely, while many other 1960's are beginning to fall back in the race.

Château La Tour-Haut-Brion, which also belongs to the Woltner family, produces only an average of eighteen *tonneaux* per annum. Very similar in style to La Mission, the quality is first-rate, but on account of the slightly richer soil, without perhaps the same finesse. Some of the older vintages of this château are quite remarkable.

Comparisons are odious, but one might perhaps compare the style and quality of Haut-Brion with, say, Lafite, feminine, graceful and superbly bred, while La Mission resembles more Latour, the latter masculine, dark, sturdy and slow to develop. After that, it is merely a question of personal taste!

Apologies are made for the considerable space devoted to the wines of Pessac and Talence, but it must be remembered that it is recognised as the number-one area for red Graves. This is by no means to say that other communes do not have fine vineyards within their confines, because indeed they do, and it will be amply proved by the tasting notes on the two good vintages which are to follow.

Given below are the principal growths of the red Graves, in accordance with the Classification of 1953 to 1959.

Pessac: Haut-Brion, Pape-Clément.

Talence: La Mission-Haut-Brion, La Tour-Haut-Brion.

Léognan: Haut-Bailly, Domaine de Chevalier, Carbonnieux, Malartic-Lagravière, Olivier, de Fieuzal.

Martillac: Smith-Haut-Lafitte, Latour-Martillac.

Cadaujac: Bouscaut.

The 1967 Red Graves
(All of these wines have a good colour.)

Olivier. (Léognan).
Attractive bouquet, good fruit, but rather green, with con-considerable acidity to lose. 9/20

De Fieuzal. (Léognan).
Full bouquet, attractive flavour, finishes well. Successful and may be ready comparatively early. 14/20

Bouscaut. (Cadaujac).
Pleasant, interesting bouquet, good fruit and body, but some greenness and a lot of acidity. 10/20

Carbonnieux. (Léognan).
Good fruit and flavour. 13/20

Malartic-Lagravière. (Léognan).
Quite a deep bouquet, but lacks charm, some greenness. 10/20

Smith-Haut-Lafitte. (Martillac).
Good bouquet, but lacks charm. 10/20

Pape-Clément. (Pessac).
Nice full bouquet, medium body, well-made, and finishes

nicely, though there is just a trace of acidity. A marked improvement was evident here. 14+/20

Haut-Bailly. (Léognan).
Attractive bouquet, full-bodied, round, complete, and well-made. One of the successes of this tasting. 16/20

Latour-Martillac. (Martillac).
Attractive full bouquet, medium body, some acidity, and not showing well at the moment. 14/20

La Mission-Haut-Brion. (Talence).
Distinguished fruity bouquet, heaps of fruit, tremendous elegance, and beautifully balanced. 18/20

Haut-Brion. (Pessac). First growth.
Full, attractive bouquet, well-made, well-balanced, great elegance, great quality. Quite different in style from La-Mission. 18/20

Domaine de Chevalier. (Léognan).
Charming bouquet, well-made, but has a touch of greenness; good, but not great. Needs two to three years. 14/20

(The points from 1 to 20 are not to be compared with those for the 1966 vintage which were tasted on the following day.)

After tasting some of these 1967's, an impression was gained that in several cases the vinification might be less good than that of other districts and also that the grapes may not have been completely ripe when they were picked. The latter may not be so much the fault of the *vignerons* as of the weather, for this is one of the few weaknesses of the 1967 vintage. In fact, the 1962 vintage was not dissimilar for red Graves, the grapes at that time were a little unripe, and to begin with, there was too much acidity in the wines, they mellowed as they matured though, and lost most of it—time is a great healer!

Without wishing to become too involved in chemistry, unripe grapes are the cause of greenness, which must not be confused with acidity, a very different matter. Some acidity is both necessary and acceptable in a wine, and in time it disappears, but greenness unfortunately remains forever.

A few of these wines were tried later with food, but they were far too young to be enjoyable. The De Fieuzal, Pape-Clément, and Domaine de Chevalier all showed up well, though I do not advise anyone to start on them yet, and the Haut-Bailly was even more backward. Since the red Graves are inclined to develop later than the others, they are certainly less attractive to taste while they are very young. The colour was good throughout.

The 1966 Red Graves

Latour-Martillac. (Martillac).
Nice bouquet, complete, pleasant, and finishes well. 13/20

Bouscaut. (Cadaujac).
Quite a good bouquet, still some tannin, rather green. 11/20

De Fieuzal. (Léognan).
Attractive bouquet and flavour, well-made. 14+/20

Carbonnieux. (Léognan).
Nice nose, well-made, good quality, but there is a trace of unripeness. 14/20

Smith-Haut-Lafitte. (Martillac).
The bouquet was all right, but the wine far too acid. 10/20

Malartic-Lagravière. (Léognan).
Rather a green nose, and tastes unripe too! 9/20

Domaine de Chevalier. (Léognan).
Attractive bouquet, good depth of flavour, distinguished, and well-bred. A fine wine with great style. 16/20

Pape-Clément. (Pessac).
Attractive bouquet, more backward than the Domaine de Chevalier, but is well-made. When it has rounded off and lost its hardness, it should turn into a good bottle. 15/20

Haut-Bailly. (Léognan).
Charming bouquet, plenty of fruit and body, and is most attractive. 16+/20

La Mission-Haut-Brion. (Talence).
Lovely deep bouquet, powerful and full-bodied, with plenty of "race." Will make a great bottle one day, but that is still far off! 18/20

Haut-Brion. (Pessac). First growth.
Fine bouquet, aristocratic, with a delicious flavour, may develop reasonably early. 18/20

La Tour-Haut-Brion. (Talence).

> Very good bouquet, strong and powerful, good quality, if of less breeding than La Mission. Considerable tannin. 16/20

Although these were blind tastings, it was just as well that the bottles had been "slightly" arranged beforehand, because there was a decided jump in quality when one came to the second half, i.e., represented by Haut-Bailly, Pape-Clément, and so on.

Tasting the 1966's proved to be an altogether more agreeable experience than the 1967's, for not only are the former a year further forward in their development, but, by and large, 1966 is a finer vintage than 1967 and the grapes were riper when gathered in. There was a trace of "verdure" here and there among the lesser 1966's, but that probably was the fault of the proprietor for picking his grapes too soon. On account of this, one cannot help feeling that some of the lesser 1966's from other districts may be more successful than their approximate equals among the red Graves. On the other hand, the finer wines such as Haut-Bailly are certainly not to be missed!

A château to watch in this district is Bouscaut, for under new ownership, almost regardless of cost, vast improvements are being made throughout the estate, and under the able managership of M. Jean Delmas, we can expect much better wine in the future, that is, once all the changes and his expertise begin to have their effect.

The Bordeaux Market

This title may lead to disappointment—first, because I find my friends wax angry when I write on any subject other than wine, and secondly, it may suggest dreary facts and figures. The latter are all right, I suppose, for hard-headed businessmen, but not of much interest to us lesser mortals who are happily guided by our more basic instincts.

What the following is all about is indeed the Bordeaux market, but the other kind—the colourful, mouth-watering, scrumptious food market in the Place des Grands Hommes. Le Marché is one of the most fascinating features of this great city, and fully deserves its reputation of being one of the finest food markets of all France. Round in shape, it is situated in a circular *place* of picturesque old houses in the very centre of the town, not far from the Grand Théâtre, itself one of the finest buildings of France.

Modern and less attractive now in appearance, for it was rebuilt only a few years ago, it sadly lacks the exterior charm of the old building, which was delightfully nineteenth century, but inside, it is every bit as good as ever it was in the past, for if ever there were a sight for sore eyes, here we have an outstanding example.

Within, all manner of good things vie with one another for attention—meat, game, poultry, fish, cheeses by the score, vegetables, fruit, flowers. Written thus, in cold print, these items sound mundane, for they are all to be found in every glittering, soul-less supermarket, but enter the Marché de Bordeaux just once and you will find an eye-opening spectacle, and so great is the effect thereof that if you are sufficiently a gastronome, you may even suffer a minor *crise de coeur,* in both senses of the word, so beware and arrive fully prepared!

Since the French are such tremendous gourmets, and Bordeaux is a great seaport on the Atlantic Ocean, perhaps the most impressive among impressive delights is the wealth and variety of the fish sector, especially if you happen to visit this market on a Friday morning. Your eyes will stick out on stalks trying to absorb all the enthralling things on display. Added to which, as at Harrods in

London, you are more than likely to meet your best friends also doing their morning's shopping.

Apart from the usual sole, turbot, skate, *loup* (sea bass), there are the *langues d'avocats* (tiny delicious soles, particular to the nearby Bassin d'Arcachon), red mullet, squid, *lotte, mule, bandoie, enconnet, rascasses*, and other fish whose names I have failed to find in the dictionary, not to forget small succulent sea trout and rainbow trout as well as the more ordinary variety.

The shellfish on display is almost incredible. I counted no less than five different kinds of shrimp, varying in colour from almost white to rosy pink, and these are all cooked with different herbs, then prawns, *écrevisses*, langoustines, clams of all sorts, colours, and descriptions, scallops, mussels large and small, live lobsters and crayfish, many of the latter gigantic in size, crabs, deep shell oysters from the Bassin d'Arcachon, as well as *belons* and *marennes*, some of the finest oysters I have ever tasted. In fact, all the ingredients which form that most delicious of all platters, *assiette de fruits de mer*. Served on a bed of seaweed with plenty of ice, this is one of the most delectable and colourful dishes imaginable, and it fairly makes my mouth water even to write about it.

Apart from the usual meats on the butcher's stalls, the selection of game available at this time of the year, early October, vintage time, is wide and exciting—pheasants, partridges with both pink or grey legs, pigeons, doves, wild duck, mallard, teal, wigeon, and so on, snipe, woodcock, and an abundance of hares and rabbits.

As well as the flowers banked on their stalls, the fruit and vegetables in vast display all around the outer circle of the market provide much of the colour, the warmth, and yes, excitement of the scene, for this is also the season of *cèps* (boletus), one of the great specialties of Bordeaux, in all their lovely autumnal shades, from fawn to brown, stout of stalk, and massive in size. In appearance these *cèps*, not unlike the giant toadstools of our childhood fairy-tale days, are cooked in butter with chopped shallots, parsley, and garlic, a true gourmet's delight. Alongside, there are *girolles*, another kind of mushroom, which are also to be found in England, but being English, we are too timorous to pick and eat.

It is not merely a question of buying beans and onions here, but which kind of bean and which kind of onion do you select; for instance, among the former there are three of four varieties, including the most exquisite *haricots*, butter, and kidney beans. Handy for the busy housewife are the hearts of artichokes, all cut and ready for cooking, and to add still further colour to the scene, huge endive and romaine lettuces in all their shades, varying from bright yellow to green. Other items to crowd the trays are peppers, gherkins, fresh horseradish (vastly superior to the bottled concoction), salsify, celeriac, fennel, and two sorts of turnips. Incidentally, while travelling by car through France on this particular journey, it seemed strange to my wife and myself that with all these fresh vegetables at hand, we should find the selection offered on the restaurant menus to be singularly limited.

Among the fruit are arranged crates of lovely fresh walnuts, so succulent at this time of the year, chestnuts, figs, melons, and grapes. Strawberries are still in evidence, as well as the delicious *fraises de bois* and fresh raspberries.

A joy to behold too are the cooked-meat stalls, where there is every kind imaginable of sausage and tongue, joints of *jambon de Parme* and *Bayonne*, all manner of other cooked dishes, such as *vol au vents* and a number of hot *entremêts* including *cocotte de lièvre*, sauerkraut, and so on ad infinitum.

Some of the most exciting things of all, perhaps, are the *hors d'oeuvres*, and of such infinite variety they would put many of the best restaurants to shame. Delicious-looking terrines and pâtés, stuffed tomatoes and artichokes, eggs in jelly, paella, ready-stuffed snails, and, in vinaigrette sauce, calves' head, small tongues, cold *ris de veau*, mussels, squid, and the usual selection of vegetables—celeriac, mushrooms, Russian salad. . . . Infinite of variety too is the selection of cheeses on their separate stalls, but much too wide of scope to enumerate here, for by this time any reader who is still with us must be at least mentally, if not physically, satiated!

The immediate result of this ocular feast is to make one wish to leave one's hotel at once and rent a house or apartment somewhere locally even for a few weeks, just to dabble and experiment with all the delectable-looking food so plentifully available. In fact, anyone who really enjoys their food could do no worse than consider this idea, for quite apart from the major interest of getting on closer terms with the greatest red wines of the world, there are other absorbing interests to be indulged in this region, such as excursions by car in all directions through the unspoilt countryside surrounding Bordeaux, where more lovely old churches and monuments abound than you would imagine, not to overlook the delicious meals to be enjoyed in the country restaurants while following these more erudite pursuits.

The Year of the Century

We have heard the cry of "wolf" so often now, that, like a fairy tale, few of us really believe it any longer!

It began with the 1959 vintage and was followed smartly, and justifiably so, by 1961, then in quick succession came 1964, 1966, and 1969! No wonder people have become sceptical. However, with that remarkable facility common to us all, called hindsight, we can at this stage assess most of these vintages with some of the scales off our eyes.

The 1959's, the origin of the trouble, received the utmost acclaim, and such was the demand from America that prices rocketed as the Bordelais suddenly realised they could not only open wide their mouths, but get away with it too. Really, one can hardly blame the growers, but never since have prices returned to what we used to consider as normal, except of course, for the unsuccessful vintages. Good as they are, it is sad that the 1959's have not quite lived up to their earlier reputation.

Going a long way back, the quality of the 1920's was such as to have been worthy of the "year-of-the-century" rating, and, given the modern skill of vinification, the 1928's might have been far less hard and thus would surely have qualified; as it was, the 1929's certainly did; they had such fantastic charm and delightful style that, in their time, they were easily discernible even at blind tastings. Next came the 1945's, and those of us who still have some left know how good they are, of such depth, such power, but they too had that aggressive tannin, and some of the good ones are only just beginning to come round.

Had the "wine explosion" in America burst but a decade earlier, the 1953's with all their seduction might well have been included in the "wolf, wolf" category. As it was, however, we had to wait until the 1959 vintage, when wine had at last become "news."

Nineteen-sixty-one was, and still is, deserving of its reputation, and will assuredly remain a landmark. Alas that it was such a small crop; but that, of course, may have contributed to its super-excellence. Alas too that people are drinking up the 1961's while they are still too undeveloped for their true quality to be fully appreciated. On account of some of the rain-drenched Médocs, 1964 is now suffering from a reverse swing of the pendulum. This is a little unfair, because a number of the 1964 Médocs are very successful, witness, amongst others, Latour, Montrose, Malescot, the fifth-growth Grand-Puy-Lacoste, and almost all the Saint-Juliens. La Mission-Haut-Brion too is excellent, and the Saint-Emilions and Pomerols have a quality which has yet to be properly recognised. This is not to say though that the 1964's are in the same class as the 1961's. More recently, with 1966, we have been blessed with a first-rate all-round vintage. Although inevitably hailed as another "year of the century," it is not quite of the same calibre as the true giants, some now, alas, of fading memory—1929, 1945, and 1961—but in a year or so, what delicious drinking these 1966's will provide.

Finally, the 1969's—I was in Bordeaux at the beginning of that vintage and quickly realised that had not the fine weather arrived as it did, in the nick of time, there was going to be a disaster, for by the end of September, *pourriture* was plentiful and on the verge of becoming rife. Further, because of the lack of sunshine during September, some of the Cabernet Sauvignon grapes had not had a chance to reach their absolute peak of maturity. Yet, this vintage too received its accolade—"the year of the century"; perhaps the small crop after the failure of the 1968's had something to do with it? That small crop was very expensive, excessively so in one or two cases. In October 1970, after tasting the 1969's, one wonders why. Although some are quite good, in general they have a disappointing colour, they appear to be lacking flesh, and in one or two instances one can even discern the effect of the fateful rain in September, for some of them taste a bit "washed out."

Well, now we come to the 1970's, and what of them? At first the press was more restrained than usual, and even French ministers had had remarkably little to say! (But now the press reports have begun to come in from Bordeaux, and here we go again—"the year of the century"—plus comparisons with such illustrious vintages as 1929, 1893, 1870, and even the year of the comet, 1811! This time, no doubt, these paeans of praise have more foundation than usual; let us hope so anyway, because there is an enormous crop of wine to be sold!)

Whatever the case may be, the 1970's are going to be very good—much, much better than the 1969's, and there is no doubt about that. No one can ever be certain at this stage, but when the climatic conditions for the vines have been so favourable, surely there should be a good conclusion. Although the vines got off to a bad start owing to the cold and late spring suffered throughout Europe, the weather which followed was so favourable that they soon recovered from the ill effects and, by the end of September, following an unusually hot summer, the grapes were as healthy, if not healthier than, any I have ever seen. There were masses of them, too, so it was clearly going to be an abundant crop.

Apart from enjoying the heavenly weather, it was fascinating to be in Bordeaux during those critical three weeks during which the vintage was being brought in and to see for oneself all that was going on. One remarkable thing, that ugly word *pourriture* was not even mentioned during this period, and that alone is a rare event, for there is usually some about somewhere!

Even at this early stage it would seem that 1970 is going to be an especially fine year for the produce of the Merlot grape, (the grape which usually ripens roughly a week before the Cabernet Sauvignon), for the Merlots were superbly ripe, and all were gathered in under excellent conditions. Thus, it seems safe to say now that, subject, of course, to the variances of individual châteaux, buyers can be assured of the quality of the Saint-Emilions and Pomerols, likewise the useful but less well-known neighbouring districts of Côtes-de-Fronsac, Bourg, and Blaye, where the same vine predominates.

The Médocs, too, should also be excellent; again the grapes looked the picture of health, though I did hear from just one source that some of the Cabernet Sauvignons could have been a shade riper, but that surely is asking for perfection! As elsewhere, there was a scrumptious abundance of them, the vines resembling fine milch cows with almost overfilled purple udders!

By November 1970 there were ecstatic reports from various château proprietors in the Médoc, but of course it is necessary to wait until the end of March, after the spring rackings, to see the whole picture of this vintage. Always a good sign, the wines are unusually dark, they are round and supple too, and so far there is no mention of any excessive tannin, which is sometimes associated with a very hot summer.

Apart from quality, it looks like being a most prolific year, and at the time of the harvest, it was being said that the quantity might be as great as in 1967. However, a word of warning may not come amiss here, for it is not often that a plentiful crop produces really exceptional quality, so let us hope that this vintage will be the exception which proves the rule! It is possible, of course, for 1953 was both superlative and abundant.

Tasting the 1961 clarets at Chateau de la Mission-Haut-Brion.

Preparations for the decanting of the double magnum of Lafite 1865. Left to right: Barney Rhodes, Bob Adamson, Walt Peterson, Larry Seibel and myself

Harry Waugh Lecture Committee
Tasting Score Sheet

The tasting score sheet which has proved so successful at wine tastings on the West Coast.

Rapt attention!

Dicussion and considration.

Voting for preference–a popular wine.

Final notes.

It's not all so serious!

The Master! Joe Heitz in his cellar.

Left to right: Joe Heitz, Barney Rhodes, Prue and myself at Joe Heitz's winery in Spring Valley.

Harvester actually picking and crushing grapes in the Mirassou Soledad Vineyards.

Transferring must from holding tanks on harvester to transport vehicle using CO_2 pressure. Pumps would cause aeration. Must is transported to the winery under a CO_2 cap.

David Pollock, the President of Chateau Latour, holding a choice bunch of grapes from the 1970 vintage.

At Chateau Latour, Jean-Paul Gardere supervising the vinification of the 1970 vintage.

Visit to America, 1971

Tastings
of French
and California Wines

30th March, 1971

A Week with Les Amis du Vin

Not only bent, but also battered as a result of a recent motor accident in Bordeaux, my wife and I arrived in Washington, D.C., at the end of March 1971, where we were met by Alfio Moriconi and without further ado were whisked off to dine with him and his delightful wife, Jocelyne, at a Spanish restaurant. Those of us who know Alfio will well appreciate his sparkling and ebullient personality and will recognise the manner with which he persuades restaurant owners to allow him to take his own wine, and by doing so, one fares far better than having to rely on any list.

We began our meal with a delightful white Burgundy, and this was followed by something actually even finer, a Corton 1962 (Domaine Rapet), an unusually dark colour for a red Burgundy, a charming bouquet, and that delicious indefinable flavour of a really fine red wine from this district—in fact, a taste one does not meet often enough; to my mind, it was infinitely superior to a Clos Vougeot which we had on a later occasion. A perfect example of the selection of a wine being more important than buying by the label.

Wednesday, 31st March

Today was highlighted by the bottle of claret we drank for lunch. Before leaving his office, Alfio asked me to choose anything I liked from his entire stock! By now, many of Les Amis du Vin will be aware of my predeliction for the 1961 clarets, but still unaware, perhaps (no doubt on account of my Scotch blood), of my extreme meanness when it comes to pulling the corks of any of my own precious bottles! There's an expression to the effect that there is no cigar so pleasant as the given cigar. To cut a long story short, I chose Pape-Clément 1961 (I have a case somewhere, but have not tasted it since it was a few months old); the colour was dark, dark, and typical of its year, a heavenly bouquet and a glorious deep and very full flavour—in fact, rich, round, and almost meaty. It can just be enjoyed now, but my word, how good this is going to be in a year or two! If you have any of it, just try to restrain yourself for at least twelve months, and if you haven't any yet, you'd best acquire some quickly!

This was not the end of this day's exploits though, for that evening at the very good Le Provençal restaurant, we began our meal with Louis Roederer Crystal 1966, the first time I have tasted this vintage, and very good it was. Next came a Meursault Charmes (Robert Ampeau), also of 1966, a full fruity bouquet and a huge full-bodied wine, very big but well balanced withal.

The Léoville -Poyferré 1964 had a good dark colour and quite a nice bouquet, but it was nothing much to write home about. There are better Saint-Juliens of 1964 in the shape of Ducru-Beaucaillou and Gloria. The Vieux Ch. Certan 1953 which followed was much more agreeable, a good colour, a fine bouquet, and a pleasing flavour, but like many 1953's has seen better days. Originally these 1953's were so charming, so fascinating, that one does not like to admit that they are growing old—gracefully, of course, but ageing all the same. As the *bonne bouche* came a 1959 Clos Vougeot, but, illustrious as its title may have been, the less said of that wine the better!

Wednesday, 1st April

Today was the day set aside for the talk and tasting of some of the wines I have described in an earlier book as the Cinderellas of Bordeaux: the Fronsadais, the Bourgeais, and the Blayais. The tasting was held in the Washington Students' Club, and there were about 150 people present.

To be brief, the classified growths of Bordeaux have become so expensive that the high prices have rubbed off even on to the *crus bourgeois* of the Médoc, once that happy hunting ground of the claret lover, but now even the *crus bourgeois* have risen greatly in price; for example, those two successful châteaux, Gloria and de Pez, are now reaching up to and sometimes exceeding the price of some of the classified growths, and for some of us, this can be painful!

So where do we look for honey? Fortunately, we still have a comparatively unexploited territory which produces such wines as the Côtes de Fronsac, Côtes-Canon-Fronsac, Côtes de Bourg, and the Premières Côtes de Blayes.

As happens with the *crus classées* of the Médoc, these wines of the Fronsadais etc. require careful selection, but the good ones, as I hope has been evident at these tastings, are not only most attractive for every-day drinking, but also are still quite reasonable in price. For how long this happy state of affairs will continue, heaven alone knows, but at least we can take advantage of the present situation. My own notes on the wines tasted are as follows:

Château Bel-Air-Coubet, 1967. (Côtes de Bourg).
> A nice fruity bouquet, light but charming, and surprisingly forward.

Château Malakoff, 1967. (Côtes de Bourg).
> A fairly full bouquet, a pleasant vinous wine with good fruit and body. Still has some tannin to lose, and so needs a further six months or so, but then it should make a good bottle.

Château la Joncarde, 1966. (Côtes de Bourg).
> A full distinctive bouquet, has fruit, body, and that extra depth of flavour so typical of its fine vintage. Still quite youthful and needs at least another twelve months.

Château de Carles, 1966. (Côtes-de-Fronsac).
> Good deep bouquet, lots of fruit, and a good depth of flavour. Still some tannin, so needs 12–18 months. Fine quality.

Château Rouet, 1967. (Côtes-de-Fronsac).
> Attractive fruity bouquet, appears on the light side after the de Carles, but this is a good wine nevertheless. Having only just arrived in the U.S., the Château Rouet was suffering a little from the journey, but I know how well it tastes on its native heath.

Château Canon-de-Brem, 1967. (Côtes-Canon-Fronsac).
> Good full bouquet, big and robust. Still has some tannin to lose, but should make a fine bottle.

Château Bourdieu-la-Vallade, 1964. (Côtes-de-Fronsac).
> A fragrant and nicely developed bouquet, good fruit, attractive flavour, ready now, but will undoubtedly improve. (This 1964 was included to demonstrate how these wines develop after a year or so in bottle.)

Friday, 2nd April

This morning we busied ourselves making tape recordings on the wines of Bordeaux in general and on a story of Château Latour. Incidentally, for lunch, with a delicious *jambon d'Ardennes,* we shared a bottle of the Château Canon-de-Brem 1967, and it showed very well, though of course it will improve greatly with some more age in bottle.

This evening we drove to Baltimore to address the Baltimore chapter. This function took place at the Woodholme Country Club, Woodholme Avenue, Pikesville, Maryland, and the proceedings were admirably organised by Mr. and Mrs. Harry Orman and their son. Altogether there were about 300 people present.

As will be seen, the wines were a "mixed bag" from Bordeaux, all quite different from one another, and this made them all the easier to discuss:

Château Carbonnieux, 1967. (White Graves).
    A good pale colour, an attractive fragrant bouquet, the flavour was clean, fresh, and dry. A well-bred, distinguished wine which would go particularly well with fish and all kinds of shellfish.

Château Giscours, 1967. (Labarde).
    A good dark colour, a fruity bouquet which has a lot of character, good fruit and a pleasant flavour, and it finishes well. Quite forward for a 1967, but needs a year or so to be at its best.

Château Lafon Rochet, 1966. (Saint-Estèphe).
    A nice deep colour, a lovely flowery bouquet. It has heaps of fruit and a delicious flavour, though there is still some tannin. This, for me, was the best wine of the evening.

    The contrast between the 1966 and 1967 was informative, because the greater depth and flavour and the greater importance of the 1966 was clearly discernible.

Château Lafleur, 1962. (Pomerol).
    The colour was very dark, the bouquet and flavour most pronounced, but it finished short and has not a long life before it. This is not really surprising, because 1962 as a vintage was not nearly so successful for Saint-Emilion

and Pomerol as it was for the Médoc. In spite of these remarks, on a show of hands this was easily the most popular wine of the evening.

Château Fonplégade, 1961. (Saint-Emilion).
The very dark colour so typical of its year, a lovely rich nose, a great big wine which still has lots of tannin to lose. It may lack finesse, but I would not mind having a bottle or so put aside for the future.

Château Mouton-Baron-Philippe, 1967. (Pauillac).
The colour was of a lighter shade than all of the others. The wine was full and fruity though, and had an agreeable bouquet; otherwise there was not a great deal to say about it. It was probably still suffering from the journey across the Atlantic. Sometimes it takes a month or so for a wine to recover from this ordeal.

There was plenty to say otherwise thanks to the diversity of the wines and the many questions put by an attentive audience. One of them which shook me a little was whether the copper sulphate with which the vines are sprayed affects the wine? This, of course, is not the case, and wine is mildly antiseptic anyway. In fact, taken with food that may be a little "off," it is reputed to prevent sickness later. While on this subject, I fear many Americans with their high standard of hygiene would be shocked by how we taste wine from the cask in France. After tasting, we spit it out on to the floor, and often when it is very precious, say, a Chambertin, the dregs of our glasses are poured back into the barrel! Nobody seems to suffer, certainly not the wine, but you must make due allowance for my backward European upbringing rising to the surface!

Palm Sunday, 4th April

Pat Pepe and Tom Meldon were waiting for me at the airport in Buffalo and swept me off to a late lunch at the Transit Valley Country Club, where we were joined by Albert Pepe, John Cottis, and Angelo Evannow. Some splendid wines had been prepared. The first, Château Carbonnieux 1944, was a revelation, for this is remarkably old for a white Graves. It still had quite a light colour, when one would have expected oxidation, and the wine itself was unexpectedly fresh.

This venerable white Graves was followed by Château Latour of the same vintage, and the latter comported itself equally well. A good colour, an old bouquet admittedly, but it was full-bodied, had a good flavour, and finished delightfully.

The last wine of all, Château Pichon-Longueville Baron, 1937, though very dark of colour, was, as I feared, still overwhelmed by that fatal 1937 tannin. I see in my notes I wrote "rigid and frigid." Thank goodness this taint of 1937 does not apply to human beings, because 1937 is the birth year of my wife!

The talk and tasting that evening was held at Hearthstone Manor, and there were about 300 people present. The subject was one of my pet ones, the 1967 clarets, and that combined with an attentive and enquiring audience made the evening all the more enjoyable for me.

After the aperitif, a nice dry N. V. Delbeck, we got down to the 1967 vintage, which is of such special interest at this particular moment. Although perhaps not quite so fine as the 1966 vintage, the 1967's with their good colour and bouquet are delightful; what is more, they may quite likely be ready before the 1966's, which will give the latter the time to mature which they deserve. This is not to say, though, that the 1967's are ready now, for if nothing else, the tasting that evening showed these wines in particular need from at least three to ten years before they will be approaching their best.

Nineteen-sixty-seven is a most useful vintage, for apart from its other qualities, there is plenty of it, and this is just as well, since the 1969's, though greatly boosted at the beginning, are not so good as they were made out to be. In view of the gap, then, between the 1967's and the very promising 1970's, this urged me to compare them with taking on gas before a long drive across the desert! This is not, of course, to say categorically there will be no good 1968's and 1969's, because there are always some good wines in a poor vintage, just as there can be some indifferent ones in the good years.

These, then, are the wines we tasted and discussed together:

1967 Vintage

  Château Lascombes. (Margaux).
      Medium colour, but then, the wines from this district are
      often lighter in colour than the Saint-Estèphes and

Pauillacs. A pretty bouquet, still very young and undeveloped, but it has an attractive flavour. Very light of body but should make a good bottle and be ready comparatively early.

Château Léoville-Las-Cases. (Saint-Julien).
Medium colour, a fine elegant bouquet, good flavour, and fine quality. It has more importance than the Lascombes and needs, say, 3–4 years.

Château Lafon-Rochet. (Saint-Estèphe).
A good dark colour, a full fragrant nose, plenty of body, and well balanced. Still very hard, so it will need 4–5 years, and then, like the 1966 from this château, it should make a delightful bottle.

Château Pichon-Longueville-Lalande. (Pauillac).
Good colour, a nice fruity bouquet, still immature of course, but this is well made. Needs perhaps 4–5 years.

Château La Gaffelière. (Saint-Emilion).
Rather light in colour, but an attractive bouquet. Full, round, and luscious, as a good Saint-Emilion should be. This too will make a very good bottle and may be ready before some of the 1967 Médocs. It was certainly easier to taste than the Médocs.

Château Latour. (Pauillac).
Last, but by no means least. As usual, the colour was beautifully dark, a very full bouquet, and heaps of fruit and flavour. Biased as I am, one cannot fail to see the quality of this wine, although it is still really rather unpleasant even to taste at this early stage in its career. It must surely be from six to seven years at least before its merits can be properly appreciated.

What struck me so much on this occasion is the tremendous spirit which has been engendered by Les Amis du Vin in the Buffalo region. All of this seems owing to the friendship and co-operation of three liquor stores, or rather their owners. It is certainly something I have never come across in England. The people concerned are Pat, Albert, and Alphonse Pepe of Hodge Liquors, Tom Meldon of Reed's Liquors, and John Cottis and Angelo Evannow of Thruway Liquors.

With the enthusiasm and co-operation of people like this, it is no wonder that Les Amis du Vin flourishes as it does all over this great and vast country. I should have liked to visit all the three stores concerned, but in view of an early flight to Atlanta the following morning, only had time to call briefly at Hodge Liquors, where there was so much to discuss we had to talk at almost double the normal speed! I only wish I had had time also to call at the other two stores, for these three merchants are clearly doing a splendid job not only for Les Amis du Vin but also for the dissemination of wine lore.

Although it seemed mighty cold to me in Buffalo, having arrived without even an overcoat, the warmth and kindness of all these Amis du Vin gave an inner glow which is hard to forget.

Monday, 5th April

Continuing on my way on this whistle stop journey, I arrived in Atlanta to be greeted at the airport by Russell McCall, an enthusiastic young merchant (who combines successfully the sale of fine wine and cheese), and by Dr. James T. King at whose delightful home I was to spend a couple of nights. It is just as well that my hostess, Martha King, is as interested in wine as her husband, for I have yet to enter another home where apart from an air-conditioned wine cellar, one of the bedrooms has been stripped of all furnishings and now contains an impressive number of cases of rare wines, headed possibly by a triple-magnum of Lafite 1961!

The tasting that evening was a smaller affair of about sixty people, limited on account of the scarcity of the fine wines to be tasted, and it took place in the splendid Memorial Art Center of Atlanta.

The aperitif, as it were, was a white Châteauneuf du Pape, clean and dry, with an attractive fruit acidity, and this was followed by two 1952 clarets, Château La Mission-Haut-Brion and Château Latour. La Mission had a beautiful dark colour, its usual fine Graves bouquet, and a mouthful of lovely flavour, whereas the Latour, equally dark of colour, with a full bouquet, still has some tannin to lose.

The two red Burgundies to be tasted were of special interest to me for they both came from the Barolet collection, which has now become so well known in the United States.

When Dr. Barolet died, he left behind him a wonderful collection of mostly pre-war Burgundies, some 30,000 bottles all told. He had inherited this fabulous stock of pre-war vintages from his father, who had been a wine merchant, but being well off, the doctor made no great efforts to sell these wines except to friends and special customers. I first heard of this treasure trove through a Burgundian broker friend who asked me to leave London as soon as possible to taste the wines which had been purchased in their entirety by the firm of Henri de Villamont of Savigny-les-Beaune.

The bottles still lay in their original bin and shrouded in the black so-called cobwebs typical of a Burgundian cellar. It was just like entering an Aladdin's cave! By the time we had pulled the corks from just one or two bottles, I realised I was on to something quite exceptional and quickly got on the telephone to my friend Michael Broadbent in London, the director in charge of Christie's wine auctions. Then following previous tastings in Geneva, Paris, and London, the Barolet collection came to light. Fortunately I had my car with me at the time, so, without asking the price, I quickly had a case each of Chambolle Musigny les Amoureuses 1934 and Chambolle Musigny 1919 loaded on board. Long ago I learnt one must never miss an opportunity! I do not think I have ever tasted finer Burgundy than those two.

After the original sale at Christie's the rest of the Barolet collection was sold by auction in Chicago and through other channels. It is doubtful if such a fine collection of old Burgundy will ever come on the market again. So here were some of the Barolet wines turning up again quite unexpectedly in Atlanta, a pleasant surprise indeed. They were Grands Echézeaux 1937, fine quality, but it needs drinking, and a quite delicious Chambolle Musigny Charmes 1934. The thing which strikes one so forcibly about the good pre-war red Burgundies is their lovely deep colour and depth of body, so much deeper than their post-war descendants.

Tuesday, 6th April

After a TV appointment with "Today in Georgia," Russ McCall took me to see his attractive new store, the Wine Shop, and sightseeing in underground Atlanta, an area fast being developed under the streets in the heart of the old city, reminiscent in a way of the French quarter of New Orleans. No wonder it has become such an attraction for tourists. My host, Dr. King, arranged a most interesting lunch in the Commerce Club of Atlanta. There were about a dozen guests in all, and there is no need to state the general topic of conversation!

We began with an unusually attractive Beaujolais Blanc of 1969, so good it could easily have been taken for a really good Pouilly Fuissé, and then came two Cabernet Sauvignons, 1964 and 1965 from Beaulieu (Private Reserve). If anything, the 1964 was the finer of the two, if not quite yet ready to drink, but they were both of a high standard.

A final dinner party was given for me in the home of Michael and Liz Terry. The cold was so intense outside I had to borrow an overcoat! I accused Russ McCall of luring me to Atlanta with promises of temperatures about seventy and here it was below freezing! One soon forgot the cold once inside the Terrys' home enjoying Liz's excellent cooking. I shall not forget the first course for a long time, crêpes with a filling of crab and lobster combined. With these we drank a splendid Corton Charlemagne 1966, Hospices de Beaune, and no less than three bottles of 1940 Latour. This is not so greedy as it sounds, though, because two of them were well over the hill, and the other, if sound, was a bit rickety on its feet; 1940 was never a great vintage, and even Latour has to give up the ghost eventually!

The next morning, half-killed by both kindness and exhaustion, I had to be helped gently onto the plane en route for California!

Meeting Les Amis du Vin has been a rewarding experience. Their interest and enthusiasm for the subject is quite remarkable, and having met so many delightful people, I shall be inclined to regard them henceforth as *Mes* Amis du Vin!

April, 1971

The Napa Valley

The Napa Valley, which of all the wine districts of California the writer is beginning to know just a little, must surely be the most fascinating, the most exhilarating grape-growing district of the world; remarkable not only for its beauty but for the vitality, the enthusiasm, the expertise, and the thirst for knowledge of the winemakers whose willingness to experiment and try out new ideas increases from year to year. This search for perfection, always present in the past, is growing to a crescendo, and is indeed truly exciting.

The concentration on the use of the varietal grape has really only been in being during the past ten years, but already it has made a vast difference to the quality of the wine and now, although this was certainly not the case in the 1950's, the different vintages are recognised for what they are and one seldom hears any more that the vintages in California are all the same, for clearly they are not!

The growers, some of the most talented and skillful winemakers of the world, admit freely that all is still new and that there is much to learn. They are not yet certain, for instance, which pieces of ground in the Valley are most suitable, say, for Cabernet Sauvignon, for Chardonnay, or Pinot Noir; this can only be found out by trial and error, that is, by actual experience. Replanting a vineyard and waiting for any proper results can take up to ten years; therefore, vines are not uprooted lightly. The vineyards of Europe have been evolved over the past thousand years, so no wonder there is no longer a rush to experiment; the European experimentation has taken place in the distant past and now mainly the successes remain. Of course, changes still continue to take place there, but in a more restrained key. But here in California, all is new, all to learn; for the vineyard owners, the soil is virtually virgin territory.

Some growers will tell you it will take thirty years before the real potential of this area can be properly assessed, others say fifty —who knows? But what is certain is that these skilled and dedicated men of the present generation are taking gigantic strides towards perfection.

For proof of this, one merely has to study the Chardonnay to see how this has improved even over the past five years. Many of the wines from this grape seem largely to have lost much of that California taste, though how to describe this taste in words is almost impossible! They seem to resemble more the white Burgundy from the Côte d'Or; in fact, before too long a time has elapsed, a number of the Burgundian growers may well have to look to their laurels. Unfortunately, the quantity made of this first-grade California varietal is still all too small. The aim here is not necessarily to make it taste exactly the same as the Burgundian variety, but to produce the best possible quality of which this vine is capable. The recently adopted habit of ageing Chardonnay in French oak seems to have made an important difference: formerly it was possible to distinguish the California Chardonnay from a white Burgundy by the bouquet alone; now it is far more difficult and at times (for this writer, at any rate) downright impossible!

The Pinot Noir still appears to be a weak link among the varietals, and the outsider is inclined to wonder why, until the clonal situation has been improved, so much of it is being planted. The answer, most probably, is commercial. All the same, one has only to taste the Heitz 1959 Pinot Noir, admittedly, a *rara avis*, to realise that with the Pinot Noir, too, success is possible.

It is clear that the Cabernet Sauvignon is strongly in the ascendancy. There are not many Everests in this world, but when one comes across summits like the Cabernet Sauvignon of Martha's Vineyard, Heitz, and of Bosche, Freemark Abbey (admittedly still of minute production in each case), the future is vastly encouraging. In this land of adventure, this new frontier, as it were, these wines represent but a minute fraction of the as yet undiscovered possibilities.

To touch on Zinfandel for a moment, a foreign visitor finds it something altogether new, and he has to accustom himself both to the bouquet and the taste in order to appreciate it properly. Of origin unknown, this vine is grown more widely than any other in California, and the results are most varied. Among the higher echelons of quality, the writer recently tasted the Louis M. Martini 1967, Napa Valley, which had a delightful raspberry flavour, and although fairly light, was completely charming, whereas alongside it stood the Parducci 1966 (Mendocino), which has a deeper colour, an attractive bouquet, was full-bodied, and quite different. In this case, it must have been either the soil or the vinification, and not so much the vintage, which has made the difference—yet each in its own way was admirable.

Even more powerful still is the 1970 Zinfandel from the Occidental Vineyard, which lies in Sonoma County, the grapes of which were transported to Ridge Winery (Monte Bello Road), resulting in a truly astonishing wine, almost black of colour. With a lovely bouquet, it has a great depth of flavour and appears to be of exceptional quality. Unfortunately, only one hundred cases are available, so for the rest of the world, quality such as this can only be described perhaps as the glint in the father's eye! It indicates, however, the possibility which still lies dormant in these California vineyards.

In order to counteract the small production of fine quality in the Napa Valley, old wineries are being brought back to life, and thus there are new names with which to contend. A good example of this is Freemark Abbey, where great progress is being made, and there are several completely new wineries where more vineyards have been planted. Prominent among these is that of Robert Mondavi, where under the dynamic control of the managing director a considerable reputation has already been gained. More recently still, there are Chappelet and Cuvaison, whose produce is now coming on the market. Changes of ownership are also having their effects, and notable among these is the Mayacamas Winery, where the quality has already vastly been improved; and it will be interesting to see what happens to the Beringer Winery, which recently has changed hands.

There are also many new vineyard owners in the valley who will be selling their grapes to the large wineries, and in most cases the old vines, which produced only rather ordinary wine, are being uprooted and replaced by the classic ones such as Chardonnay, Pinot Noir, and Cabernet Sauvignon. All of this will help to uplift the general quality. It will, no doubt, take these newly planted vines some ten years to approach their best, but then, what excitement there will be! How one wishes one could be a young trainee winemaker with all his life before him, for it will be during his lifetime that the potential of these California vineyards will be recognised throughout the world.

Although admittedly on a lesser scale, the electric feeling now vibrant in this California air puts one in mind of what must have been the "fever" of the gold-rush days, for it appears to be the ambition of nearly everyone in these parts to own a vineyard or even a piece of a vineyard in order to produce grapes, not just grapes as such, but of the best quality. Coupled with this romance—and a delightful romance it is—is the possibility of living in one of the most beautiful valleys imaginable, where the air is so pure and the scenery so striking.

It can be a chastening experience for the English wine merchant to come to California, for suddenly he realises (at least, this one does) how little he knows about vines and viticulture. For example, until only a few years ago, the term "varietal" was an entirely foreign word to him and he had to enquire exactly what it meant! The vine names Cabernet Sauvignon, Merlot, Riesling, etc., are all well known to the European, but in Europe these vines are grown in widely different areas; here in California one sees them, and many others as well, growing cheek by jowl on the same estates. Here too one learns what 100-percent Cabernet Sauvignon tastes like, for in Bordeaux, apart from Mouton-Rothschild perhaps, all the Médocs have a good proportion of other grapes in their make-up. Similarly with the Chardonnay, which in Burgundy is always matured in oak casks; in California one has the two methods of upbringing. In the former manner, maturation is in huge redwood vats, and then there is the more modern method of maturing in Limousin or Nevers oak casks, just as is done in France.

Incidentally, some of the varietal names of California can be confusing, for instance, White Pinot and Pinot Blanc are two quite different varietals, but White Pinot is synonymous with Chenin Blanc, because both derive from the same stock. To make matters all the more difficult, some wineries produce both a White Pinot and a Chenin Blanc, but more often than not in this case the Chenin Blanc will be a slightly sweeter wine.

The Merlot grape is a comparative newcomer on this California scene. In the Médoc of Bordeaux the power of the noble Cabernet Sauvignon is toned down by the judicious blending with Merlot, etc., but there is no hard-and-fast rule as to the proportions in which this is done. It is only during the past ten years or so that the Merlot vine has been planted here, and then on the initiative of the University of California at Davis, that fairy godmother of all California wine growers.

If a European visitor may be permitted to comment, the Cabernet Sauvignon of California does strike one as being perhaps a little fiercer, though that is possibly an unattractive description, than the red wines of Bordeaux. This seems to be owing more to the character of the grape itself than to the soil, the climate, or the wine growers, so perhaps here too a little blending with the Merlot could be beneficial. Hazarding a guess, it may well be that in the past, originally Médocain proprietors tried only Cabernet Sauvignon in their vineyards and then by trial and error found that the addition of a little Merlot improved the final result. No doubt such blending has already been tried by a number of growers of which this writer is unaware, but the only instance which so far has come to his notice is at Freemark Abbey, where the Cabernet Sauvignon (Bosche) of 1968 has about 10 percent of Merlot in the blend. The result is striking, for this wine is a splendid achievement. Here, unfortunately, we have an example of the experimental stage of this area, for only sufficient of this wine has been made for "directors' " consumption! There is none for sale! The vines which produce this particular Merlot are already some seven years old, and the 1970 vintage is most unusual, to say the least. The colour is as dark as the best of red Bordeaux of the same vintage (that is saying a great deal), the bouquet is delightful, and the intensity of flavour remarkable; in fact, this is a most impressive wine. One can imagine that when blended with the 1970 Cabernet Sauvignon, it can only add colour, intensity of flavour, and a delightful softness to the final result.

If and when the Merlot has made its reputation here in California and is accepted generally in the Napa Valley, one's descendants may even see the California equivalent of fine Saint-Emilion or Pomerol, though under what name it would appear is for the future to decide.

Here I have dealt mainly with the Napa Valley, but in many ways even more exciting things are happening elsewhere in California. For example, the planting of ungrafted varietal stocks in virgin soil around Soledad, Monterey County, coupled with mechanical harvesting, cries out for further attention.

One's imagination boggles at the thought of what is happening in Monterey County, where 7,000 acres have already been planted out with pure varietal vine stocks. The planting has been taking place during the past decade, and once these vines have reached maturity, it will be fascinating to compare their produce with that of the normal budded stocks.

Added to this, the mechanical harvester has come on the scene, an intrusion of modernity which might horrify the purist, but it appears to be successful. For example, the particular machine used by Mirassou Vineyards gathers in only the ripe berries, leaving the unripe ones behind, and largely prevents oxidation, that deadly enemy, especially of white wine. It is reckoned that just eight seconds elapse between the time the grapes are picked and the time they are enclosed in the reception tank containing CO_2 so as to avoid all risk of oxidation. Then back at the winery there is only a further eight seconds' exposure to the air from the time the grapes leave the reception tank until they enter the press!

It can be dangerous to be put off by innovation, for when at Château Latour we installed stainless-steel fermentation tanks in 1963, there was much muttering and rubbing of chins. As it transpires, it has proved extremely successful, and the fermentation is controlled better than ever before. Since the cost of labour is one of the sobering factors in the production of wine in California, it is to be hoped this mechanical harvesting will prove successful. Should this be the case, it may take many years for the system to be adopted generally, for to make it possible, the rows of vines have to be planted farther apart than they are at present.

Floating as I do on my ethereal cloud of enchantment for all that is happening here in the wine industry, I am all too often brought up short when talking to friends in, say, Chicago or New York. They say, "Yes, that's all very well, but the wines of California are so expensive, and there is better value to be obtained by buying a well-known red Bordeaux at a similar price."

It may well be true at this particular juncture, but with the vast improvement which is evident even from one year to another, while the quality of the great French wines remains more or less static and, regrettably, in some cases is diminishing, that of California is fast going up, though it may be long after many of the present generation are dead before ambitions are fully realised. For example, one has only to consider the Chardonnay of California, the wine at the moment which seems to be making the most rapid progress, for if the quality continues to improve at the present rate, all is possible. As to the red wines, the improvement in quality of some of the 1968 and 1970 Cabernet Sauvignons from one or two of the smaller wineries is so exceptional that this can only be but a portent of what is to come.

The Day to Day Wines of California

At the risk of repetition, I must write further about the day to day California wines, by far the most intriguing aspect on the wine scene of California. This inexpensive stuff, though "stuff" is an unfair word to use, commonly known as "jug" wine, is the type which is sold in half-gallon and larger jars, and is produced by the wineries which specialise so successfully in mass production. I still believe it is here that the quality and value for money is so astonishing.

In England we have what are called the branded table wines; a little of it comes from France, but by far the greater proportion is from Spain and Portugal. It is shipped over in containers, is bottled in England, and usually sold in litre bottles. Though it costs more than its California equivalent (this is not necessarily the fault of the suppliers, but of high taxation), the quality is far inferior, the wines lacking all the charm and freshness of the California counterpart.

Again, through high taxation and the loss of the Algerian source of supply, the quality of the vin ordinaire of France, for which we all used to have such an affection, also leaves much to be desired when it comes to a question of comparison. The American consumer, no doubt, takes these "jug" wines for granted; they have always been there, and perhaps it is not noticeable how much their quality has increased over the past decade. It may be, too, that he does not appreciate his good fortune?

Even if one has a good cellar, one does not necessarily wish to drink fine wines every day, and this is exactly where these "jug" wines come in so admirably—for everyday drinking. For "gracious living," if one may be permitted to use a hackneyed and perhaps a rather doubtful term, the most attractive way to serve them is by the use of a decanter, which can provide a delightful form of table decoration. It does not necessarily have to be very expensive, and the search for pretty ones can be amusing. What can be more enchanting when you enter your host's dining room, or even the other part of the sitting room, as happens in my apartment in London,

113

than to behold on the table a decanter of white wine and another of red! The colour of the wines alone adds lustre to the scene and gives one an agreeable sense of anticipation.

Here are some notes on them when they were tasted in May 1971. These, in some respects vary from the same wines tasted a year ago with Les Amis du Vin. It seems that I have been more tolerant in my assessment than my American confreres.

The prices are those ruling per half-gallon in California, and where possible, the price per bottle is translated alongside. If purchased by the gallon,* these prices per bottle would be reduced even more.

Red Wines

> *Italian Swiss Colony Burgundy.* (Napa, Sonoma, Mendocino). $1.99 half-gallon ($0.79 per bottle).
>> Dark colour, quite a powerful fruity nose, good fruit, and easy to taste. Good quality.

> *Paul Masson Burgundy.* $3.29 half-gallon ($1.32 per bottle).
>> Good colour, pleasant bouquet, although a trifle rough, plenty of fruit and impact. This should be good with red meat.

> *Guild Tavola Red.* $1.59 half-gallon ($0.63 per bottle).
>> Medium colour; nice rather light bouquet; on the light side, and mildly sweet. Useful for all normal occasions.

> *Gallo Hearty Burgundy.* $1.89 half-gallon ($0.76 per bottle).
>> A lovely dark colour, very good bouquet, a great big meaty wine, in fact a proper mouthful. This is well named, for it is indeed a hearty "slap-on-the-back" wine. How Gallo does this at the price is beyond me.

---

* For English readers, the American gallon is smaller than the British. There are six bottles to the English gallon but only five to the American. This is why a bottle of wine in America is often called a "fifth."

Almadén Mountain Red Claret.

$2.78 half-gallon ($1.11 per bottle).

> Medium colour, a fruity bouquet, on the light side, but has a pleasant flavour.

My favourites among these five reds were the Italian Swiss Colony and the Gallo, and these appear to be remarkably good value.

This Hearty Burgundy style of wine is sold by a number of the big wineries, and it is proving immensely popular.

Non-vintage Varietal Red Wines (also sold in Europe):

Paul Masson Rubion Baroque.

$1.99 per bottle.

> Good colour, a pleasant bouquet, full-flavoured, and finishes nicely. This is a cleverly blended "burgundy-type" wine which has only recently come on the market; it deserves to be successful.

Almadén Zinfandel.

$1.89 per bottle.

> Medium colour, attractive bouquet, on the light side, but a good flavour, and it has considerable charm.

Christian Brothers Pinot Saint George.

$3.00 per bottle.

> Medium colour, a big fruity bouquet. Plenty of fruit and body. This is a wine which should improve greatly with more age in bottle.

> (The Pinot Saint George varietal is not to be confused with Pinot Noir, because they are entirely different varieties.)

White Wines

Guild Tavola White.

$1.59 half-gallon ($0.63 per bottle).

> Pale colour, fresh, but slightly scented bouquet, full, and fairly sweet.

Italian Swiss Colony Premium Chablis.
$1.99 half-gallon ($0.79 per bottle).
> On the label are printed the words "Napa Sonoma Mendocino," which means that the grapes came from these three districts. A nice pale colour, fresh bouquet, a pleasant medium-dry flavour, finishes well.

Gallo Chablis Blanc.
$1.89 half-gallon ($0.76 per bottle).
> Good colour, a pleasant fragrant bouquet, an attractive flavour which is similar to the bouquet. Reminiscent, in a way of the style of Johannisberg Riesling. It is easily one of the largest sellers of this type, and it is truly remarkable how Gallo continue to keep up the standard of quality.

Almadén Mountain White Chablis.
$2.78 half-gallon ($1.11 per bottle).
> Good colour, clean nose, and it has a good fresh, rather distinctive flavour.

Franzia California Chablis.
$1.29 half-gallon ($0.52 per bottle).
> Good pale colour, a fruity bouquet, and agreeable fruit acidity. Astonishing value.

Paul Masson Chablis.
$3.29 half-gallon ($1.32 per bottle).
> Pale colour, a nice fragrant bouquet, good flavour, and quite a dry finish. Good quality. It gets its character from the number of choice varietals in its make-up.

All of the above had their own individual character and are of surprising value for the money.

Getting away from the old-fashioned system of generic names, some of the great wineries are substituting them with non-vintage varietal wines. Here are three successful examples:

Christian Brothers Pineau de la Loire.
$3.00 per bottle.
> Good colour, a very fragrant bouquet, it seemed slightly spritzig, which is attractive; a medium-sweet but interesting flavour.

Paul Masson Emerald Dry.
$1.99 per bottle.
>   Very pale colour, a nice fresh bouquet, a delightful flavour coupled with attractive fruit acidity. No wonder this is one of the best sellers.

Almadén Gewurztraminer.
$2.39 per bottle.
>   Pale colour, a pretty Traminer nose; in fact it smells strongly of its varietal, and finishing well, it has a most interesting spicy flavour.

(These three wines are all available in the European market.)
The realistic New Yorker or Chicagoan may consider this to have been written with rose-tinted spectacles, but if one has the good fortune to spend a month or so each year in California, and in daily contact with its many and varied wines, it is not easy to restrain one's enthusiasm.

Montrachet, the Great White Burgundy

The Berkeley chapter of The Wine & Food Society must surely be the best-informed group of wine lovers to be found anywhere in the world. With only three wine merchants amongst its membership of thirty-two, the members belong largely to the medical profession. Many of them are vineyard owners in the Napa Valley, who sell their grapes to the important wineries; furthermore, as a hobby, some of them make wine for consumption at their own tables. An unusual and delightful feature of this chapter is that women are members in their own right, and, given equal opportunity, are proving just as good at tasting as the men.

Owing to its situation, the possibilities of the group are almost unique, for not only are all the finest wines from Europe readily available, but literally on their doorstep, as it were, lie all the vineyards of California, where such exciting progress is being made. The group meets monthly in different members' homes, each person bringing his own set of glasses, thus avoiding domestic problems for the hostesses concerned.

On this particular evening, at the home of Dr. and Mrs. Marvin Smoller there was Montrachet from six different growers, with in addition a Chevalier and a Bâtard-Montrachet. The wines had been assembled by Darrell Corti, the brilliant young wine merchant of Sacramento, who is to be congratulated, for, under any circumstances, it is an unusual feat to gather together at the same time so many Montrachets of the same vintage. Genuine Montrachet is hard to come by!

Although great in renown, the vineyard of Montrachet, being only about eighteen acres in extent, is anything but great in size. In this particular instance, Mother Nature has been lavish over quality, but rather mean when it comes to quantity. This vineyard, which produces perhaps the finest white wine of the world, lies half in the commune of Puligny-Montrachet and half in that of Chassagne-Montrachet.

Unfortunately, this small plot of ground is divided up amongst about a dozen different proprietors, the most important of them being the Marquis de Laguiche, Baron Thénard, and the firm of Bouchard Père et Fils. The quantity produced is minute, about 23,000 bottles, which is nothing when one considers world demand: the greater part of this is shipped to America. In good vintages this masterpiece has a rich, almost overwhelming bouquet, with a richness and depth of flavour which is astonishing. If of a good vintage and cellared under the right conditions, Montrachet will last for many years.

These, then, are my notes on the wines, which, of course, were tasted blind. *(See next page)*

With the exception of the Romanée-Conti and Bouchard Père et Fils wines, the quality of the rest of the Montrachets was disappointing, especially when one considers their high price.

1966 Montrachet and Other Fine Wines

Wine	Characteristics	Preference Mine	Group
Montrachet Romanée-Conti $24.95	Good pale colour, fine, full rich bouquet, a great big rich wine, excellent quality	1	1
Montrachet Marquis de Laguiche $21.00	A nice pale colour, but too much sulphur on the nose, it came through on the taste as well. On light side, quality medium for such a wine	5	5
Chevalier-Montrachet Bouchard Père & Fils $12.50	Good colour, a fine fairly rich bouquet, has depth as well as good fruit and flavour	2	4
Montrachet Bouchard Père & Fils $18.34	The colour was a shade darker, but a very nice rich bouquet. Full-flavoured, well-balanced, nice fruit acidity, good quality	3	2
Montrachet Jacques Prieur $16.50	A nice pale colour, the bouquet perhaps a little less refined, a well-balanced wine with a nice finish	4	7
Montrachet Boillerault de Chauvigny $20.00	Colour already turning slightly brown, a poor, tired bouquet, the wine thin and sharp, not to my liking	8	6
Montrachet Baron Thénard $18.34	A nutty nose, but not quite so fragrant as it might be, the taste was nutty too, but finished on the sharp side	6	8
Bâtard-Montrachet Louis Poirier $6.00	A disappointing bouquet, the flavour begins better than it finishes, that is, with considerable acidity	7	3

Four Exceptional White Wines

Until 1971, I had not even heard of the small Chalone vineyard, perched at 2,000 feet in the Gavilan Mountains, Monterey County. The soil, sparse and reddish brown, is underlined by limestone. The production is only about 600 bottles an acre, and in 1969 5,173 bottles were made, each one numbered. The wine is matured in French oak barrels, which makes the bouquet almost undistinguishable from white Burgundy. It has a special Burgundian flavour too, which puzzled me, and it has a nice dry finish. Unusually good quality.

1969 Chalone Pinot Blanc.
Attractive bouquet and a delightful flavour, excellent quality.

1969 Chalone Pinot Chardonnay.
Pale colour, a delightful bouquet which erroneously I mistook for a white Burgundy. Hindsight can be helpful, for the taste also resembled a wine from the Côte de Beaune. This may largely be thanks to the fact that the wine was matured in small oak casks. It is only recently that the use of small oak casks has become fairly general in this district, and unquestionably the result is proving beneficial.

1969 Souverain Pineau.
Pale colour, fresh clean fragrant bouquet, clean and fairly dry, refreshing and attractive. This vineyard was made famous by Lee Stewart, and after some seventeen years at the helm, it has just been sold. His wines have been of great quality, but since the new owners are devoted wine lovers, there is no fear that the standard will be lowered.

1968 Heitz Pinot Chardonnay. (Zinfandel Associates.)
Pale golden colour, pronounced varietal flavour, full and fruity, nice aftertaste, fine quality. (This particular wine has figured in tasting notes in my previous books and it has lived up to expectations.)

The Grand Cru Club:
A Tasting of 1964 Claret

There are two clubs, the Grand Cru Club and the Premier Cru Club, centred on the Bay Area of San Franscisco, which were founded for the purpose of studying the great wines of Bordeaux. To make it more interesting, four other châteaux have been added to the list: Mouton-Rothschild, Pétrus, Cheval Blanc, and Ausone.

There are eight members of each club, all of whom are experienced tasters, and to give an example of their expertise, while I was present at a tasting of the 1962's in April 1969, my host, Dr. Rhodes, put a name to six out of the eight, and he capped this when tasting the 1959's later on, for on that occasion he got them all right! As will be seen, it is not always the first growths of the Médoc which come out on top!

The Grand Cru Club tasting on this evening was held at the home of Dr. Robert Knudson in San Francisco. The members and guests were: Dr. Harry Drescher, Dr. W. Dickerson, Dr. Bernard L. Rhodes, Dr. Robert K. Adamson, Dr. J. Tupper, Mr. W. Peterson, Mr. Karl Petrowsky, and myself.

The meal was prepared and cooked by our host, and each course was served on priceless Royal Crown Derby plates; the spoons and forks were from his well-known collection of Hester Bateman silver. Such was the setting!

The first course consisted of asparagus vinaigrette, cold cauliflower in a béchamel sauce, radish and a stick of fennel; then came a chicken consommé, followed by beautifully cooked fish, special to this coast, called ling cod. With the former we enjoyed first an excellent magnum of Deutz 1961 and then Château Pontac Monplaisir 1967, an attractive white Graves. This château, which takes its name from a Marquis de Pontac in the seventeenth century, is not too well known, but it produces good-quality wine.

We ate roast leg of lamb, slightly pink inside, just as they eat it in France, alongside the eight *Grands Seigneurs* and followed on with a selection of cheeses which Harry Drescher had had specially flown in from Paris.

The fruit course was so good it must be described—a slice of papaya (with limes), a melon at its best, the finest-tasting pineapple the writer has ever come across, and huge firm strawberries, glistening in their scarlet glory. Incidentally, this is the season here for both strawberries and asparagus, and California is noted for the quality of both. Then came the splendid cookies for which Ray Dickerson is so rightly famed. With these last two courses we compared Château Guiraud 1955 and Château Climens 1955. Both were excellent, and yet so different; of the two, the Climens proved the more popular.

When one ponders over it, this is not a bad meal for a bachelor to produce, and what's more, with no outside help whatsoever! All the same, the purpose of the evening was the wine and not the food. We were to put the wines in order of preference and to try to recognize which was which. No mean task! As usual, Dr. Rhodes distinguished himself by getting six out of eight correct!

(See next page)

To find volatile acidity in the 1964 Pétrus was disconcerting, and since this is the second faulty bottle from the same case, later on I checked the wine with the château proprietor in Bordeaux. This particular case must have suffered from bad storage, because the 1964 Pétrus in Bordeaux is not only perfectly sound but splendid into the bargain!

At previous blind tastings of the 1964 vintage by the Grand Cru Club, Cheval Blanc had come out on top with Latour second. The other tasting club, the Premier Cru Club, had the same results in 1969-70, but with Pétrus averaging third.

1964 Vintage

The Wine	Characteristics	My Placing	Group Placing	Points
Lafite	Good colour, nice nose with fruit, medium body, well-balanced	3	4	40
Mouton-Rothschild	Medium colour, fair nose, medium body, mellow, some acidity still to lose	6	6	51
Cheval Blanc	Quite a nice colour, nice nose, fine big and round, good fruit and flavour	2	2	20
Margaux	Good dark colour, good nose, plenty of fruit, some tannin	4	3	33
Pétrus	Deep colour, full rich strong nose, bit of volatile on nose, unattractive; some acidity at finish	8	7	62
Haut-Brion	Fair colour, not much nose, good fruit, some acidity to lose; sharp finish	7	5	42
Ausone	Brown colour, odd nose, old in comparison, big wine, harsh finish	5	8	68
Latour	Deep colour, good nose, big and fine, a big wine still backward and undeveloped; some acidity to lose	1	1	18

A Galaxy of 1945's

Hosts: Mr. and Mrs. Larry Seibel, San Francisco.

Guests: Dr. and Mrs. B. L. Rhodes
Mr. and Mrs. Karl Petrowsky
Mr. and Mrs. Gary Park
Mr. and Mrs. Harry Waugh

Although it was not exactly his birthday, the dinner was arranged to celebrate his twenty-fifth anniversary, for Larry Seibel was born in 1945. As will be seen from some of the wines consumed, this was more than an ordinary vintage, and the cooking of Angie Seibel, his pretty young wife, was well in accord with the purpose of the meal. Apart from collecting fine wine, Larry Seibel has already amassed an important collection of books on the subject.

The Fare:

Quiche Lorraine: the perfect appetiser, so light that one forgot its presence. In accordance with the agreeable American custom, this dish was served with the Champagne, before we sat down to table.

Oxtail soup: embellished mildly with Rainwater Sack Madeira, this made a suitable "lining" for what was to follow.

Tomatoes stuffed with finely sliced ham and a piquant mayonnaise.

Leg of lamb served with a delicious mint cream sauce and with fresh green beans with toasted almonds.

Cheese: an assortment of mixed California and French.

Poached oranges in liqueur syrup.

Our host set us all to work by making us name the wines, few of which we got right! But after the third or fourth tasting, we did catch on to the fact that all of the wines were going to be of the same vintage.

The Wines: 1945 vintage.

Champagne, Gonet, recently disgorged.
Although the age was slightly discernible, the very pale colour and freshness were accounted for by the recent disgorging.

Mountain Folle Blanche, Louis Martini.
This was tasted after the champagne, and we found it difficult to place! Considering its great age, this white California wine had some admirable qualities.

Forster Freundstuck beerenauslese.
A pretty golden colour and a fabulous sweet rich bouquet, a splendid flavour too, yet not too sweet for the tomato dish, with which it was served. Over the course of time this beerenauslese has lost a good deal of its original sugar. What disturbed us all was the green bottle, giving the impression that it might have been a Moselle. The green colour of the glass was doubtless owing to the shortage of bottles at the end of the war, when anything available had to be used.

Château Mouton-d'Armailhac.
Dark colour, a good Cabernet Sauvignon bouquet, on the dry side, but still quite good. This was the wine served at Torquay, England, during the Second World Convention of the Wine & Food Society.

Château Mouton-Rothschild.
Dark colour, the unmistakable nose of Mouton (that is, when you are lucky enough to guess it right!), that typical cedar nose, or what the Americans call eucalyptus. Fine, full-bodied, and well-balanced, probably at its best now.

Château Latour.
Dark colour, a lovely expansive bouquet, full-bodied, with a fine flavour, but with some tannin, will doubtless improve. Very fine quality.

Beaune-Grèves (Avery).
A good dark colour and a big powerful wine.

Bonnes-Mares, Domaine Belorgey.
   Also a good colour, a charming fragrant bouquet which
   improved with exposure to the air, a delightful taste, a
   really fine red Burgundy.

Château Rieussec.
   A deep golden colour, a full sweet bouquet, rich, round,
   and lovely, still in perfect condition.

Sandeman Vintage Port.
   Good colour, a fine "firm" bouquet, good fruit and body,
   but is beginning to dry up a little.

Nineteen-forty-five can indeed be called one of the vintages of
the century because it was such a good all-rounder. As may be seen,
its wines from widely dispersed areas have kept splendidly over
twenty-five years. Perhaps the champagne was cheating a little
on account of its recent disgorgement, but apart from that, the red
and white Bordeaux, the Rhine wine, the red Burgundy, and the
port had all stood the test of time remarkably well. The only subsequent vintage which was really worthy to be hailed as the year
of the century is 1961, but with weaknesses where Rhine, Moselle,
and vintage port are concerned, this can hardly be called an all-
rounder.

A Visit to Freemark Abbey

Our hosts were Mr. and Mrs. Brad Webb, Mr. and Mrs. Carpy, Mr. and Mrs. Jaeger, Mr. and Mrs. Laurie Wood, and Mr. and Mrs. Luper. Besides my wife and myself, the other guests were Walt Peterson, Ken Kew (director of Esquin's, one of America's leading wine merchants), and Mr. and Mrs. Jack Davies, the creators of Schramsberg Champagne, recognized by connoisseurs to be one of the finest produced in the United States.*

Although it may have a religious-sounding name, Freemark Abbey has no connections of that nature. It is a recently resuscitated winery whose first vintage was 1967, and much of the produce comes from the 300 acres of vineyard owned by the directors.

In accordance with modern thinking, the number of varietals planted is limited to Cabernet Sauvignon, Pinot Noir, Chardonnay, and Johannisberg Riesling, and the ambition of the directors is to produce the finest quality of which these "aristocratic" vines are capable! The winemaking is in the capable hands of Jerry Luper, a young but well-trained enthusiast. Behind him he has all the knowledge, expertise, and experience of Bradford Webb, a noted biochemist and one of the most able winemakers of California.

The enthusiasm and dedication of all concerned at Freemark Abbey can only be described as ardent, so doubtless considerably more will be heard of this winery in future. These are some of the wines we tasted:

1970 Vintage from the wood

> *Pinot Chardonnay.*
>> A most distinctive bouquet, the wine is fresh and fruity, with a nice dry finish. Still in its nursery stage, this will probably be bottled around April 1972, and if one may judge by the way it is progressing, it should turn out very well.

* This Champagne was the only wine taken to Peking by President Nixon when he visited China in 1972.

Pinot Noir.
> A pleasant bouquet, and though not a big wine, it has a nice flavour.

Cabernet Sauvignon.
> Medium colour, a nice nose, again not a big wine, but it finishes well.

Cabernet Sauvignon (Bosche).
> A good colour and a lovely concentrated bouquet, good depth of flavour. With Martha's Vineyard, this is one of the finest Cabernet Sauvignons I have come across.

Merlot (from Zinfandel Associates).
> A very dark colour indeed, delightful bouquet, and a lovely full concentrated flavour. This is most unusual and most impressive. (It should prove wonderful for blending with Cabernet Sauvignon)

Wines in Bottle

1969 Johannisberg Riesling.
> Fresh and fragrant, with a pleasant dry finish, but it has a touch of what I call the California flavour, though how one defines that is beyond me!

1968 Johannisberg Riesling.
> A blend of wine from the vineyards of Chuck Carpy and Laurie Wood. Colour, an attractive light golden, a delightful spicy, honeyish nose, and a delicious taste not unlike that of a Rhine wine.

1968 Pinot Chardonnay.
> A typical fragrant Chardonnay nose, a lovely taste, with a whole gamut of flavour.

In my last book I described this as a "whacking great wine," and now, some two years later, so it has turned out. It is full of delightful flavour.

1968 Cabernet Sauvignon (Bosche).
> Mr. Bosche sells his grapes to a number of wineries, and the name has established a fine reputation.

A beautiful deep colour, a fine fruity bouquet reminiscent slightly of black currants. This wine has considerable body and depth and is unusual in that it had 10 percent of the 1968 Merlot added, the Merlot coming from the same source as the 1970 vintage. Unfortunately only sufficient of this wine was made for directors' consumption, but it is a good foretaste of what may lie in the future.

25th April, 1971

Ridge Vineyards

This winery, perched at some 2,300 feet high on the Montebello Road, overlooks part of the vast suburban sprawl of the San Francisco Bay Area, but in all other directions the view of the surrounding hillsides is most impressive.

Although I had known about 'Ridge' for some time, this was the first occasion I had actually visited the winery. There are in fact two wineries, and our host, Dick Foster, led us first to the old one situated at the summit of the hill; literally cut out of the rock, it was built some eighty years ago.

The red wines there were quite astonishing, and here are some of the details:

1970 *Zinfandel* (the grapes came from a vineyard in Occidental, situated in the Sonoma Valley).
An extraordinarily deep colour, a lovely bouquet, an enormously powerful wine with a superb flavour. It is quality such as this which excites one about the future of these wines of California.

1969 *Zinfandel* (Montebello Ridge, 1100 Ft.).
A deep colour and a bouquet reminiscent of blackberries, full-bodied, but it was spoiled for me by a slightly bitter finish.

(This is not to be confused with the other Montebello Zinfandel, which is now in bottle.)

1970 *Cabernet Sauvignon.*
Again a colour almost black, the bouquet so intense and so rich that it matched the splendid concentration of the flavour. As is to be expected, there is some tannin, but the wine is well-balanced and should make a great bottle.

1968 *Cabernet Sauvignon* (about to be bottled).
A good deep colour, a powerful bouquet, and heaps of fruit. Plenty of tannin too, which gives it a rather dry finish.

If I had the good fortune to live in this land of plenty, I would quickly put my name down for some of the 1970 Zinfandel and the 1970 Cabernet Sauvignon!

Descending to the lower winery, we were entertained by the directors and their wives: Mr. and Mrs. R. Foster, Mr. and Mrs. D. R. Bennion, Mr. and Mrs. H. Crane, and Mr. and Mrs. C. Rosen. We were also introduced to a new member of the Ridge organisation, Paul Draper, co-winemaker with Dave Bennion, a highly qualified young man who has studied not only in Bordeaux but has directed winemaking in Chile.

Amongst the wines we tasted from the bottle were:

1968 Ridge Zinfandel (Geyserville grapes).
   Good colour, attractive nose, lots of fruit, and considerable charm.

1959 Cabernet Sauvignon.
   A beautiful dark colour and a superbly rich wine. No wonder it has gained such a reputation.

(This was one of the early successes from this vineyard, and it was the quality of this wine amongst others which encouraged Dave Bennion to give up his post at Stanford Research Institute and to take to winemaking in a professional manner. When one considers the quality of the 1970 Zinfandel and Cabernet Sauvignon, one realises how beneficial this decision has been for the lovers of California wine.)

Finally our hosts opened for us a bottle of the 1968 Zinfandel Essence, a lovely, in fact delicious, dessert wine made from individually selected bunches of botrytised grapes picked at about 35 degrees Balling in November. These bunches were sorted one by one by Mrs. Bennion, Mrs. Crane, and Mrs. Rosen with sticky, absolutely freezing fingers!

Dinner with the Petersons

On this beautiful Sunday we tasted the following wines with Walter and Frances Peterson.

Charles Krug 1947. (Cabernet Sauvignon).
> A lovely dark colour, a lovely full Cabernet Sauvignon, almost Médoc nose, which grew and grew. So difficult to distinguish from a great Bordeaux, really fine.

Château Rouget 1945. (Pomerol).
> Very deep colour, a great scented sweet nose, huge rich, almost sweet wine. Formidable!

Vosne-Romanée Beaux Monts 1953. (P. Ponnelle).
> Great finesse on nose, well-balanced, lovely flavour, finishes beautifully, wonderful condition for a 1953.

Chambertin 1945. (P. Ponnelle).
> Rich nose, a great big wine, very fine quality. These two are exceptional Burgundies.

La Tour Blanche 1937.
> Not too rich, but very good.

Quinta do Noval 1931.
> What a treat to have this rare wine again, one which you hardly ever come across in England. The quality was tremendous!

Mayacamas

The Mayacamas Winery was built in 1889 by John Henry Fisher, an immigrant from Stuttgart (where he was a sword engraver) and a San Francisco pickle merchant. Bulk red and white table wines were made, and there was a small distillery. Vineyard plantings were of Zinfandel and "Sweetwater" grapes. Fisher sold the property after the turn of the century, and the winery fell into disuse. In 1941, after several changes in ownership, Jack and Mary Taylor (he of England, she of California) acquired the empty stone winery, distillery, and the ancient, declining vineyards. The winery was renovated, the distillery made into a home, and the old vines were torn out. The Taylors replanted the vineyards to Chardonnay and Cabernet Sauvignon and gave the winery the name Mayacamas (Fisher had called it Mount Veeder Vineyards).

In 1968 the Mayacamas Vineyards and Winery property was sold again. Now, under the control of Robert and Elinor Travers, it is specializing more and more in the wines of Mayacamas-grown grapes, Chardonnay and Cabernet Sauvignon. Other wines are sometimes made when top-quality grapes are available.

Mayacamas is the name of the mountains which separate the Napa and Sonoma valleys, where the vineyards and winery are located. It is a Spanish adaptation of an Indian word meaning "howl of the mountain lion." Cougars and bobcats still roam this range, and the name inspired the Mayacamas label design of two lions rampant. The winery is situated in superb country, still unblemished by the hand of man. At 2,000 feet it is one of a number of hilltop vineyards which seem to flourish in California.

I first visited this property in the most torrential downpour imaginable on a spring day in 1969 and mentioned some of its wines in *The Pick of the Bunch.* On the second visit, in April 1971, the weather was kinder, and after the tasting we were able to enjoy an alfresco lunch on the terrace in front of the Travers' house. This terrace overlooks a small but enchanting valley with wooded slopes on the left, but on the right the skyline is dominated by dramatic volcanic cliffs, now partially covered by trees and bushes. The bird life is vocal, to say the least, and high in the air soar the vultures which, no doubt, inhabit the rocky crags. This is a scene not to be forgotten.

The delightful young owners, Bob and Nonie Travers, are grubbing up the surrounding undergrowth and are planting out new vineyards as fast as they and their small labour force are able. As mentioned earlier, they are in the forefront of the growers who intend to reduce the varied assortment of varietals and in future to concentrate mainly on the few vines they consider most suitable for their particular soil.

With their purchase of the vineyard from their predecessors, they "inherited" Bob Sessions, a talented young winemaker. Together the two "Bobs" form a splendid young team, and it is easy to predict a promising future for Mayacamas.

These are some of the wines we tasted:

Wines in Wood

1970 *Chardonnay.*
> A lovely pale colour, a fine Chardonnay nose, plenty of fruit, yet fresh, with a nice dry finish. This wine, which has lots of promise, will be bottled around November 1971.

1970 *Chenin Blanc.*
> A good pale colour, an attractive bouquet, a very nice flavour, and a dry, good finish. There is plenty of breeding here.

(The previous owner sold a White Pinot from these identical vines, so no wonder there is confusion over these names. It might help the poor consumer if some *appellation contrôlée* could be exercised in this respect.)

1970 *Cabernet Sauvignon* (from vines averaging 7–8 years old).
> A splendid dark colour, a fine rich bouquet, similar, in fact, to that of a good red Bordeaux. This is a big strong wine with lots of tannin and some acidity, but there is plenty of time to lose that before it is fully mature!

1969 *Cabernet Sauvignon.*
> Very good colour, a fruity bouquet, full of fruit and flavour (a nice curranty taste), and it finishes well. This should make a good bottle.

Facing the fabulous view, we lunched in the spring sunshine off wild duck and fresh asparagus, and these are the wines we tasted with our most succulent repast.

1964 Pinot Chardonnay.
Unusually pale colour for its age, a well-bred bouquet, and a good flavour.

1967 Cabernet Sauvignon.
A good dark colour, with lots of fruit, and it showed particularly well with the cheese.

1968 Zinfandel (still in wood then, but bottling date was June 1971).
Very, very deep colour, almost black, a full bouquet, and a glorious rich flavour. No wonder, since its strength is 17 percent! The limit is 14 percent, so special permission had to be sought from the authorities to sell this wine.

This is what Dr. Richard Peterson of Beaulieu Vineyard has to say on the subject: "I called Bob Travers to get some information about it. He told me that it was a happy accident. He'd had some trouble during the crushing season and had fallen behind schedule. These Zinfandel grapes overripened to an average of 29 degrees Balling before he could get them picked and crushed. By that time, many of the individual berries had shriveled to become natural raisins! The natural acidity remained high, however, which is the real happy accident. When Bob saw this, he realized that he had a chance to make a truly different, but possibly quite good red wine. Without the acid, it would have been impossible.

"He fermented the must to complete dryness, which itself certainly was no easy feat—the final product contained 17 percent alcohol. Very few yeasts can survive and continue to ferment in a 17-percent environment! Such a heavy wine will undoubtedly require many years' bottle age to achieve its peak of softness. . . ."

Fortuitously during this visit to California, Walt Peterson's Wine Sampling Club held a tasting of old vintages of Mayacamas Pinot Chardonnay, and since it is seldom that one comes across such a long range of vintages from one property, this seems a good place for the findings to be recorded.

At times, at blind tastings such as this one, the organisers have a habit of slipping in a wine from Europe, or vice versa, and very often the result is quite revealing. On this occasion, the tasters were warned that a 1966 Montrachet (Bouchard Père et Fils) would be included, but as will be seen from the notes, not everyone picked it out! According to the book, it should have stood out head and shoulders above the others, so clearly the difference was not as definite as it might have been. Not only do customs like this put the tasters on their mettle, but the result also indicates that wines from Europe do not always stand out from the others, as might be expected.

A Range of Vintages of Pinot Chardonnay from Mayacamas

Year	Characteristics	My Placing	Points Against	Group Placing
1956	Dark colour, old and nutty, round and fat and sweet. Rather good	5	100	9
1968	Pale colour, nose a bit musty, young, light, very dry (acidity)	7	62	1
1969	Pale colour, nose very California, young, dry but attractive too, California taste	8	89	5
1952	Some colour, nice nose (older), some age but good	3	84	4
1959	Fine nose (fresh), clean, dry, good flavour, a bit hard at finish	4	92	6
1966 Montrachet	Very good nose (breed), good fruit and flavor	1	74	2
1966	Nice nose, attractive flavour	2	98	7/8
1967	Dusty nose, gone 'appley'	12	98	13
1964	Query nose? Tastes better than it smells	9	98	7/8
1955	Poor nose, no good	10	77	3
1958	Dark colour, old but sweet and rich/old still all there	6	101	10
1951	Dark colour, very old nose, maderise	13	134	12
1957	Odd nose (corky), has fruit, but a sharper finish (slightly corked)	11	123	11

Mirassou

This is the story of a family and of the oldest vineyard which has remained under single ownership since it was founded in 1854. There may be even older wineries, but in these cases the ownership has changed hands. The story has been told many times, but briefly, the founder, Louis Pellier, came from Cognac, finally settled in Santa Clara Valley, and planted a small vineyard on the western slopes of Mount Hamilton southeast of San Jose. Later on, his brother Pierre joined him, bringing with him vine cuttings from Bordeaux.

In 1884 one of Pierre Pellier's four daughters married a neighbouring vintner, Pierre Mirassou, originally from the Basque country of France. This was the beginning of the Mirassou dynasty. Until quite recently the family policy has been to produce good-quality wines which were sold to the large wineries, unaged and unbottled, only a small proportion being kept aside for home consumption, for local sale at the winery, and perhaps for exhibition at wine fairs.

Now the fifth generation of Mirassous (five of them) is in command, and in 1966 the whole policy was changed, new brooms sweeping clean! Instead of selling the majority of the wines to other vintners, the grapes are crushed, fermented at the winery, and the wine is now sold under the Mirassou label.

As so unfortunately is happening all over the world, urban development is fast encroaching upon agricultural land; thus, the Mirassou vineyards at Santa Clara County are being firmly pressed in just the same manner as all those fine lost vineyards which lay around châteaux Haut-Brion and La Mission-Haut-Brion, now encompassed by the suburban sprawl of Bordeaux. Bricks and mortar have taken their relentless toll! So it is in the Santa Clara Valley, where lovely orchards of apricot and other fruit trees are being grubbed up daily, only to be replaced by unattractive building estates.

With both courage and foresight the younger generation of Mirassous have purchased and laid out 1,000 acres of admirable vineyards, some eighty miles farther south, near Soledad in Monterey County. This land was virgin soil for vines and had never been infected by phylloxera, but just in case there would be any danger, an operation called "ripping" took place, and the ground was dug to the depth of from ten to twelve feet so that it could be properly immunised. The object was to be able to plant the pre-phylloxera vines without the usual grafting onto the native root stocks. These vines were planted some ten years ago, as from 1961 onwards, they are now maturing nicely, and every year the quality of the wine will improve. Previously it had taken some three years to select these vine stocks (all pure varietals) in order to ensure the best possible quality.

In company with other wineries in Monterey County, Mirassou has adopted mechanical harvesting, and it seems with most successful results. This means, of course, that the rows of vines have to be planted farther apart, but somehow it does not appear to affect the ultimate quantity of wine made.

This particular subject is of such interest that, by kind permission of Mr. E. A. Mirassou, his essay on the matter is included. I quote hereunder as follows:

A great step forward in the improvement of quality in table wines was taken at Mirassou Vineyards in 1969. This was accomplished by the use of a system of "Vineyard Crushing" of mechanically harvested grapes. In the vineyard, the bitter grape stems are left on the vine and the grapes are crushed into a must (seeds, skins, and juice). The must is then sterilized and placed into a closed stainless-steel container in an atmosphere of CO_2, the natural gas of fermentation. This system performs the first step of winemaking, formerly accomplished at the winery, within seconds from the time of picking.

The result of this "Vineyard Crushing" is a wine that has captured the fresh bouquet and aroma of the fruit and has eliminated any possible deterioration or oxidation during the initial stage of winemaking. We have compared wines made in 1969 and 1970 from both the "Vineyard Crushed" and the handpicked, winery-crushed grapes with the following results: the essence of the grape is consistently more pronounced in the "Vineyard Crushed" wine and the freshness and fruitiness has remained to enhance the wine and add to its ageability.

We believe this step forward in the production of quality in wine is as important as that step taken many centuries ago, when the winemaker first used a glass container and cork, instead of a ceramic jar with a goatskin cover. The glass and cork then allowed the winemaker to improve the wine by aging it in the bottle.

Within the last ten years, many agricultural crops have been harvested using newly developed methods of mechanical harvesting. Most of these methods have stressed the reduction in cost per ton of harvesting with little consideration for quality. We at Mirassou Vineyards, along with other California winemakers, have insisted on also improving the quality of the product.

Healthy, mature fruit, whatever the variety, is at its peak of perfection the moment it is removed from the mother plant. Within minutes after being picked, the fruit starts to deteriorate and oxidize, which results in a loss of food value and the natural flavor. One method of arresting this deterioration of the fruit is by harvesting before maturity. This method, however, results only in added eye-appeal and does not capture the quintessence of perfection as designed by nature.

We believe it is impossible to improve on nature in winemaking. Since this process is a natural one, the winemaker can only act as a guide. At Mirassou Vineyards, the grapes are harvested at their peak of ripeness and are kept at this peak until fermentation begins. This protection of the grape aids in the retention of its natural flavors, acids, and aroma. It also deters such factors as bitterness from stems and oxidation from air or foreign particles. Thus, the essence of the natural product is preserved by our system of "Vineyard Crushing."

The development of the mechanical grape harvester began in 1959. At that time, Mirassou Vineyards started to work on a harvester using the vacuum principle. Between 1960 and 1964, Gallo Winery, also working on the vacuum principle, succeeded in assembling several working models. About the same time, Cornell University in New York State was harvesting vitis Labrusca grapes in the eastern states with their newly designed harvester. Also in the early 1960's the "Sycle Bar" method of harvesting grapes was developed by the University of California at Davis.

All of these methods had undesirable features. Among the problems encountered were: breakage of the berries, damage to the vine causing an excessive number of leaves and limbs to enter into the harvester, and too many grapes left on the vine.

Between 1961 and 1965, the Wine Advisory Board financed many contracts with the University of California. The departments of viticulture and enology at Davis, California, began working on the development of methods of mechanical harvesting. They also experimented with longer stems on the grapes and stems that would break more easily to facilitate the mechanical harvesting. Then, about 1967, Davis came up with the idea of training grapes on the two-wire, horizontal trellis. The harvester companies developed the vertical impactor machines which did a satisfactory job of harvesting these vines. During 1968 and 1969, the transverse impactor and the pivotal striker were developed. These developments enable the machine to pick a high percentage of grapes. In many varieties, however, individual berries, rather than the total bunch, were picked, which resulted in many of the berries being broken. This meant, of course, more rapid deterioration and oxidation of the fruit. The deductive answer, therefore, was to crush the fruit in the vineyard immediately after picking.

In 1970, Mirassou Vineyards harvested 75 percent of their 1,000 acres in Monterey County using a new method of "Vineyard Crushing." To accomplish this, a mechanical harvester designed by the Up-Right Harvester Company was used. Two small crushers and two specially designed tanks with a 500-gallon capacity were mounted on the harvester like saddle bags. At the end of each vine row, the harvested and crushed grapes were emptied from the saddle bag tanks, with the pressure of CO_2, into an enclosed tank truck which immediately transported the juice, seeds and skins to the winery. Thus, the grapes did not come in contact with the air, from the time they were removed from the vine until safely fermenting at the winery.

This system improves the efficiency of handling, reduces costs, increases productivity, and most importantly, improves the quality and control of the end product. In view of these results, we believe that within a few years most harvesting of wine grapes will be done with a system of "Vineyard Crushing."

Mechanical harvesting can be especially important in the crushing of white grapes, for it is white wine which suffers most from oxidation. With this new method, as stated previously, it is reckoned that only eight seconds elapse from the moment the grapes are picked until they enter their CO_2-filled container on the machine, and a similar period at the winery before they go into the fermentor. It is claimed that only the ripe grapes are picked, the unripe ones being left on the vines. With the introduction of mechanical harvesting, alas, much of the gaiety and glamour departs from the vineyards, but it will certainly help to keep down the cost of production, for by this method two men can now accomplish the work of 125.

Ray Krause, Mirassou hospitality director, explained all these details to Belle Rhodes, my wife, and myself at the winery in San Jose where we were joined for the tasting by Dan Mirassou, a member of the dynamic younger generation. Wine is still made from the 300 acres of Santa Clara County vineyards, but one of these days, the latter will doubtless succumb to relentless concrete and the horrors of human expansion.

As for the vineyards around Soledad in Monterey County, the first harvest was in 1966, and this is pointed out on a special neck label; the 1969 vintage, for example, is called the "Fourth Harvest, Limited Bottling," each bottle being numbered; and the date of bottling is also given: "September 1, 1970."

These are some of the wines we tasted:

1969 Pinot Chardonnay.
          Fourth Harvest (Monterey, hand-picked).
          Bottled September 1st, 1970. Aged in small Limousin.
          Very pale colour, nice fresh bouquet, clean and very dry,
          good aftertaste.

1969 Johannisberg Riesling.
          (Santa Clara, hand-picked.)
          Pale colour, nice clean bouquet, fresh, with a good flavour.

1970 Johannisberg Riesling.
          (Monterey, machine-harvested.)
          Pale colour, a most fragrant nose and a delightful flavour,
          it has a nice fresh finish, the flavour not unlike that of a
          German wine.

1970 Gewurztraminer.
          Fifth Harvest (Monterey).
          Pale colour, attractive, Traminer nose, tasting as it smells.
          Good quality.

1970 Chenin Blanc.
          (Monterey, machine-harvested.)
          Full, slightly sweet bouquet, medium dry, medium sweet,
          but good quality.

1967 Petit Sirah.
          (Santa Clara, hand-picked.)
          Good dark colour, a nice full bouquet, a big rich rather
          grapey wine, quite a mouthful, in fact, made from very old
          vines.

1967 Zinfandel.
          (Santa Clara, hand-picked.)
          Pretty bouquet, plenty of fruit and has a nice finish.

1966 Cabernet Sauvignon.
          First Harvest (Monterey, hand-picked from five-year-old
          vines).
          Pleasant varietal nose, some acidity, which no doubt will
          diminish, but good considering the age of the vines.

(This wine was kept for 2½ years in 50-gallon Limousin oak barrels. From 1970 onwards all the Monterey County wines have been

machine-harvested. During 1968 and 1969 experiments were conducted on a few acres.)

Later on we were taken to lunch at an excellent restaurant in Santa Clara called Lorenzo's, where the "patron," an Italian called Lorenzo, cooked a delicious meal for us with his own hands.

Chappelet

Situated high up in the hills of the Napa Valley lies Chappelet, surely the most striking, the most modern, and the most unusual winery in the world. Set like a gigantic gem in superb unspoiled wooded country, it seems to blend itself into the very ground. Conceived by an artist and not an architect, it defies proper description.

The greater part of the vineyards of the Napa Valley are planted on flat ground, but here at Chappelet the vineyards slope in all directions, similar to those on the hillsides of the Côte d'Or of Burgundy, all of which tends to give the setting an added charm. Unlike the majority of vineyards, visitors come here only by request, hence the difficult approach road winding up the steep hill through the woods which appear to be infested by wild deer, some of which you are almost bound to see either on the way up or down. Attractive as they may look by the roadside, these deer are a real problem for the wine growers, because they cause immense damage; they seem to be particularly partial to vine leaves, and even more so to grapes. The deer fences which forcibly surround these hillside wineries are quite a costly capital item.

As you enter the winery, you gasp, such is the effect upon you of this vast, almost cathedral-like building, which seems to support itself without pillars, yet remains entirely functional. In one corner there is an impressive line of stainless-steel fermentation tanks (Mueller Co., Springfield, Missouri), each jacketed by an eighth-inch-thick cooling sheath which contains glyco; I am told this is highly efficient.

I first met the young owner, Don Chappelet, in 1969 at an alfresco lunch and tasting at Joe Heitz's winery in Spring Valley. At that time his winery had yet to be built, but the produce from his vineyards was made into wine and cared for by no less a person than Joe himself. Now Don Chappelet was here proudly to show us his remarkable property. We also met his skilled winemaker, Phil Togni, who had been for some years at Château Lascombes and had also studied enology at famous French institutes such as that at Montpellier.

The policy at Chappelet is to restrict the planting to Johannisberg Riesling, Chenin Blanc, Chardonnay, Cabernet Sauvignon, and Merlot. It is also very evident that the idea of quality stands supreme here, and although the quantity may never be great, this is one of the new wineries from which one can expect great things in the future.

Here are some of the wines we tasted:

Johannisberg Riesling 1969.
> Very pale colour, a nice fresh bouquet, elegant and fruity, exceedingly dry; in fact, one of the driest Johannisberg Rieslings I have tasted so far.

Johannisberg Riesling 1970.
> Very pale colour, this has a stronger varietal bouquet and is a little richer, with more fruit.

Chenin Blanc 1970. (13.7 percent).
> Delightful bouquet; in fact, a most intriguing gamut of smells, a rich but clean flavour, with a pleasant finish.

We also tasted the same wine which had been kept in Nevers oak for six weeks, and already it was slightly different in character; then the same wine again, but this time from a cask made of Limousin oak; the latter had a stronger flavour. This is what is so fascinating about California; nearly everyone is experimenting, everyone trying to see how they can make things even better.

Cabernet Sauvignon 1969. (from cask).
> Good colour, an agreeable fruity bouquet, plenty of body and plenty of tannin, will need time to mature. This wine was made from five-year-old vines and had 2 percent Merlot blended with it. The small percentage of Merlot is accounted for by the fact that that is all there was available, but as time passes and all these young vines come into full production and grow to "man's estate," we shall be hearing much more of the Chappelet vineyard.

7th May, 1971

With Les Amis du Vin in San Francisco

Early in April 1971 while I was in Washington, D.C., Alfio Moriconi suggested that I should get in touch with Bill Hickey, the San Francisco director of Les Amis du Vin, and through him in due course Prue, my wife, and I received an invitation to dine with Dan Chapin at the University Club at the summit of Nob Hill.

Although I have not seen anything like as much as I would wish of this fascinating city of San Francisco, it was a great pleasure to enjoy vicariously the thrills experienced by my wife, Prue, whose first visit this was. The precipitous streets (so long as you do not have to walk up them), the cable cars, and the ever-changing views are a constant source of delight. Actually, as I sat at the dinner table I looked out on what was for me an altogether fresh scene, a view looking along the Bay Bridge towards Treasure Island. Our fellow guests were Mr. and Mrs. Hickey and a wine merchant called Tony Wood.

For dinner we ate excellent Dungeness crab and roast chicken, and with this we drank Chablis La Fourchaume 1967, two bottles of Château Margaux 1953, of which the first was surprisingly old and decrepit but the second was much better. All the same, from this experience it would seem that this once so lovely wine has seen better days. Our spirits were restored though by the excellent bottle of 1962 Musigny Vielles Vignes (Comte Georges de Vogüé).

Feeling no pain by this time (as may be well imagined!) we set out for the Stanley Burtons' lovely home on Telegraph Hill, where the tasting of a number of vintages of Château Latour had been arranged for about twenty members of Les Amis du Vin. Among them I was delighted to meet again Dave Bennion and Paul Draper, the two able winemakers at Ridge Winery.

It is always interesting as well as educational for me to see a range of vintages of Château Latour because so often am I asked how such and such a vintage of the château is faring, because I myself have none since 1959 in my own possession; at present-day prices, I have to be content with lesser fry. A tasting such as this, then, gives one an opportunity to assess the merit of one vintage

146

against another, but also how Latour itself fared in those years and how the wines are behaving now.

As was to be expected, the 1949 took pride of place but the surprise however was the 1955, because this has turned out to be a slightly disappointing year for a number of châteaux. The 1955 emerged with flying colours, full-bodied and sturdy with considerable character. All the same, I did not expect it to beat in popularity the more famous 1961, though, of course, the latter, still so severe and buttoned up, has a splendid future in prospect.

The disappointment was the 1952, a year of which at the time we all expected great things. Being unduly greedy, I would have preferred instead to have tasted the 1953 Latour in order to compare it with the 1953 Margaux we had tried earlier in the evening at dinner, but such opportunities occur all too seldom. Ever since this great vintage of 1953 came on the scene, the 1953 Latour has been the odd man out among the first-growths community. It may be now when some of the famous châteaux are sliding gently downhill that the robust Latour may come into its own, but this can only be tested by trying them all together. This makes one wonder who, if anybody, has all the first growths of that year still in their possession.

The following are my notes from the Burtons' tasting:

Vintage Château Latour

1966 Medium-dark colour, intense very young nose, full, fierce, and powerful, heaps of fruit. Needs five years or more.

1964 Deep colour, distinguished nose, developing well. Well-balanced, full-bodied, still lots of tannin. Needs five years.

1962 Very dark colour, full fruity nose, beginning to develop but still a bit fierce, masses of fruit, some tannin. Needs three to four years.

1961 Very dark colour, huge bouquet, almost overwhelming. A huge wine, still undeveloped, full of tannin. Ten to twenty years?

1959 Very dark colour, fine full bouquet. Deep and full-bodied, has developed well and is ready to drink. Lovely meaty flavour. Still some tannin. Four years perhaps?

1955 Very dark colour, full cedar bouquet, which is well developed, round with heaps of fruit, but still some tannin. Here is the real Latour flavour. Three to four years?

1952 Dark colour, powerful yet rather severe nose, with a trace of cedar or what the Californians call eucalyptus, very dry. Plenty of fruit, but at the same time somewhat hollow. Still considerable tannin. Query, will the fruit outlast the tannin?

1949 Good dark colour, rich fragrant cedar bouquet, lovely flavour, most of the tannin and immaturity is now discarded. Latour showing its true self, but it may improve still further.

Dinner with the Rhodes

When I visited Lee Stewart in 1964, I was so impressed by his 1961 Cabernet Sauvignon that there and then I bought and paid for a case, hoping somehow it could be shipped to England. The case never arrived, and I had given up hope, until during my next visit to Souverain in 1969. Lee told me he had found it impossible to ship one single case to England. This provided a splendid opportunity to reciprocate some of the Rhodeses kindness to me, so I handed the case over to them and on this splendid evening we drank it amongst the others. Here is yet another proof of the possibilities of the great wines of this district.

The Wines:

> 1970 *Souverain Green Hungarian.*
> Fresh, very fragrant nose, lovely fruit acidity.

> 1970 *Souverain Flora.*
> Hybrid of Gewurztraminer and Semillon. Slight smell of Traminer, good fruit, but too much acidity for me.

These wines were served with tomatoes stuffed with Dover Sole, herb sauce and fish aspic—really excellent!

> 1970 *Souverain Cabernet Sauvignon.*
> Good colour, very rich nose, smells of some fruit, is it plum? Very good fruit, which is encompassed by acidity.

> 1961 *Souverain Cabernet Sauvignon.*
> A fine deep colour, going brown at edges, a lovely rich nose, a huge rich wine, superb quality. Took it for a great Cabernet Sauvignon 1947! The first time I have actually drunk it, and it's *marvellous.*

The Cabernet Sauvignons were accompanied by beautifully underdone steak and carrots; fresh spinach salad with water chestnuts, crisp bacon, onion, herbs. *- herbed croutons !?*

149

1959 Suduiraut.
Very great elegance, not too rich, just right.

With gorgeous coffee-layer ice-cream cake.

1950 Croft.
Full and as good as any 1950 I have ever had.

At Yountville

We spent our last Sunday in California in fine style, for Harry See had invited the Rhodes, Prue, and myself for lunch at his home at Yountville in the Napa Valley. A short time ago Harry built this delightful house on the edge of a lake, or what is really a reservoir, for the irrigation of his vines. Besides his son, also Harry, the other guests were Mr. and Mrs. Joe Heitz and Mr. and Mrs. William Darney.

Knowing my predilection for seafood, our host had provided a magnificent spread of entirely West Coast specialities. To begin with, served in what resembled small egg cups with one or two bay shrimps, were the minute Olympia oysters for which San Francisco is so famous. On top of this delicacy, it was suggested we should ladle a spoonful of local caviar!

In Europe, on the extremely rare occasions when one is offered caviar, it is served more or less by the thimbleful, but here in California the portions are decidedly generous; at least that has been my fortunate experience! Once or twice before I have mentioned the California variety from the Sacramento River, which is so good that unless you actually taste the Beluga alongside, you would hardly know the difference.

These tidbits were followed by cracked crab, which on this occasion was served with no less than three different sauces, mayonnaise, vinaigrette, and crabfat sauce. Never before had I even heard of the last-named, but it was delectable.

Harry See has a property here of some 320 acres, of which about 40 percent are freshly planted with vines. It runs alongside the Napa River, and on the other side is bounded by the enchanting hills, such as you only see in this immediate neighbourhood; they remind you of a kind of fairy dreamland. When these vines reach maturity in, say, ten years or so, they will undoubtedly contribute to the quality of the Napa Valley produce of the future.

Later, we drove to Spring Valley to spend the rest of the day with Joe and Alice Heitz. This is a highlight of any visit to California, for here you taste what is possibly the finest quality the district can produce. Joe Heitz is undoubtedly among the three outstanding winemakers. In fact, I regard him rather as I do Henri Woltner of Château La Mission-Haut-Brion in Bordeaux. When I visit Joe, no punches are pulled; he lets me taste his entire range, and at the same time invites candid criticism. He is on fairly safe ground there, though, because being such a skilled winemaker, it is difficult to restrain one's enthusiasm.

As will be seen from the following tasting notes, using his exceptional skill and knowledge as a winemaker, he selects wines from many wineries and brings them to maturity on his own property and then sells them under his own label. He has the originality to indicate on the label the source of wine or grapes, as the case may be. For instance, U.C.V. means the grapes from the University of California Vineyard; Zinfandel Associates is a vineyard belonging to a syndicate comprising Doctors Rhodes, Adamson, and others, and, of course, there is Martha's Vineyard. Cabernet Sauvignon of the quality of Martha's Vineyard could almost be described as a first growth of the Napa Valley. Certainly it is among the very best red wines produced in California, or, for that matter, the United States.

While we are on the subject of Cabernet Sauvignon—and I am sure I have mentioned this elsewhere—the average Cabernet Sauvignon of California often has a tiny trace of fierceness which you do not find in the red wines of Bordeaux. Perhaps this is the reason why formerly the growers matured their Cabernet Sauvignon in huge wooden casks for three or four years before bottling. All the same, it would be interesting to know what pure unblended Cabernet Sauvignon from either Latour or Lafite would taste like!

Incidentally, while in Bordeaux in July 1971 I found that a proprietor of one of the classified growths, Château Lafon-Rochet, had kept aside a cask of unblended Cabernet Sauvignon and one of Merlot, just to see how they would develop individually, and then, later on, of course, they will be blended with the rest. The Merlot was soft and charming and far less astringent than the Cabernet Sauvignon, the latter being much more powerful, with considerably more tannin.

These are the wines which I tasted that day:

Pinot Blanc 1970. (Lindcrest vineyard).
    Good pale colour, flowery, fragrant bouquet, good flavour.

Pinot Blanc 1970. (Stony Hill vineyard).
    Good colour, most attractive bouquet, has a little more depth than the Lindcrest. These two Pinot Blancs have the

same sugar content and have been treated in exactly the same manner, so the difference must be a matter of the soil. The Stony Hill wines usually develop a bit later than other white wines of the same kind.

Pinot Chardonnay 1970. (U.C.V.).
Very pale colour, fine flowery bouquet, light and clean, needs time to develop.

Pinot Chardonnay 1970. (Zinfandel Associates).
A shade darker, full round bouquet, ripe and fruity, this will make a good bottle.

Cabernet Sauvignon 1970. (Martha's Vineyard).
A splendid dark colour, the bouquet reminiscent of black currants! This is a great big wine which is still full of tannin.

1968 Cabernet Sauvignon. (Regular).
Good colour and a most attractive bouquet, has charm, and is rounding off nicely. Bottled around January 1972.

1968 Cabernet Sauvignon. (Martha's Vineyard).
Very deep colour, full, but still undeveloped bouquet. A huge fruity wine, one can almost eat it!

1969 Cabernet Sauvignon.
Good deep colour, lovely bouquet, good fruit and body, still undeveloped.

1969 Cabernet Sauvignon. (Martha's Vineyard).
Colour almost black, full, almost curranty nose, a huge, full-bodied wine.

Wines already in bottle

1967 Cabernet Sauvignon. (Martha's Vineyard).
Good deep colour, concentrated bouquet, a big full-bodied wine, but there is still a little acidity to lose. Will be sold in 1972.

1966 Cabernet Sauvignon. (Martha's Vineyard).
Very deep colour and very full bouquet. A great big wine which I preferred to the 1967, though this was not every-one's opinion at the tasting. I was reminded that I had

also preferred it when tasting last year. It was bottled
about a year ago.

While dining with Tom and Martha May during this visit to
California, they served this very wine, and it showed up remarkably
well, though it was full young. I imagine it needs four or five years
more to be at its best.

Later, at dinner, fellow guests were the Sebastianis. August is
the noted wine grower at Sonoma whom I mentioned in *Bacchus
on the Wing*. It was nice to see him again.

Joe started us off in fine style with a lovely magnum of his Pinot
Chardonnay 1968 (Lot Z82). Then for my benefit he opened a bottle
of 1917 Zinfandel, Castlerock Mountain, Repsold, and it was most
interesting. The colour was good, and it had kept very well, better
than many a red Bordeaux of its age. With our cheese we shared a
magnum of Joe's Cabernet Sauvignon 1962. (This was before Martha's Vineyard appeared on the scene.) A good deep colour, heaps
of fruit, and very good to drink now. As a *bonne bouche* Joe gave
us his Alicia, a speciality which he makes in the same manner as
one would a Barsac, but from Chardonnay grapes.

20th May, 1971
With the Wine and Food Society in New York

We arrived in the late afternoon in time to change for a dinner given by the directors and management of the New York Wine & Food Society at the Harmonies Club. This gave us a splendid opportunity to meet the New York members and their wives, as well as a group from the Baltimore chapter, many of whom were old friends from the last world convention held in Torquay, England.

Gastronomically the evening was also most interesting, for it was a seafood affair and never before in the United States have I been exposed to so great a variety—delectably exposed, I hasten to add. How I enjoy the American habit of offering a first course while you are still standing up, and may I add, in view of the inborn hospitality of the citizens, while one is still capable of standing up!

Actually, we drank only Taittinger Champagne (only that!!!) to begin with, but what did we eat with it? No less than smoked salmon, fresh clams on the shell, three different ways of cooked clams, steamed baby lobster, and also steak tartare. If you are about to embark on a vinous evening, there is no better "tummy lining" in the world than steak tartare. On this occasion it was a particularly good mix!

The vinous target of the evening was a range of six vintages of Johannisberg Riesling from that genius of a wine grower, Dr. Konstantin Frank. He must be a genius indeed if he can produce such good wine when he has to contend with such an inclement climate! To be absolutely honest, I found some of the wines a little too sharp for my particular palate, but in view of the climate, I can readily understand this. The two vintages I liked were the 1967 and the 1962.

With the wine we consumed a gamut of seafood, clam soup, soft clams dunked in their natural broth, and broiled lobster, all quite delicious. After the meal I discoursed courageously on the wines of California, of which I do not pretend to be in any way an authority, merely an enthusiast.

The following day we paid a visit to Sam Aaron of Sherry Lehmann and then lunched in Central Park West with Leonard and Bonny Birnbaum, where among the guests I was enchanted to find

155

my dear friend Poppy Cannon, with whom I did a wine progression, as mentioned in my first book, *Bacchus on the Wing,* also Charles Mandelstam, a lawyer, and vineyard proprietor of the Côte Rotie in France.

That evening was the occasion of my talk to the members of the Wine & Food Society on Château Latour and this took place in the vast Waldorf Astoria Hotel. This I at least enjoyed, if no one else. There were many questions, which is always satisfactory. Later Howard and Marie-Elaine Meighan took us for a "reviver" at the Four Seasons, and later we dined delightfully at the 21 Club.

The last day was spent mainly at the telephone, everyone was out, or away (it was raining outside too) but the gloom was lifted while I lunched with Margaret Dorsen, who looks after the public relations for the wines of Bordeaux and Alsace. The restaurant was the Madrigal on 53rd Street, where, as a starter, I ate some of the best soft-shelled crab of my life, but as to the wine, I made the mistake of letting the sommelier suggest Calon Ségur 1964. Only when I tasted its curious sweetness did I remember *les evenements* of the vintage of 1964! I should have known better.

France,
1971 Visit

Dining in London Clubs

The expression "a London clubman" was in common use in the days before the war but seldom does one hear this today—it epitomised a part of London life which is fast disappearing. Nevertheless, London has always been and still remains, a man's world, just as Paris is a woman's world and in spite of women's lib and all that, for heaven's sake let us cling to this, our last stronghold!

The clubs, those sanctuaries of the male preserve, are a delightful if diminishing part of the London scene. Three of them date back to Georgian times and they stem from the old London Coffee Houses, taking their names from the erstwhile proprietors, namely, White's, Boodles and Brooks's.

The first I ever belonged to was the Cocoa Tree in St. James's Street, also one of the old original Coffee Houses but now defunct and long pulled down and, as a very young man, I remember the fear and trembling with which I entered its portals. The very thought brings back to me the smell of the old leather of ancient armchairs and sofas, the imitation trunk of a palm tree which formed a pillar in the middle of the Smoking Room, also alas, the prehistoric plumbing when infrequently, I stayed the night. I cannot remember ever dining in those far off days. My sorties to London were more concerned with the fair sex, so my dining, wining and other activities took place elsewhere, though this was not nearly so dashing as it may sound, for in those far off days "le plupart de jeunes filles étaient sans raproche," or is it that I was rather slow?

My next club, the Wyndham (also defunct) was situated in the north-west corner of St. James's Square, a lovely old 18th century building, which happily still stands, though now sacrificed to vulgar commerce. Members were told that it was from the balcony of this house that the first news of the victory of Waterloo was announced. Inside, mingled with an agreeable atmosphere, there was excellent plain English food to be had, for it was noted for its cuisine; although this may be difficult for some visitors to believe, at its best, English cooking takes quite a lot of beating! At lunch time, the chef, Mr. Wicks, attired in spotless white, used to appear in the coffee room to see that all was well. I can see his chef's apron still, for around it was strapped a belt containing a fearsome array of carving knives.

From those days there are unforgettable memories of delightful bibulous dinners in the company of friends of my own age, followed by games of "boozey" billiards. I can safely say we never actually damaged the cloth but at times must have got mighty close to it, for by that time we were usually on our second glass of vintage port! The meals consisted of dishes such as plovers' eggs (in springtime) or Dover Sole followed by grilled steak or something similar, and incidentally, for those Americans who have not visited London, how good Scotch beef can be, so much better than the Charollais variety about which they make such a fuss in France. The only beef I personally have tasted to equal it has been in Chicago, but "chacun à son gout"!

What claret were we drinking in those gloomy years just before the war when the spectre of Hitler and his brownshirts loomed so heavily over us? For best, it must have been the 1920's and 1924's and how good they were and as for red Burgundy, we were terribly spoiled with the 1923, 1926 and 1929 vintages. At that time, the backward 1926 clarets were altogether too tough to be really enjoyable, the already famous 1928's hopelessly rigid, frigid, or whatever it is, and the blissful 1929's were also really too young to drink.

But the Port, oh, the vintage Port, that with a fine Havana cigar was part of the background of our evenings at the Wyndham, rare events admittedly on account of our slender purses—a huge glass of, was it the Taylor 1920, or the Cockburn 1896? I know we had both on tap and both sold for what nowadays would be a derisory price. There can be few clubs in the world these days which have a great forty year old vintage port for the asking!

The poor Wyndham closed its doors for the duration of the war, never to re-open independently, but since by that time I was a relatively elderly but undistinguished soldier, I joined the Guards Club and that led to some of my best years of claret and port drinking, not of course, during the war because one was seldom in London, but during the years just afterwards.

In the late forties, the 1928 clarets were still undrinkable and the much vaunted 1934's sadly disappointing. Before the war, I had sold the 1934's to all my best friends, expecting them to be marvellous, but somehow, with the exception of the Saint-Emilions and Pomerols, they never really made the grade, but at least my friends saw a healthy capital appreciation.

So what did we have? The 1929's—what else? Verging on six-teen years old and absolutely in their prime, they were magnificent, never before nor since have I tasted their equal. Their bouquet was so delightful and so distinctive that even I at times, could guess the vintage! What a flavour they had and what charm! Later on, in their heyday, the 1953's were also in the same sort of bracket, but I don't think they ever matched the 1929's. Outstanding among them were Léoville-Poyferré and Rausan-Ségla, two châteaux which might do a lot better in these modern days. Pontet-Canet was a masterpiece and still is, but you need the good fortune to be invited to the château to enjoy it. The last bottle I drank of 1929 Calon-Ségur was delicious too and the Latour isn't doing so badly either! But the port, again, oh, the port, for this was the time when the 1927's really came into their own, at just about 20 years old. There was a remarkable choice at the Guards Club in those days, we began with the Sandeman and moved on to the Graham, then to the Fonseca and finally the Taylor, so far as I can remember, all bottled by my old firm Harveys and all of them fabulous. It was ridiculously cheap too for it is the tradition in a good club always to give the members the benefit of a favourable purchase. Very occasionally nowadays one is offered a 1927, but at some forty years old, it is, to me, at any rate, only a shadow of what it used to be twenty years ago. Eheu fugaces!

What about the present day though, because that is what I am supposed to be writing about! Once nostalgia steps in, away we go! The London Clubs have changed greatly since the war, burden-some taxation has had its depressing effect so it has been a struggle for many of them to keep open, but in spite of that the more popu-lar ones still have long waiting lists. Formerly, they were strictly a male preserve, but sometimes females are now graciously per-mitted to participate, either in their own right as members of the Ladies' side, as, for instance, in Boodles and the Guards Club; in others, such as Brooks's, they are only allowed to poke their noses in on Friday and Monday evenings, much to the displeasure of certain members—the thin end of the wedge and all that!

The Ladies' side of Boodles is particularly attractive, pleasant surroundings, very good food and moderately priced wine. Here, though, you are likely to fall in with old friends and that may mean falling into trouble over vintage port, to which under other circumstances, you might not have succumbed!

The Coffee Rooms of the traditional London Clubs (presumably they take this name from their former Coffee House days) are always packed at lunchtime, though no longer are you permitted to drink your post-prandial coffee there. One of the main features at lunch is the good "cold table," where spread before you, is a wide selection of smoked salmon from Scotland, smoked trout, potted shrimps, cold lobster and patés galore. English caterers seem to be over fond of the everlasting liver paté; seldom, as in France, does one come across a good terrine. Then there is the unsurpassed cold salmon and the best time to enjoy this in England is between the end of January and the end of May, thereafter the taste is less good, but you can always switch to sea trout which is similar and remains succulent until the end of the summer. Also on the "cold tables" are to be found briskets of beef, tongues in their natural shape, cold legs of lamb and joints of roast beef, though at times it is difficult to find the roast beef sufficiently rare. I reckon you cook your beef much better in America than we do in England.

The hot dishes consist of the usual steaks and chops, liver and bacon, kidneys and bacon, but seldom sweetbreads. The "plat du jour" can be quite diverse, fish cakes, sometimes very good, roast lamb, roast beef, boiled silverside and dumplings, a traditional English dish this, if ever there was one. Then in winter-time there is steak and kidney pudding and this means great wedges of delicious but "fattening" and no doubt, indigestible suet on your plate!

To accompany this food at lunch-time, quite a lot of wine is drunk, either by the glass or "en carafe." For those who order something finer and many do, the claret or red burgundy is always decanted.

The cooking in these male preserves may not be of the same high standard as at the Jockey Club or the Nouveau Cercle in Paris, but, by and large, with some weaker brethren admittedly, it is a fairly good average. It must be remembered that, in England, we probably have some of the finest primary produce in the world and so it remains until some of our chefs get at it! For instance, the fresh vegetables which should be our pride and joy, are, in reality, one of our besetting sins, because even in the most exclusive establishments, they are usually hopelessly overcooked. We have to console ourselves with the thought that there are other things which make up for this lapse from grace!

Some clubs are busy at dinner time, others not so much, but they all have their own atmosphere and individual character. Prominent among them is the Garrick, renowned for its food, but it is also famous for what might be termed its picture gallery. There are pictures everywhere, the staircase in the main hall is crowded with fascinating portraits of past members and theatrical personalities over the past two hundred years, including one of Garrick himself and in the dining room, among a number of other paintings, there are several Zoffany's.

While on this subject, on the walls of the first floor dining rooms of the St. James's Club (one of the few fine 18th century houses still standing on Piccadilly) hang the famous paintings of the Dilettante Society. It can be highly agreeable to dine here on a long summer's evening and look out through the tall windows on to the verdant grass and beautiful trees of Green Park. Each club has its own special charm and if you happen to be an admirer of elegant staircases, there are particularly fine ones to be found in the St. James's, Brooks's, White's and the Garrick.

In White's, where you eat and drink very well, you dine on the first floor in the large, lofty red walled room which looks delightful by candlelight and there on the walls hang huge portraits of past monarchs, all former members of the club, as well as one of the Duke of Wellington. One of them was painted by Goya. White's has an amusing club device or coat of arms which was designed by an 18th century member, instead of the usual motto underneath, carved in large letters is the word "CLARET"!

In Brooks's, the one time haunt of Charles James Fox, the drinking of claret is such a tradition that it accounts for about 80 percent of the total consumption, aided of course, by a little vintage port! Here, in winter time, you eat your grouse, partridge or whatever it is, by the aid of candlelight. The splendid Georgian silver candlesticks have been the property of the club since it was founded some 200 years ago. Private dinner parties of the first order are held on the first floor in the finely proportioned, barrel ceilinged Subscription Room, with insets high up on the walls reputed to be the work of Angelica Kauffman. This is the room where the Regency Bucks used to gamble and a coloured print by Rowlandson depicts this scene, and, as a matter of further interest, the original gaming tables still stand there.

Another great claret club is Boodles, whose house, a piece of delightful architecture, stands opposite to Brooks's on the east and more sunny side of St. James's Street. Founded in 1762 its warm interior is enhanced by the almost unequalled Adam's "Great Saloon" on the first floor overlooking St. James's Street. It is here that the private dinners take place and for which Boodles has gained such a reputation. The cooking throughout, in the Coffee Room and also on the Ladies' side, is of a high order and the wine cellar must be one of the finest, if not the finest, of any club in London. Boodles is especially noted for its "club claret," inexpensive yet well selected, the wines, always of good vintage, are bought some years in advance and laid down in the cellars below, so that they will be as perfect as possible when eventually their turn comes. The head wine butler at Boodles, who has retired after 35 years' service, remembers members who drank one and even two bottles of vintage port to their own cheek but, of course, they drank no cocktails beforehand and probably took just a glass of a light claret as an opener.

Perhaps one of the most fascinating of all these is Pratt's, a proprietary club, which merely consists of a basement in Park Place, just off St. James's Street and is only open in the evening. As you go down the stairs, you enter the main room, brim full of character, its walls hung with stuffed fish and other trophies of the chase and it is in this delightful atmosphere that you order your pre-dinner drinks. There is but one table in the small adjoining dining room, for which you have to wait your turn because it will only seat about ten people and then you sit where the club steward indicates. Though the food is essentially simple, the conversation which is general, can be sparkling. In his time Sir Winston Churchill was a prominent member, so in surroundings such as this, Pratt's must be one of the most interesting of all places in which to dine.

As may be expected, famous clubs like these have long waiting lists, in fact for one of them I had to wait about fourteen years before my name came up for election! Usually they have reciprocal arrangements with their American counterparts, for instance, both Boodles and Brooks's interchange with the Knickerbocker Club of New York and Boodles also with the Somerset Club of Boston, Mass.

There are, of course, a number of other noted clubs in London, too many to mention here! These cater to the Arts, politicians, members of the armed forces, sailing enthusiasts, the Universities and other interests. Naturally, the standard of cooking varies from one to another, but in all of them you can feed in congenial surroundings without irreparable damage to your purse.

24th January, 1971

A Claret Tasting: Château Malescot

On three successive evenings during the week commencing January 4th, the members of the International Wine & Food Society assembled at the London headquarters in Edgware Road, to discuss half a dozen vintages of red Bordeaux, as exemplified by Château Malescot-Saint-Exupéry, a third-growth Margaux and, if one can judge by the quality of its wine, a château which does not appear to be nearly so well known as it deserves.

The vineyard took its name from Maître Simon Malescot (attorney to the king) in 1697, but it was already functioning as a vineyard under the direction of the Demoiselle Escousses. A succession of owners followed, each contributing their share of improvements. In 1827 Malescot became the property of Comte Jean-Baptiste de Saint-Exupéry, and from this date onwards it has been known as Château Malescot-Saint-Exupéry. This man, incidentally, was the great grandfather of the famous writer.

The cellar buildings were enlarged and modernised in 1871 by a M. Fourcade, and in 1885 a M. de Boissac rebuilt the château in the style of Louis XV.

Since 1955 the estate has been in the hands of the Zuger family, and under the skilled and meticulous care of Paul Zuger and his son Roger, the vineyard is now producing wine which is worthy of the best of Bordeaux. This was amply brought out by the quality of the vintages we tasted.

To emphasise the pride and integrity of the owners, there was no 1963 vintage at Malescot, the wine being sold simply as Médoc on the Bordeaux market and, in the other indifferent vintage, 1965, only the best of the stock, i.e., about 25 percent, was château-bottled.

The meetings were embellished by the presence of Roger Zuger, whose charm and fluent English captivated the members. By means of a duologue between M. Zuger and myself, the six vintages were discussed in turn, and these are a rough consensus on the notes on them.

Château Malescot-Saint-Exupéry, Margaux

1967 (London-bottled).
Medium colour, pleasant bouquet, not yet developed, attractive flavour, but very light. This should develop early.

1966 (château-bottled).
Good colour, full bouquet, plenty of fruit, and much bigger than the 1967. Still has some acidity to lose.

1964 (London-bottled).
Medium colour, good nose, pleasant flavour, but not nearly so good as the château-bottled version of this wine; the latter is outstanding.

1962 (château-bottled).
Good colour, lovely bouquet, which is developing beautifully, the real fragrant Malescot bouquet, for which it is so noted. A lovely "aromatic" taste in addition.

1961 (château-bottled).
The very deep colour, so typical of this fine vintage. A lovely scented bouquet and a great full-bodied wine. Its original quite considerable acidity has now worn off, leaving a little tannin. When the tannin has disappeared, this should be a lovely rich wine. Ready perhaps in a few years' time, and it should go on improving for a very long while.

1959 (château-bottled).
Good colour, lovely well-pronounced bouquet, with just a trace of the "cedar" smell which is to be found in other great clarets, a delightful flavour, and there is still plenty of life ahead.

19th June, 1971

Three Great Vintages for Red Bordeaux

Among the myriad of "vintages of the century" so freely lavished upon us since the last war, there have in fact been but two, which were really outstanding—1945 and 1961. The younger of them, 1961, has been written about fairly thoroughly but so far we have had little opportunity to rub shoulders properly with the elder dignitary. In fact, it is all too seldom that one comes across the 1945's now, because most of them have been drunk up long before they were ready. This vintage *hors classe* had but one defect, an excess of tannin, and that is why, only now, a quarter of a century after its first appearance, the wines are becoming enjoyable to drink. A similar vintage perhaps, but now only of academic interest, is 1870, which for a brief flash has suddenly come back into the news.

Down in the cellars of Glamis Castle in Scotland, an ancient stronghold of historic association with Mary, Queen of Scots, over the years there has lain untouched a cache of magnums of Château Lafite 1870, and these will be auctioned at Christie's on June 24th. People may say it is nonsense to enthuse over something which is over a hundred years old, and rightly so in most cases, but in this particular instance, the wine is superb.

Although packed with quality, the 1870's were so full of tannin that for many years they were quite undrinkable. In consequence, one reads that the great English enophiles of the post-First World War period enjoyed them hugely in the 1920's and 1930's. Incidentally, this was a coterie of great authorities on wine whose like has never been seen since, for included among their number were Francis and Charles Walter Berry, the two distinguished partners of Berry Brothers of St. James's Street, London; Colonel Ian Campbell, author of *The Trailing Tendrils of the Vine* and a noted wine importer whose brother and son both won the Victoria Cross (Britain's greatest award for gallantry); Maurice Healey, who wrote *Stay Me with Flagons*; and the late André Simon of literary and gastronomic fame. Since I did not move in such august wine circles in those days (in fact, I did not join the wine trade until 1934), it was not until the 1950's that I was able to judge for myself the merit of the great Lafite 1870, and I drank my last splendid bottle

167

(bottled by Harvey's) in 1966. That, I feared, was the end of it, for me at any rate, but on June 2nd, Michael Broadbent gave a dinner for a small circle of friends in Christie's board room, where with appropriate but beautifully cooked food, as the *pièce de résistance* we decanted and consumed one of these fabulous magnums from Glamis Castle. The colour of the wine was so deep, the bouquet, so superlative, and the flavour, so magnificent, that we were all confounded. (The magnum was decanted immediately before we drank it.)

It makes one commiserate with the long-dead owners of the 1870's who have been outlived by their wine and who perforce had to drink much of it up long before its time. Since the Lafite has lasted so remarkably, one cannot help wondering how, in view of the notable longevity of Latour, the 1870 vintage of that château can have fared. Only once has it ever passed my lips, and on a tragic occasion too, because it had been criminally decanted about two hours before the meal, and by that time it had virtually given up the unequal struggle.

Now it is the turn of the 1961's, which also are not being given the chance they deserve. Just imagine what Latour 1961 must taste like now, yet it is being "gobbled up regardless"! Fortunately, for us all, since 1945 the methods of vinification have greatly improved; otherwise the 1961's might easily have been as full of tannin as the 1945's or, who knows, even perhaps the 1870's.

One of my weaknesses has been collecting wine, but with all the inconveniences of a London flat there is little room for storage, although some comfort is derived from there being less risk of burglars! Having a fairly good idea of what it was all about, I began my collection of the 1961 clarets in January 1962 and have never regretted it since, but I am not drinking any of them yet except for one or two *crus bourgeois*, the 1961 Fronsadais and the lesser wines from Pomerol and Saint-Emilion. The finer ones are being reserved for the time when they can appear in their true glory.

To size all this up, then, when it comes to the great but tannic vintages, the 1870's took about fifty years before they became drinkable, but with more modern progress, the 1945's, similar in style, will have taken roughly 25 to 30 years to reach their best, and at a rough guess it may take the 1961's, say, 15 to 20 years. Thus progress in the vinification of hard vintages has been necessary, but there is a warning concealed behind all this; the Bordelais must take pains to avoid changes which are too sweeping, for they have all too clearly before them the sad post-war experience of red Burgundy, which is but a ghost of its pre-war predecessor, and one can only hope the point has already been taken.

Now we come to another dinner which took place in a private room at Lockets Restaurant, London, on June 18th. Our host was Joseph Berkmann, one of London's most brilliant restaurateurs. Among the guests were Peter Sichel of Sichel & Co.; Louis Vialard, proprietor of Château Cissac, Bordeaux; and Philippe Cairol, who had come specially from Burgundy. The English wine trade was represented by Michael Broadbent, Alan Taylor-Restell, Jack Hill, and John Brackenbury.

The purpose of the meal was to compare blind a dozen representatives of the 1945 vintage, and it was an achievement on the part of our host to assemble together so many examples as long as a quarter of a century after these wines were made.

From time to time it is agreeable to be able to enthuse over English cooking, and all that one need say on this occasion is that it was a pleasure to watch our guests from France all nodding their heads and smacking their lips. Taillevent is perhaps my favourite restaurant in Paris, and with regard to this meal at any rate, I can honestly say a comparison of the two would not be unfair. The menu was as follows:

prawns in jelly
summer green-pea soup
roast best end of lamb with fresh mint sauce
new season's turnips
braised spring onions
new potatoes
choice of cheese
fresh raspberries with raspberry sherbet

(For the benefit of the purists, we did not fall to the blandishment of the mint sauce!)

Since these notes really concern claret, the excellence of the 1949 Bollinger (magnum) and the two white Burgundies of Comte Lafon, i.e., Meursault Perrières 1966 and Montrachet 1966, which preceded the red wine, will not be enlarged upon.

The twelve glasses set before each of us were quite an awesome sight, for our task was not only to assess the wines, but as best we could, to place them in order of merit. For me, at any rate, on such occasions there is a fatal temptation also to endeavour to guess the names of the wines concerned. This is a temptation I have to resist, because once I start guessing—and guessing it is in my case—it throws out the rest of the assessment. On this occasion, though, the Mouton was delightfully obvious—it had such a typical Mouton bouquet and flavour—and (luckily for me) so was the Latour. I thought at least I would be able to spot the Saint-Emilion, Clos Fourtet, from among all the Médocs, but failed, of course. Also, I expected to find that number 6, the Léoville-Barton, would be something more august than it was, a good mark this for English bottling.

The following tasting notes are my personal ones.

Twelve Apostles of the 1945 Vintage

Château de Pez, cru bourgeois. (Saint-Estèphe) (bottled in England).
> A good full bouquet, a full-bodied wine which stood up well amongst its peers.   My placing 10th,   group placing 9th,   points 134.

Clos Fourtet, grand cru. (Saint-Emilion) (château-bottled).
> A good deep colour, good bouquet, not much body, and a little hard, nothing special by comparison.   My placing 12th,   group placing 11th,   points 151.

Château Saint-Pierre-Sevaistre. 4th growth, (Saint-Julien) (château-bottled).
> Good rich bouquet, round with a pleasant, if unusual, flavour.   My placing 8th,   group placing 12th,   points 155.

Château Beychevelle. 4th growth, (Saint-Julien) (bottled in England).
> A dark colour, the bouquet a little more severe than some, but there is lots of fruit, as well as some tannin. Good quality, this is a wine which should continue to improve. My placing 9th,   group placing 8th,   points 132.

Château Léoville-Las-Cases. 2nd growth, (Saint-Julien) (château-bottled).
> Deep colour, also quite a severe bouquet, quite a big wine, but there is still too much tannin, needs time, say 2 or 3 years.   My placing 7th,   group placing 7th,   points 131.

Château Léoville-Barton. 2nd growth, (Saint-Julien) (bottled in England).

> A delightful bouquet, a huge wine of great quality, a good mark here for English bottling. My placing 2nd, group placing 4th, points 77.

Château Pontet-Canet. 5th growth, (Pauillac) (bottled in England).

> Something odd about the nose, has fruit, but could have more middle. This has suffered from bottling, because if you drink this wine at the château it is immensely better, i.e., fuller and much richer. My placing 11th, group placing 10th, points 146.

Château Palmer. 3rd growth, (Saint-Julien) (château-bottled).

> Good deep colour, delightful bouquet, beautifully balanced, great quality. My placing 3rd, group placing 6th, points 102.

(The first bottle at my end of the table was badly corked, and there was only enough left from the good bottle for Peter Sichel and me to taste. Some of the others less fortunate may have put it down on account of the corked bottle, hence 102 points.)

Château Margaux. 1st growth, (Margaux) (château-bottled).

> Deep colour, most elegant bouquet, beautifully made, and most attractive, though there is still some tannin. Doubtless this will improve. If you are fortunate enough to have some of this in your cellar, try it again in, say, 1974. My placing 6th, group placing 5th, points 89.

Château Latour. 1st growth, (Pauillac) (château-bottled).

> Very deep colour, a simply fabulous cedar bouquet, also fabulous fruit and flavour. For me this stood out among all the rest. Great now, but will improve still further. My placing 1st, group placing 1st, points 32.

Château Lafite. 1st growth, (Pauillac) (château-bottled).

> A huge nose, this wine full of finesse and breeding, has great quality. My placing 5th, group placing 2nd, points 54.

Château Mouton-Rothschild. 2nd growth, (Pauillac) (château-bottled).

> Magnificent cedar nose, masses of fruit and flavour, this fine wine has a most pronounced character. My placing 4th,   group placing 3rd,   points 62.

As will be seen, some of these 1945's still have a certain amount of tannin, so there is really no rush to drink them up. The well-advised possessors, for well-advised they must have been still to have some 1945's in their cellars, can now open a bottle from time to time to enjoy with a discerning friend.

The 1908 Cockburn vintage port was so outstandingly good that it was terribly difficult to resist a second glass, but I had before me the thought of rising next day at six a.m. to start off for the Côte d'Or by car. So well chosen was the meal and so good the wine that the early rise was achieved without the least inconvenience.

A Great Vintage:
1970 Saint-Emilions and Pomerols

It is not in every vintage that conditions are really favourable for the wines of Saint-Emilion and Pomerol. The Merlot vine predominates in these districts, and although it fares miraculously well when the climatic conditions are good, being of a frailer constitution than the sturdy Cabernet Sauvignon, it suffers more from adverse weather.

It must be acknowledged that the weather in the region of Bordeaux is not always as benevolent as one would hope, but there, of course, lies half the pleasure and all the challenge for the claret lover. No one ever knows what will happen each year and how the set of weather conditions will affect the resultant wine. In consequence, no two vintages are absolutely alike; therefore, every fresh one requires a separate assessment. Apart from the general situation, one has also to take into account the many and varied facets which come into play.

Let us, then, make a kind of profit and loss account of the last eleven vintages from the districts of Saint-Emilion and Pomerol:

(See page 174)

Sec p. 185

Loss		Profit	
1960	Poor, the Pomerols were a shade better than the Saint-Emilions.		
		1961	Outstanding.
1962	Disappointing, but again the Pomerols were a little better than the Saint Emilions.		
1963	Useless		
		1964	Very good indeed.
1965	Useless		
		1966	Very good indeed.
		1967	Very good (on the whole, the 1966's were better).
1968	Useless		
1969	Disappointing, but one or two good wines were made.		
		1970	Outstanding.

The above could be broken up still further by indicating all the years when the Pomerols were more successful than the Saint-Emilions and vice versa, also the vintages when the Saint-Emilions and Pomerols were more successful than the Médocs, and again vice versa. For example, 1962 was certainly a success for the Médoc, but with a few possible exceptions, not nearly so good for the Saint-Emilions and Pomerols. The latter districts got their own back in 1964 when they produced full-bodied quite rich luscious wines, while some of the Médocs, but not by any means all, were extremely disappointing.

Nineteen-sixty-six, a fine vintage, was a success in both camps, but in 1967 the Saint-Emilions and Pomerols may prove to be a short head in front, because when they were picked, the Merlot grapes were ripe, whereas the Cabernet Sauvignons of the Médoc, which usually ripen about a week later, had not, in all cases, fully matured.

Nineteen-sixty-eight was a pretty good disaster everywhere, and 1969 is certainly not the vintage it was originally claimed to be. The weather during September that year had been so bad that had it not changed at the last moment to enable the grapes to be gathered in under excellent conditions, one shudders to think what might have happened!

Now we come to 1970, one of those vintages for which we all pray so fervently. An assured success for the wines of the Médoc, it may turn out to be exceptional for those of Saint-Emilion and Pomerol, because weatherwise it was a miraculous year for the Merlot grape, and since the Merlot predominates in these districts, we have much to be thankful for.

Once again I would like to express my thanks to M. Jean-Pierre Moueix for preparing for me a really remarkable tasting of some of the leading châteaux from these two districts. This tasting took place at the end of June 1971, a little early perhaps to make a thorough assessment (three months later might have been better), but the anticipation and eagerness to get at them was difficult to resist.

The very first effect, the colour, was most impressive; along the sideboard in the tasting room overlooking the broad River Dordogne, ten glasses were arrayed, each half-filled with almost black-looking Saint-Emilion. A good colour is one of the predominant features of the 1970 vintage, but seen like this, the very dark colour in these glasses was quite dramatic.

Saint-Emilion 1970

Château La Clotte.
> Very deep colour, pleasant nose, round, full, and well-made. A little tannic. 15+/20

Clos Fourtet.
> Very deep colour, deep nose, a great big wine with some tannin. One to buy. At last, after many years of disappointing quality, Clos Fourtet has taken a turn for the better. Once again this may well be a château to follow. 18/20

Château Moulin-du-Cadet.
> Very deep colour, deep nose, good fruit, and well-made. 16/20

Château Bel-Air.

Very deep colour, deep nose, good fruit and quality. However, it does not have much character and is not outstanding. 15/20

Château Fonroque.

Very deep colour, good nose, good fruit, flavour and body. Good quality. 17/20

Château Pavie.

Very deep colour, but not much nose. Good fruit, but less round; somewhat disappointing at the moment—rather closed up and not showing well. Before making final judgment, this should be tasted in about six months' time. 15+/20

Château Figeac.

Very deep colour, excellent nose. Round, with lots of character. Good quality, a little green perhaps, but good quality nevertheless. 18/20

Château Magdelaine.

Very deep colour, great finesse on nose. Very good quality, has great elegance and breeding. 18/20

Château La Gaffelière.

Very deep color, great finesse and elegance in bouquet. Excellent, deep, full-bodied. One to buy—outstanding for this vintage. 19/20

Pomerol

Château Le Gay.

Deep colour, good nose, and a delicious taste. 13/20

(13/20 may appear a low rating, but it is only comparative in relation to the others, for this is a fine wine, one I would be delighted to have in my own cellar.)

Château Bellevue.

Deep colour, good nose, even more delicious. Has both charm and finesse. Super quality. 16/20

Château de Sales.

Deep colour, fine nose. Has quality, good fruit and flavour. 14/20

Château Beauregard.
> Deep colour, good nose. Has good fruit and flavour. 15/20

Vieux-Château-Certan.
> Deep colour, distinguished nose, good quality. 14/20

Château Feytit-Clinet.
> Especially dark colour, fine nose. Great big, round wine, excellent. 18/20

Château La Conseillante.
> Dark, dark colour, fairly good nose. Good fruit, and very well-bred. 15/20

Château Lagrange.
> Very dark colour, very good nose. Full, round, and fine quality. 16/20

Château Latour-Pomerol.
> Dark, dark colour, very good nose. Very well-bred, beautifully balanced, and good fruit. 19/20

Château La Fleur-Pétrus.
> Dark colour, excellent nose. Round, full, well-balanced, and well-made. 19+/20

Château L'Evangile.
> Very dark colour, elegant and distinguished nose. Huge, big, round wine. Excellent, very fine, but Trotanoy, below, is twice as powerful. 19/20

Château Trotanoy.
> Very dark colour, full and deep nose. Fine quality and well-made. 19+/20

The Three Great Wines

Château Cheval Blanc. (Saint-Emilion).
> Very deep colour, very deep bouquet. Big and powerful, beautifully bred. Splendid. 19/20

Château Ausone. (Saint-Emilion).
> Good colour, elegant bouquet, but thin in comparison with the others. Lovely deep flavour, fine quality. 18/20

Château Pétrus. (Pomerol).
    Wonderful colour, very deep bouquet, enormous, won-
derful quality. Magnificent! A masterpiece! 19+/20

Even Ausone is good in 1970 but the other two, Cheval Blanc
and Pétrus, are *hors classe!* The bouquet of the above three wines
will develop much more. How sad that one should have to say this
about Château Ausone, whose performance has been so disappointing for so many years, particularly since the potential of this
famous vineyard is so great.

    Nineteen-seventy, as I had fully expected, has proved to be an
unusually good vintage for the wines from the right bank of the
river Dordogne. The Saint-Emilions are excellent, but, if possible,
the Pomerols are even more successful. This can be seen just from
the colour alone, for it is the darkest I have seen for many years.

    Every now and then there is an outstanding vintage for the
wines of Pomerol, and 1970 is surely one of them. Just after the
war I was lucky to be introduced to two exceptional vintages by
Edouard Cruse, a real devotee of this district. These were 1945 and
1947, and I can remember still the fabulous wines I bought for Harvey's at that time, among them La-Croix-de-Gay 1947 and Cheval
Blanc 1947. Alas, in my cellar, I have none left of La-Croix-de-Gay
1947, and only a bottle or so of the Cheval Blanc. For many years
now the latter has been regarded as the greatest post-war wine
of all.

    Recently in August 1970 at the hospitable table of Eddie
Penning-Rowsell, the well-known writer on wine, we enjoyed a
bottle of La-Croix-de-Gay 1947, which he must have bought from
me some twenty years ago, English-bottled and a little brown in
colour; it was miraculous, and without having the famous Cheval
Blanc 1947 alongside, it seemed every bit as good, if not better.

    The 1949 Pomerols were also very good, but apart from that,
1970 may prove to be the best vintage for Pomerol since 1947,
including 1961, and that is indeed saying something.

The 1967 Vintage, Once Again

A blind tasting in Bordeaux, the tasters being Patrick Danglade, Jean-Francois Moueix, and myself.

Once again, and yet this time with a difference. All we were told beforehand was that it was the 1967 vintage and that the wines had been paired in their communes. In each pair there would be a *grand cru classé* alongside a first growth or the equivalent thereof. For me this was an original way in which to taste wine.

1967 Wines

Belair. (Saint-Emilion). Grand cru.
   Pale colour, full fragrant bouquet, good fruit, but a bit hard. 14/20

Ausone. (Saint-Emilion). First growth.
   Pale colour, charmingly scented bouquet, fairly full with a very nice flavour. 16/20

Margaux. (Margaux). Grand cru.
   Good deep colour, good full bouquet, an individual but attractive flavour. Needs time. 16/20

Brane-Cantenac. (Margaux). First growth.
   Good colour, well-made, medium body, fine quality. Preferred this to the Château Margaux. 17/20

Pichon-Longueville-Baron. (Pauillac). Grand cru.
   Medium colour, attractive bouquet, good fruit, still hard and undeveloped. 16/20

Latour. (Pauillac). First growth.
   Deep colour, nose still undeveloped, still hard, but very good quality. 19/20

Mouton-Rothschild. (Pauillac). Grand cru.
   Quite a good color, very good bouquet, full and round, a big wine. 18/20

Pichon-Longueville-Lalande. (Pauillac). First growth.
> Quite a good colour, attractive bouquet, lighter, but has charm. 15/20

La Conseillante. (Pomerol). Grand cru.
> Good colour, very good bouquet, medium body, and a little hard. 13/20

Pétrus. (Pomerol). First growth.
> Dark colour, fine bouquet, full fruity taste, a big wine. 19/20

Haut-Brion. (Graves). Grand cru.
> Good colour, attractive nose, good fruit and body, lots of tannin still. 18/20

La Mission-Haut-Brion. (Graves). First growth.
> Very dark colour, nose undeveloped, a huge wine, plenty of tannin, fine quality. 18/20

Clos Fourtet. (Saint-Emilion). Grand cru.
> Good colour, quite a good bouquet, complete, but needs time. 15/20

Cheval Blanc. (Saint-Emilion). First growth.
> Very good colour, fine bouquet, delightful flavour, full of charm, great quality. 19+/20

With the exception of Margaux and Brane-Cantenac, it was not too difficult to discern which of the two was the *grand seigneur*. In our blind tasting, both Patrick Danglade and I preferred the Brane-Cantenac to the Margaux, and looking up my notes of the previous year, I see that Brane-Cantenac had fared well on that occasion too.

The last time I tasted this vintage, in October 1970, I had preferred the Pétrus to the Cheval Blanc, but on this morning, the Cheval Blanc was a good half-length ahead of all the others. During their youth, wines are inclined to run like horses in a race, sometimes they are a neck in front, sometimes a neck behind. On form Pétrus 1967 is a better horse than its "white" rival, so could it have been a bit off-colour that morning? Happily Latour, which had run disappointingly in the October stakes, was back on its old form.

At Clos Fourtet, where the wine has been disappointing for vintage after vintage, there is new management, so as from the 1970 vintage much better things can be expected. If only the same thing could be said about Ausone, a château with tremendous possibilities, the quality of whose wine remains consistently well below its proper level.

The Fronsadais

Situated strategically as it is at the confluence of the rivers Isle and Dordogne, a historical significance has been literally forced upon the district of Fronsac; thus, since early times, it has constantly been the scene of military activity.

It seems it was quiet to begin with, for the Gallis Biturigis are known to have held a market there, and later the Romans built an altar. But in 700, when Charlemagne came to conquer the Gascons and settled to prepare his army to cross the broad River Dordogne, which in those days must have been a serious military obstacle, the site became known as the Frankish Camp. Later on, a fortified stronghold succeeded the wooden palisades of Charlemagne, and it was here that during the ninth century the local inhabitants took refuge from the Normans and, for safety's sake, removed and enclosed therein the bodies of Saint Geneviève and Saint Emilion.

During the three hundred years of the English occupation, Fronsac became a bastion against the enemy, and twice a year its inhabitants watched the passing of the English wine fleet en route for Albion. The importance of this city was enhanced by the absence in England of any customs duty, an advantage designed to foster the trade of the province of Aquitaine.

After 1378, when the Seigneur de Fronsac was beheaded for treason, the Grand Senechal de Guyenne, Thomas Felton, decided that henceforth the fortress should only be garrisoned by English soldiery and under the command of an English commander. The château thus came into the possession of the English crown, and it was there that the archives of the province were deposited, and there they remained until 1451, when they were transported to the Tower of London. These Gascon Rolls, as they are known, which are intact, have since provided immensely valuable information regarding the history of those far-off times. After the departure of the English, it took a long time to readjust the market for the sale of wine. However, in 1514 there is a record of 500 *tonneaux* going to Spain.

Besieged several times during the wars of religion, in 1623 at the order of Richelieu the fortress of Fronsac was finally razed to the ground. Subsequently, some of the governors of the duchy of Fronsac (the smallest in France) led a somewhat chequered career. For instance, one of them, Hercule d'Harzillimont, used to stretch a chain across the Dordogne to hold up the river traffic, thus forcing the ship's captain to pay tribute and at the same time insisting that he also pay deference to the château by firing a gun salute; hence possibly the origin of the name Canon-Fronsac. It is interesting to note that a number of vineyards still incorporate the word "Canon" on their château labels. These, incidentally, are among the most expensive! D'Harzillimont also pillaged the neighbouring countryside and amongst other places burned to the ground the houses of Plainpoint and Mayne Vieil, two properties still noted for the excellence of their wine. He was finally arrested by Louis XIII, whom he was foolhardy enough to visit while the latter was in Bordeaux. Courageous to the end, just before he was beheaded he said to the bishop who begged to let him blindfold him, "Monsieur, if you were in my place, would you not wish to do as you pleased?"

Cardinal Richelieu purchased the lands of Fronsac in 1633 so as to leave them to the children of his youngest sister. In the eighteenth century his great-nephew, whose resounding titles were Marechal Duc de Richelieu, Duc de Fronsac, and Governor of Guyenne, built a folly on the Tertre, the spectacular high hill overlooking Fronsac. There he organised sumptuous *fêtes galantes* to which he invited all the ladies of the neighbourhood, the latter being little aware that the slabs on the floor were made of *glaces indiscrètes!*

Of such an intriguing past, there now remains only the Tertre, still dominating this smiling corner of France, surrounded as it is by entrancing hillsides whose vine-clad slopes produce such delectable wine. The quest for quality in this region dates back to as long ago as 1700, when the seigneur of the duchy decreed that any *vigneron* who picked his grapes before the official date would not only be ducked in the lower ditch, but have his crop confiscated into the bargain!

After the rather dull flatness one becomes so accustomed to in the Médoc, this small wine district situated only about a mile northwest of the town of Libourne is almost surprisingly beautiful. The delightful vineyards are planted on steep hillsides overlooking truly enchanting reaches of the broad winding river. In all, there are seven different communes: Fronsac, Saint-Michel de Fronsac, La Rivière, Saint-Germain La Rivière, Saint-Aignan, Saillans, and a part of Galgon. The district is also divided into two separate areas from the point of view of *appellation contrôlée*—Côtes-Canon-Fronsac and Côtes-de-Fronsac.

These wines, and particularly those from the Côtes-Canon-Fronsac, have a wealth of flavour and an unusual richness which is most attractive. With a good deep colour, they are sturdy and full-bodied and have been described as having all the charm of red Bordeaux, combined with the vigour of Burgundy; intriguingly, one note on them adds "with all the truculence of "Burgundy"!

The reason why they are not better known may perhaps be ascribed to the fact that they used to take too long to mature, and, in this respect, were not unlike some of the *crus bourgeois* of the Médoc. However, in the last twenty years or so, the method of vinification has been greatly improved so as to encourage this some-what resistant type of wine to develop earlier. Consequently, only four years after its production, one could begin to enjoy the successful 1964's from this district; this is not, of course, to say that the 1964's will not continue to improve in the bottle, because indeed they will. There are a number of châteaux in the Côtes-Canon-Fronsac which produce fine wine consistently, and among them are Château Vrai-Canon-Bodet-La-Tour, Château Canon-de-Brem, Château La Chapelle, and Château Grand-Renouil.

The wines from the Côtes-de-Fronsac may lack some of the depth and splendid richness of those from the Côtes-Canon-Fronsac, but being still more reasonable in price, they represent remarkably good value for everyday drinking. Such remarks may make the Côtes-Canon-Fronsacs sound expensive, but this is by no means the case, for although their quality often resembles that of the lesser growths from Saint-Emilion and Pomerol, they are only about half the price. Good châteaux to follow from the Côtes-de-Fronsac are Rouet, Plainpoint, La Dauphine, Mayne Vieil, Las-tère, Tasta, and De Carles.

As well as its vineyards, this region is also embellished by a number of notable houses, in particular châteaux Gaby, Rouet, and La Dauphine. These are attributed to the famous architect Victor Louis, whose *pièce de résistance* perhaps is the Grand Théâtre in Bordeaux. Château Rouet has been in the hands of the family of the present owner, Roger Danglade, since the eighteenth century, and down in the garden below the house there is a genuine hermit's cave which is officially regarded as a historic monument .

It is really still too early to make a true appraisal of these wines, for, sadly, two of my favourites from this district, Châteaux La Dauphine and Canon-de-Brem, have not quite finished their fer-

See p. 174

mentation. That is the trouble with a popular vintage; one is too eager to get at it! Patience is a virtue! Making due allowance for their immaturity, however, this is certainly a vintage in which to invest in the wines of the Côtes-de-Fronsac and Côtes-Canon-Fronsac.

The Merlot is the predominant vine of the districts lying on the east bank of the river Dordogne, i.e., Saint-Emilion, Pomerol, the Fronsadais, the Bourgeais, and the Blayais. It is not so hardy, of course, as the Cabernet Sauvignon, and so suffers more in bad weather, but every now and again conditions occur which are especially favourable for it, and the vintage of 1970 is certainly one of them. If it is of any encouragement, the local growers of the Fronsadais regard their 1970's as of better quality even than 1961, and that indeed is saying something.

The colour of the 1970 vintage in this region is striking, as dark as anything I have seen for many a year, and that is always a good sign. The bouquet is delightful, and the wines are packed with fruit. For those who have not yet ventured into the realms of the Fronsadais, it is a good moment to begin, for I do not think they will be disappointed. These Cinderellas of Bordeaux are still comparatively unknown, therefore reasonable in price.

Since the classified growths of the Médoc have become so expensive, with the *crus bourgeois* following hard on their heels, it is these good, but still comparatively unknown wines, which are assuming an ever greater importance.

These are the notes on a blind tasting arranged for me by my friend Roger Danglade, the proprietor of Château Rouet.

1970, tasting at Château Rouet

Château Rouet. (Côtes-de-Fronsac).
   A deep colour, pleasant nose, light, charming, fruity, pleasant taste. Ready to drink early. Has not yet quite finished its fermentation, so it is still too early for proper marking.

Château Reychotey. (Côtes-de-Fronsac).
   Very deep colour, fine bouquet, heaps of fruit and body. Finishes nicely. Some tannin. 17+/20

Château Lastère. (Côtes-de-Fronsac).
   Very deep colour, excellent delightful bouquet. Has fruit and deep body. Very good quality. A wine to buy. 19/20

Château Tasta. (Côtes-de-Fronsac).
> Fabulous colour! Excellent bouquet, even finer than Las-tère above. Deep body. Solid, beautifully made. Tannin excessive at the moment, but magnificent. A wine to buy. 18/20

Château La Dauphine. (Côtes-de-Fronsac).
> Fine deep colour, almost perfumed bouquet. Medium body but charming. Still fermenting a little, so it is too early for firm marking.

Château Lariveau. (Côtes-Canon-Fronsac).
> Fabulous colour, good nose not giving much. Round, full-bodied. Has not yet quite finished its fermentation, so it is still too early for firm marking.

Château La Chapelle-Lariveaux. (Côtes-Canon-Fronsac).
> Fabulous colour with a fragrant bouquet. A huge wine packed with fruit. Some tannin. Exceptional quality. A wine to buy. 19/20.

Château Canon. (Côtes-Canon-Fronsac).
> Dark, dark colour, fragrant bouquet, but it is a bit disappointing. 16/20

Château Canon-de-Brem. (Côtes-Canon-Fronsac).
> Deep colour, delicious and delightful bouquet. Plenty of fruit and body, though difficult to taste at the moment. Has not yet quite finished its fermentation, so it is still too early to assess properly.

Château Vray-Canon-Bodet-La-Tour. (Côtes-Canon-Fronsac).
> More fabulous colour still. Good bouquet. Well-balanced, well-made, with good fruit and considerable tannin. A wine to buy. 18/20

It is still a little early to taste the above, some of which were still fermenting.

As with the produce of Saint-Emilion and particularly Pomerol, this is a year to go nap on the wines of Côtes-de-Fronsac and Côtes-Canon-Fronsac. From this tasting, these are the wines I recommend:

Côtes-de-Fronsac.
> Rouet; Reychotey; Tasta; Lastère.

Côtes-Canon-Fronsac.
Vray-Canon-Bodet-La-Tour; La Chapelle-Lariveaux.

I would have liked also to recommend two of my favourites, La Dauphine and Canon-de-Brem, but at the moment neither of them have quite finished their fermentation.

Côtes de Bourg

Here are my notes on a blind tasting held in Bordeaux chez Duclot.

Château La Joncarde, 1966. (Côtes de Bourg).
Good colour, nice nose, attractive pleasant flavour. 17/20

Château Falfas, 1966. (Côtes de Bourg).
Good colour, very fruity nose. Plenty of fruit and good flavour. 16/20

Château Rousset, 1966. (Côtes de Bourg).
Good deep colour, full attractive bouquet. Round with plenty of fruit, it is complete and well-made, finishing nicely. A success, in a good vintage, from this district. 18/20

Château La Joncarde, 1967. (Côtes de Bourg).
Medium colour, nice nose. Has fruit, but is rather disappointing in comparison with the others. 13/20

Château Falfas, 1967. (Côtes de Bourg).
Good colour, distinguished fine nose. Plenty of fruit but a little oxidised. 12/20

Château Rousset, 1967. (Côtes de Bourg).
Medium colour, medium nose. Quite good with plenty of fruit. This, too, is oxidised. 12/20

Château de la Croix Millorit, 1967. (Côtes de Bourg).
Medium colour, nose has character but is not great. Medium body and medium quality. 14/20

Here lies the advantage of a blind tasting, for had I seen the label I might easily have been influenced more favourably!)

Château Rousset, *1966 tasted blind against Château Liversan,* 1966 (Médoc).
These wines are both château-bottled, but Liversan was found to be not in the same class as Rousset.

2nd July, 1971

A Visit to Mouton-Rothschild

(A blind tasting at Château Mouton-Rothschild, Pauillac, with M. Jean-Paul Gardere. Our hosts were Messrs. Cottin and Sionneau.)

The glasses and bottles were laid out on a table placed at the far end of the *cuvier*, surely one of the most attractive in the Médoc, or anywhere else for that matter, the majestic vats providing the perfect setting for such an occasion. Not only is it a pleasure, but a great experience to taste in the company of that splendid man, Jean-Paul Gardere, who, together with Henri Martin, runs Latour so efficiently. Jean-Paul is a man whom one could easily describe as the very salt of the Médoc earth.

It was also a great privilege to have an opportunity to taste a range of vintages from both Mouton-Baron-Philippe and the great Mouton-Rothschild; instructive, too, because the individual character of each property was so well defined, though one must admit there seems to be quite a kinship between them in style, but naturally the Mouton-Rothschild is more important.

The unusually dark colour, the heavenly bouquet, frequently embellished with a hint of cedar, so characteristic of this château (or eucalyptus, as my friends from California like to insist), the richness, the great depth of body, and powerful masculinity of this great wine are the very essence and stamp of Mouton-Rothschild, making it one of the masterpieces of this world.

Now, in the form of Château Clerc-Milon, there is a newcomer to this illustrious family, for Clerc-Milon is a vineyard of great potential. The soil and situation are especially good for the cultivation of vines. Therefore, with all the skill of the management of Mouton, it will be fascinating to see what the vintages from this château will be like in, say, the 1980's, once the new ownership has begun to make its mark.

Knowing their wine so well, our hosts M. Lucien Sionneau and M. Philippe Cottin did not participate in the tasting, so at our request, beginning with a range of Mouton-Baron-Philippe, they set out the glasses so that we would not know which was which. What struck us immediately, of course, was the good dark colour of all the wines. Grading is on a scale of 1 to 10.

Mouton-Baron-Philippe 1966.

A dark colour, nice winey bouquet, good fruit, and most agreeable, with a delicious characteristic flavour. It is still closed up, and on account of its youth, it was not fair perhaps to taste this against the others, but certainly it will make a good bottle.

Mouton-Baron-Philippe 1962.

Good colour, the darkest of all. Full, rich bouquet, and it has a lovely round flavour, quite rich and of good quality. Still not quite mature, and if I owned any bottles of this 1962, I would keep them for another year before trying them again. 8/10

Mouton-Baron-Philippe 1961.

Deep colour and a very good rich bouquet. Nice rich flavour too, very ripe; in fact, there is a *roti* taste; one can almost taste the 1961 sunshine here! 10/10

Mouton-Baron-Philippe 1959.

Good colour and a fine distinguished, almost perfumed bouquet. A big wine, full-bodied, well-balanced, with a flavour that lasts. This must be delicious to drink now! 9/10

Mouton-Baron-Philippe 1953.

The colour beginning to turn a little brown, but the bouquet ageing slightly is fine and harmonious. Though smooth, mellow, and well-developed, nevertheless it is on the downward slope; therefore, if you have any left, enjoy it now! This is nothing unusual, because, by now, most of the 1953's have seen better days. 7/10

There was a short pause after tasting the above, and before we moved on to the *grand vin* Philippe warned us he had included an off-vintage and asked us to pick it out! It would have been too shaming if one had failed in such company! However, on reading through the notes, I see I failed at the time to mark points against each wine, but this is the order in which I placed the vintages.

Mouton-Rothschild 1966.

Dark, dark colour, with a youthful bouquet. It has heaps of fruit but is very, very young and undeveloped. Not really possible to judge at the moment. It is not its fault that it was placed sixth!

Mouton-Rothschild 1962.

> Dark, dark colour, a lovely big full bouquet. Rich and round, with a delightful flavour. This will undoubtedly improve with more time in bottle. Fourth.

Mouton-Rothschild 1961.

> Dark colour, and a distinguished rich bouquet. A huge robust wine which one day will turn into something magnificent. Clearly the best of the group, and it pleases me when I remember I bought it in both bottles and magnums in 1962! I shall not touch it for several years yet. First.

Mouton-Rothschild 1959.

> Dark, dark colour, with a well-bred cedar bouquet. This is sweet, round, full, and seductive; the flavour is delicious. Delightful now, but all the same, it still has some way to go. One does not often have the opportunity to taste the great 1959's, but this must surely be among the best. Second.

Mouton-Rothschild 1958.

> Good colour, but an older and thinner bouquet. Although it has fruit and body, it lacks the roundness and charm of the others and is not in the same class. If you have any, drink it up! Fifth

Mouton-Rothschild 1955.

> Good colour with a wonderful cedar, typical Mouton bouquet. Mature, ripe, harmonious and well-balanced, fine quality but it has passed its best. There is no immediate rush to drink this up, but it is a 1955 and the 1955's will not keep for ever. Third

The above were a really magnificent array of splendour, so the criticisms must be considered as merely relative. Finally, before proceeding to lunch we went into the main *chai* to taste the 1970 vintage. This is clearly going to be a success. Not only does it have the usual deep colour of Mouton but also the extra deep colour of its year, the bouquet is very full and the wine itself round and complete. Will undoubtedly make a great bottle.

Then inside the chateau, there followed the most Lucullan meal imaginable; here is the menu:

Pilaf aux Langoustines

Poulet Roti aux Herbes
Pommes-de-Terre Anna
Haricots Verts

Salade
Fromages
Glace aux Fraises

Mouton-Cadet Blanc
Mouton-Baron-Philippe 1961
Mouton-Rothschild 1949
Mouton-Rothschild 1918
Mouton-Rothschild 1880

The *pilaf aux langoustines* was out of this world, so a second helping was irresistible, and the Mouton Cadet went very well with it.

For the sake of brevity, however, here are my notes on the other wines:

Mouton-Baron-Philippe 1961.
> Notes similar to the tasting, lovely to drink now, but this will improve further.

Mouton-Rothschild 1949.
> Good colour, a glorious typical Mouton bouquet, that unmistakable Mouton nose (easy to say when you know what the wine is!), rich, full, and beautiful. A very great bottle.

Mouton-Rothschild 1918.
> Good cedar bouquet, had fruit, but was somewhat dry and still a little hard.

Mouton-Rothschild 1880.
> Naturally the nose was old, but it was also rich and round, similar in fact to the flavour, which was full-bodied, round, rich, and really beautiful. This was a great treat!

3rd July, 1971

Les Forts de Latour

When Château Latour came under English control in 1963, none of us had heard of *les forts,* and it is only by chance that this most suitable name has turned up. It was found that through the generations, or perhaps centuries, the original borders of the Latour vineyard had been in part eroded away, and it was only by buying back these small pieces of land or through exchanges with vines elsewhere that the title deeds came to light. On these title deeds it was discovered that some of these plots of land were described as Les Forts de Latour.

The name derives, it is thought, from the time of the English occupation of Aquitaine in the Middle Ages, when an English fortress or stronghold stood on the exact site where the present *chai*, or winery, is situated.

According to French law, it is only permissible to sell wine with full *appellation controlée* so long as the vines from which it is made are four years old or more (in California, it is three years), but it is not really until the vine attains the age of from eight to ten years that it begins to fulfill its promise. Thenceforth, being in full production, the quality continues to improve and the quantity remains roughly the same until it is about twenty-five years old, but from that time, the quantity produced begins to diminish.

In the case where quantity rather than quality is concerned, the vines are pulled up when they are about twenty-five years old, for to keep them is no longer commercial. However, at Latour, the soil being what it is, even the young vines will produce quality equivalent to that of a second growth. Although the bunches become fewer, the quality continues to improve until the vine reaches a great age, and that is why at Latour there are numbers of vines which are sixty years old or more. The lifespan of a vine is roughly the same as that of a man.

For some time, the management had considered producing a second wine, similar to Les Carruades de Lafite, and this would come from the younger vines on the estate. Consequently, this idea was put into practice, beginning with the 1966 vintage. At the same time, it was also decided that the wine would be château-bottled.

One of the characteristics of Latour is that it usually takes longer to develop than most other wines, but getting better and better with age, it often outlives them. It is hoped, therefore, that the public fully appreciates that it is a pity to open a bottle of a fine vintage before it has had time fully to develop. For example, many 1962's have been delicious to drink for several years, but good as Latour is, it will get better and better with a few more years in bottle.

Coming, as it were, from the same stable, it was feared that once it was offered on the market, Les Forts de Latour might be consumed almost immediately in the restaurants of the world, and before it had had time to show its true worth. It was decided, therefore, that the 1966 vintage, bottled in 1968, would not be sold until it had had at least a few years to mature in bottle, and that is why none has so far appeared on the market.

Since there is not much stock of the 1966 vintage, the 1967 will be offered at the same time, and this will most probably be during the course of 1972. By that time the 1966 will have had almost four years in bottle, and the 1967, a slightly lighter wine, about three.

Although they will undoubtedly continue to improve, people in Bordeaux are now beginning to drink the 1966's, and they will soon follow suit with the 1967's. Ideally, of course, it would be preferable to hold on to these two vintages of Les Forts de Latour for another two years, for this would give them an even better chance to demonstrate their quality. It is hoped, therefore, that once they have reached, say, the American market, that the public will not be in too much of a hurry to drink them up!

Here are some tasting notes on Les Forts de Latour, taken during a visit to the château.

> 1970 *Vintage.*
> A beautiful colour, good bouquet, though still undeveloped, round with plenty of fruit, this will surely make a good bottle.
>
> 1969 *Vintage.*
> Medium to good colour, and quite a nice bouquet. Plenty of fruit, is well-made, and can be considered very good for its year.
>
> 1968 *Vintage.*
> Medium colour, again quite a nice nose. Medium body,

and although it has fruit, it could be fuller. Certainly satisfactory, considering 1968 was such a poor year.

1967 Vintage.
Quite a good colour, good full bouquet, ample fruit, and some tannin.

1966 Vintage.
Good colour, an attractive bouquet which has developed nicely. Heaps of background here, and it should prove a pleasant surprise.

4th July, 1971

A Cru Bourgeois: Château Cissac

When one thinks of the Médoc, nearly always one's mind gravitates to the classified growths, but since the incursion of the American market on to the Bordelais scene, these are becoming alarmingly expensive; this is by no means the fault of the Americans, but simply a question of supply and demand.

Fine as they are, the first growths have long since gone beyond the reach of most English claret lovers and are in danger of doing the same in the United States, except that in that vast country there always appear to be more and more well-to-do newcomers arriving on the vinous scene.

All the same, some of my friends in California who, after every good vintage, used to buy the first growths, gave up after the 1964's and in their place are now laying down the second and other classified growths, and there must be many other people who are doing the same. As the demand for the classified growths has risen, so have the prices, and these increased prices are now rubbing off onto some of the *crus bourgeois.*

For generations the *crus bourgeois* have provided a steady and dependable source of supply for the English devotees of claret, not only among the more impecunious, but also those who, although they have been able to afford the great wines, have really enjoyed these less spectacular growths for everyday consumption.

Their number is legion, but their quality can vary greatly according to the soil and the calibre of the owner, and to pick out the successful ones can provide an exciting challenge for the connoisseur. You can be fairly certain of quality with a Rolls Royce or a Cadillac, but it is not so easy when you have to choose among the smaller cars.

Certain châteaux, such as Gloria, De Pez, and Lanessan, produce such good wine vintage after vintage that their names have become almost household words, but the price they are fetching is already causing some complaint!

There is, however, a *cru bourgeois* which also produces good quality consistently but nevertheless still remains comparatively

196

unknown and whose wine is still reasonable in price. This is Château Cissac, whose vines, although in the commune of Cissac, grow close to those of Château Lafite.

The charming one-story château was finished in 1670 and has all the simplicity and unpretentiousness which many of the grander nineteenth-century châteaux of the Médoc so sadly lack. Behind the house there is a pleasant terrace from which in summertime you overlook a garden ablaze with roses. This is the home of Louis Vialard, whose family has tended the vineyard and inhabited the house for one hundred years. The Vialards are one of the very few old Médocain families which still actually live the year round in their family home. The role of most Bordelais châteaux nowadays is mainly for entertaining visitors, and few are inhabited except during the summer months.

After all these generations of *vignerons,* Louis Vialard, whose great-grandfather and grandfather were the managers of Château Lafite, must surely have the ruby-coloured wine of the Médoc running in his veins. There are no new-fangled methods here at Château Cissac, and no short-cuts are employed in the making of the wine, hence the good dark colour and its full-bodied fruitiness.

The first vintage that I can remember tasting from this château was 1955; now some 1955's, although delightful to begin with, are beginning to go downhill, but this is certainly not the case with the 1955 Château Cissac, though admittedly it came from a magnum. While others with far more illustrious names are failing, it had such a good colour, such good fruit, and evidence of further improvement, that I determined to investigate further.

These are my notes on some more recent vintages which I tasted at the château.

Château Cissac

1969 Medium colour, nice fruity bouquet, good fruit and body. Quite a big wine for its year. Should be ready fairly soon.

1967 Good colour, pleasant bouquet, medium body. Well-balanced, with plenty of fruit. Still young, but will make a nice bottle.

1962 Deep colour, lovely bouquet. Plenty of depth and quality.

1960 Good dark colour, full bouquet, plenty of fruit and body.

Some 1960's are beginning to go back a little, but this one is still at its best.

1959 Deep colour, delightful bouquet, rich and full-bodied, really good.

Finally we tasted the 1970 vintage from the cask—good deep colour with an attractive bouquet. It is round, full, and well-balanced. Louis Vialard says this is not unlike his 1961, and, in fact, claims it is the best wine he has ever made.

10th July, 1971

The Côte Chalonnaise and Southern Burgundy

After browsing on the Côte d'Or, the south-bound gourmet has a choice of ways, the new stretch of the autoroute connecting Paris with the Riviera, or the enchanting country road, N. 481, which runs through the Côte Chalonnaise; there should be little doubt, however, as to which he should take!

After a few minutes' drive then from Chagny, you enter the district of Rully, known principally for its white wine (Chardonnay grape), most of which is used for sparkling Burgundy. Although scarcely known, this still white wine can be surprisingly good, and should you ever visit that good restaurant Lameloise in Chagny, you will find Rully on the wine list. Its selection is to be recommended, not only for the quality, but also because the price will be kind to your purse!

Adjoining lies the district of Mercurey, where both red and white wines are made, though it is more noted for the former. This good medium-bodied wine is made from the Pinot Noir grape, and its style is often described as being halfway between that of the Côte de Beaune and Beaujolais.

The road meanders southwards along vine-clad hillsides past the small and comparatively unknown region of Givry (red and white wine, but principally red) until you come to Montagny, where, as in Rully, some delightful white Burgundy is produced, not dissimilar from that of the Côte de Beaune. Made from the Chardonnay grape, the quality of Montagny is such that it deserves greater recognition. This is also a road for the camera fiend, because all along, and close to the wayside, stand splendid old châteaux, having as their *tête de cuvée* the Abbey of Cluny.

Finally, before reaching Mâcon, the road climbs over a range of hills to present you with the spectacular scenery of the Pouilly Fuissé area, where the rock of Solutré and Le Rocher Vineuse provide such an impressive background. The renown and undoubted quality of Pouilly Fuissé (Chardonnay grape), has made the demand greater than the supply; nevertheless, this excellent dry white wine adds a lustre to the gastronomy of southern Burgundy.

The wine takes its name from the two villages of Pouilly and Fuissé, and it is from this small area whence the finest quality emanates. Since, of recent years, the genuine Pouilly Fuissé has become so expensive, merchants are now marketing more freely the produce of adjoining districts, such as Pouilly Vinzelles and Pouilly Loché. If maybe a little lighter of body, these are very similar in style to Pouilly Fuissé and when well bottled are very much to be recommended.

In actual fact, the Pouilly Fuissé district lies in the Mâconnais, noted for its large production of both red and white wine, of which about 60 percent is red. Both Mâcon blanc and the red Mâcon are agreeable, inexpensive wines, but whose quality does not pretend to match that of Pouilly Fuissé and Beaujolais.

The Beaujolais

Although still relatively unappreciated by the gastronomes, this most beautiful of the wine districts lies virtually in the heart of France, not too far from Switzerland and latitudinally just north of the wine district of Bordeaux. Beaujolais is to be found within the confines of southern Burgundy and, being some eighty miles south of the Côte d'Or, its vineyards sometimes have the advantage climatewise over those of its more northerly and fashionable neighbour, but neither mode nor fashion are of any importance insofar as Beaujolais is concerned, for although at times it can rise to great heights, it is at heart a country wine, indeed a peasant wine, which one quaffs down gaily, but does not sip!

The district takes its name from the little town of Beaujeu, once the principality of the dukes of Beaujeu so noted in French history. Bounded on the west by the Monts du Beaujolais, with the flat valley of the river Saône on the other side, it stretches from near Mâcon in the north almost as far south as the great city of Lyon. This truly delightful countryside, composed of enchanting hills and dales, is clad in summer with a raiment of green leaves which turn to golden red in the autumn, and the surroundings are so beautiful as to leave one almost breathless. In spite of its proximity to Lyon, the countryside remains unspoiled as yet by the developer's hand and still unsullied by tourism; even the Kodak signs are few and far between! The rolling hillsides are planted with a vine called the "Gamay Noir au jus blanc," which thrives in the granitic soil, and the resultant wine is so fruity, so full of freshness and exhilaration, that it is a joy to drink.

It was in the late thirties that public attention was first drawn to this region through the publication of the best seller *Clochemerle*, a racy, and, for those days, slightly salacious account of the village life of the district. Although centred on a fictitious village called Clochemerle, the story is reputed to be about Vaux-en-Beaujolais, situated idyllically up in the hills and where at the Salle de Dégustation you can sample the latest vintage and then repair for a delicious lunch at the local restaurant, called, naturally enough, l'Auberge Clochemerle!

During this summer of 1971, the *bons viveurs* of France are drinking the 1970 Beaujolais, the quality of which is well above the average, as vintages go, for this unusually beautiful region; 1969 was far superior to 1968, and when well selected, many of the 1970's are as good as, if not better than, the 1969's. Unlike the produce of most other famous districts, these red wines, sometimes described as precocious, are at their best while they are really young. Local gourmets who prefer to drink their Beaujolais lightly chilled are inclined to regard a two-year-old wine as over the hill and passé.

The more humble, lighter, and less expensive wines come from the southern sector not far from Lyon, but *les grands vins* —and, in good years, *grands vins* they are indeed—commence roughly along the lattitude of Villefranche and reach northwards until they join the white-wine area of Pouilly Fuissé, which lies just south-west of Mâcon. Thus the local inhabitants are favoured with both red and white nectar with which to embellish their excellent regional cooking.

Beaujolais, the true Beaujolais, and not the creature which so often masquerades under this alluring name in England and elsewhere, is fresh, charming, and fruity. The freshness, the fruitiness, and charm, its most endearing qualities, are only captured by being bottled within six months, and often less, after the vintage. There are one or two exceptions to this rule, however, because some of the bigger wines, such as Moulin-à-Vent, need more time to mature in the cask and so are often bottled a month or so later, but not much more than that.

In order to avoid the extra duty on wine bottled abroad, it has been the custom in England to ship the major part of the importation in bulk, and this usually takes place about a year after the vintage, by which time the wine has lost much of its inherent freshness. However, welcome changes are taking place, because a few enlightened importers are now following the custom of the growers in the Beaujolais and are bottling their wine much earlier.

Yet another change seems to be impending, and this time it emanates from France. Since the varying quality of Beaujolais to be found on the English, German, and Dutch markets does not meet with the approval of the more serious growers and negociants, there is a movement afoot locally to ensure that ultimately all Beaujolais sold for export must be bottled within the district itself. No doubt a few years will have to elapse to enable negociants with bottling plants in other parts of France to adjust their business and also local growers and negociants to adapt themselves to bottling all their stock. This will, of course, have repercussions, Beaujolais in England will become more expensive, but at least one will know what one is buying. The indifferent wines now sheltering under the label of Beaujolais can easily be sold under brand names. To quote a common saying, "You get what you pay for!" Beaujolais is no longer one of the cheaper wines, and this fact has to be faced.

Not all of the above affects the United States market, the greater part of whose French wine arrives either bottled at the domaine or château, and this is preferable, for if nothing else, it favours authenticity. All the same, it is bound to affect the American consumer a little, because, inevitably, there will be less traffic in tickets of *appellation controlée*, so the authenticity of all wines exported from this region will be re-inforced.

There are, in fact, two types of Beaujolais. First, *le vin de l'année*, a light, joyous affair which appears in the bistros of Paris as from November 15th onwards. Like a gaily painted butterfly, it flits across the vinous scene to gladden our hearts during the gloomy winter months, but also like a butterfly, its span of life is brief. It is better not to keep it after March following its vintage, but by that time, the finer wines of its year are beginning to come on the market. In fact, by the time this book is printed, the *vin de l'année* of 1971 will have come and gone! Originally only a French speciality, the *vin de l'année* is now being shipped to both the United States and Britain, where it has become quite a fashionable wine to offer one's friends.

Secondly, there is the finer, fuller variety, usually from the more illustrious areas known as Beaujolais Villages, which is put into bottle any time from January to May of the following year, that is to say, within some six months of its birth. There are some twenty-seven of these villages whose communal wines are entitled to be sold as Beaujolais-Villages, and of which the produce is carefully controlled. Among them, of course, are the famous names, *les grands crus* of the Beaujolais: Chiroubles, Saint-Amour, Chénas, Juliénas, Moulin à Vent, Fleurie, Morgon, Côte de Brouilly, and Brouilly. A small amount of white wine also comes from this district and is achieving a degree of popularity; some of this Beaujolais Blanc is excellent, but also, much that is not so good. The best comes from those vineyards bordering on Pouilly Fuissé and preferably is domaine bottled.

There have been four good vintages recently for the red wines of the Beaujolais, 1966, 1967, 1969, and 1970, although the first two mentioned, or perhaps even three, are now regarded by the local cognoscenti as having whiskers on them and who consume, and enjoy best, the wine of the previous year.

Should the reader ever consider visiting this inviting country-side, it is better to choose a time immediately following a good vintage; for example, had you gone there in 1969, all you would have found to drink in the numerous excellent little restaurants in and around the countryside, would have been the 1968 vintage, and that, in my opinion, was thin, rather hungry stuff! This year, 1971, it is quite a different matter, for the 1970's are excellent, and *now*, and not any later, is really the time to enjoy them. No doubt, by the time this chapter gets into print, the 1970's will already be regarded as past history in the Beaujolais district and the eyes and palates of all connoisseurs will be turned upon their successors, the 1971's, whose quality at the time of writing still lies in the lap of the gods.

Although a few of the more fortunate continue to indulge in it, the cost of travelling in France has, to say the least, become some-what expensive, and one of the items which has risen most is the price of table wine in the restaurants. The famous names have soared, so that only the very rich can afford them, but the price of Beaujolais remains comparatively reasonable. Therefore, when you order a first-rate Beaujolais in a smart restaurant, the bill at the end will not come as so great a shock as it would had you ordered, say, a bottle of Chambertin or a good second-growth red Bordeaux.

In Romanêche-Thorins, in the heart of the Beaujolais, not far from Moulin-à-Vent, there is a firm which takes its name from its founder, Georges Duboeuf, and within the space of but one decade, the name of M. Duboeuf has swept across the gastronomic scene of France.

In a land of connoisseurs, this talented young man (and a per-fectionist to boot) has a palate far above the average, and that is why, following each vintage, such an unusually large proportion of the wines he has bought are awarded gold medals and similar awards at the official exhibitions. For instance, of the 1969 vin-tage no less than thirteen wines of M. Duboeuf's stock were awarded gold medals. His busiest time, for tasting, that is, follows immediately after the vintage, when, for a period of about two months, on an average he tastes up to two hundred samples a day.

The proof of this is to be found in M. Duboeuf's tasting room, skilfully fitted out with cabinets where the samples are kept chilled to exactly the right temperature for tasting. There, instead of just one Beaujolais-Villages, there are three of four quite different ones to be tasted, likewise Fleurie, Morgon, and so on, for they all come from different growers.

If only for reasons of authenticity, domaine bottling is superior to bottling elsewhere; also, the less wine is moved about, the less chance there is of its being affected by oxidation. Unfortunately, unlike the majority of château proprietors in the Bordeaux area, few of the growers in the Beaujolais possess the necessary equipment for domaine bottling.

M. Duboeuf, however, who specialises in domaine bottling, has been able to overcome this difficulty by devising his own mobile bottling plant. At the appropriate moment, each wine lying in its original cellar is analysed by a competent wine chemist and then is fined. When it is ready for bottling, he despatches one of his mobile bottling plants to the domaine concerned, where it is piped direct from the casks in the cellar into the plant standing in the courtyard. Here it is subjected to the customary light filtering, is bottled and cased on the spot. Under these circumstances the handling of the wine is as perfect as possible, and there is an absolute guarantee of authenticity.

His methods of sale also differ from those of the usual negociant, because apart from La Maison de Truffe, that mouth-watering establishment in the Place de la Madeleine in Paris, he sells his wine mainly to the great *restaurateurs* of France, names connected with the finest gastronomy of the world. Since there is insufficient fine wine available, his policy is not concerned with mass sales, but is restricted to supplying only a distinguished clientele.

At the exhibitions held soon after the 1970 vintage in Mâcon and Villefranche, M. Duboeuf's wines won no less than twenty-six prizes; among them there were nine gold medals.

For those who are contemplating gastronomic treats in France during the coming twelve months, here is a list of just a few of his wines and the names of the renowned restaurants where they are to be found, a perfect example of how gastronomy is linked with fine wine. It may be that by the summer of 1972, some of these stocks of 1970 will be exhausted, but if the quality of 1971 as a vintage is satisfactory, the 1971's will be appearing in their place. Incidentally, in poor vintages, which, like the poor, are always with us, M. Duboeuf never offers a quality superior to Beaujolais-Villages.

For visitors to London, a selection of his wines is to be found at the Minotaur, Au Jardin des Gourmets, Genevieve, l'Opera, and Lockets restaurants, and they are retailed exclusively by Jackson's of Piccadilly.

(See pages 207-208)

The Beaujolais is also blessed with splendid regional cooking, and it is hard to think of any district in France where the local wine blends better with the food. Situated, as it is, in the gastronomic centre of France, and therefore of the world, the Beaujolais area is a worthy upholder of the great French tradition, for there are quite a number of quiet, unsophisticated, but fine restaurants dispersed among the vineyards, and these, fortunately for us, if not for their proprietors, have so far been overlooked by tourism. A visit is to be recommended if only to savour and enjoy the mouth-watering *poulet à la crème* with or without *morilles*, which the local chefs prepare so admirably. This, remember, is the district so noted for its regional delights—the famous *poulets de Bresse*, the hams of Morvan, *andouillettes, quenelles de brochet* from the nearby Saone, and, of course, the Charollais beef, the finest in France, not to overlook other more common or garden specialties such as snails, frogs' legs, and *terrines de campagne*.

For the traveller by car, a good place to stay is the Hôtel Les Maritonnes in Romanêche-Thorins, which has a rosette in the *Guide Michelin*. Within easy reach from there, the choice of good restaurants in the district itself, there is Le Beaujolais at Blaceret, the Vieux Cep in Fleurie. Then farther afield you have Le Chapon Fin at Thoissey, Troisgros at Roanne, Paul Bocuse outside Lyon, and, if you study the *Guide*, many more than our frail frames can stand!

To quote from the *Guide Michelin*, this is indeed an area *qui vaut le detour*.

1970 Vintage
Where to Find Them in France

Beaujolais (Saint-Laurent)
> Premier Prix au Concours des Beaujolais à Ville-franche
> Premier Grand Prix au Concours de Mâcon

Available at: Le Chapon Fin, Thoissey
> 2 Rosettes *Guide Michelin*

Beaujolais-Villages (Jambon)
> Premier Prix au Concours des Beaujolais à Ville-franche

Available at: Auberge de l'Illhaeusern, Alsace
> 3 rosettes *Guide Michelin*
> Relais de l'Empereur, Montelimar
> 2 rosettes *Guide Michelin*
> Petite Auberge, Noves
> 2 rosettes *Guide Michelin*
> Ty Coz, Rennes
> 1 rosette *Guide Michelin*

Fleurie (Bernardot)
> Premier Grand Prix au Concours des Vins à Mâcon

Available at: Lasserre, Paris
> 3 rosettes *Guide Michelin*
> Cafe de Paris, Biarritz
> 2 rosettes *Guide Michelin*

Morgon (Descombes)
> Premier Prix au Concours de Villefranche

Available at: Pot au Fer, Asnières
> 2 rosettes *Guide Michelin*

Moulin-à-Vent (Labalme)
> Premier Grand Prix des Beaujolais au Concours de Villefranche
> From among over 1,100 entries this was adjudged the best wine of the year.

Available at: Les Maritonnes, Romanêche-Thorins
> 1 rosette *Guide Michelin*
> Le Vert d'Eau, Angers
> 1 rosette *Guide Michelin*

1970 Vintage *(continued)*

Juliénas (Pistorezi)
  Available at: Le Chapon Fin, Thoissey
          2 rosettes *Guide Michelin*
        Le Petit Brouant, Nice
          1 rosette *Guide Michelin*
        La Mère Poulard, Mont Saint Michel
          1 rosette *Guide Michelin*
        Leon de Lyon, Lyon
          1 rosette *Guide Michelin*

Côte de Brouilly (Geoffray)
        Premier Prix au Concours de Villefranche
         Medaille d'Or au Concours de Mâcon
  Available at: Brazier, Lyon
          2 rosettes *Guide Michelin*
        de la Poste, Avallon
          2 rosettes *Guide Michelin*

Beaujolais Blanc (Co-opérative de Chaintré)
        Premier Prix au Concours de Villefranche
  Available at: Flavio, Le Touquet
          1 rosette *Guide Michelin*
        Les Mouscardins, Saint-Tropez

Pouilly Fuissé (Duboeuf)
  Available at: Troisgros, Roanne
          3 rosettes *Guide Michelin*
        Louis XIV, Paris
          1 rosette *Guide Michelin*

Mâcon Blanc (Corsin)
        Medaille de Vermeil au Concours de Mâcon
  Available at: Georges Blanc, Vonnas
          2 rosettes *Guide Michelin*
        Auberge Bressane, Bourg
          2 rosettes *Guide Michelin*

Vintage Port

Here is a subject upon which I hesitate to expand. All my life I have loved vintage port, but like a rejected suitor, it does not love me! Being one of those unfortunate creatures, a town dweller, I have to beware of it, but if I were bucolic and could indulge in country pursuits, my cellar would contain many a tempting bottle.

As it is, this delectable post-prandial drink has to remain merely a temptation to which I can succumb from time to time. A good vintage is always available at my club though, and there it lurks, like Satan himself, awaiting my downfall, but every now and again when I do weaken to its blandishments, for some obscure reason my guilty conscience gives me a twinge of pleasure. The suffering comes later!

During some correspondence with Ronald Avery on this subject of vintage port, the variation of bottling among different firms arose, and Ronald suggested that he would bring with him from Bristol three of four samples of his own bottling of the 1960 vintage so that we could compare them with the identical wines also from their original bins, in the cellars of Jackson's of Piccadilly. The tasting duly took place in my London flat, and to help us we had Derek Gannaway of the Wine Society, a real devotee of vintage port who had brought with him a bottle of Taylor and Sandeman of the same vintage.

This, then, is what we tasted (blind), together with our opinion on the wines:

1960 Vintage Port

	Cockburn
Jackson's	Nice nose, plenty of fruit, good flavour. Second
Avery	A bit bolder and firmer, stylish and elegant. First

	Dow
Jackson's	Good bouquet, very good flavour; if anything, a shade firmer than the other. Equal
Avery	Similar to the above, but perhaps a trifle fuller. Equal

Graham

Jackson's   Slightly darker in colour, good bouquet, powerful, and fine quality. First

Avery   Good colour, good fruit, fine quality. Second

Sandeman

The Wine Society (one bottle only)   Good colour and a nice taste, but perhaps a little spirity on the nose.

Taylor

The Wine Society (one bottle only)   Good colour, fine bouquet, a great velvety wine, marvellous quality.

Avery's Special Reserve

This is a wine which Ronald Avery bottles in every good vintage, and if the quality of this example is anything to go by, there is a lot to be said for it!

Good colour, an attractive fruity bouquet, heaps of fruit, and a good "grip." Very fine quality.

Insofar as the bottling of the wines was concerned, we were all in agreement, the Avery bottling of the Cockburn being better than the Jackson. On the Dow, we could find little difference, but with the Graham, the Jackson bottle was better, so really the honours were even. This does emphasise, however, Ronald's point that there can be a difference in bottling between one firm and another.

When it came to placing the wines in order of preference, we were not so unanimous, because Ronald had a partiality towards the Cockburn, which he placed second after the Taylor, with Dow third.

Derek Gannaway and I were in accord, with Taylor first, Graham second, Avery Special Reserve third, Dow fourth, Cockburn fifth, and Sandeman sixth, except that he placed the Dow above the Avery Special Reserve.

When I drink vintage port, I like it to have a good "grip," and on this occasion, the Taylor, Graham, and Avery's Special Reserve had that quality.

Vintage port is a somewhat pernickity creature; it objects to being moved about unduly; a modicum of movement does little harm, but the more it is moved, the less it likes it, so when the time comes to drink it, the feebler becomes its welcoming handshake.

When buying an old vintage, it is therefore important to look into its past life, and, if possible, learn its history; better still, of course, to taste it yourself beforehand!

(It is interesting to record that on the following day the Sandeman's spiritous nose and palate had completely disappeared and in fact was showing rather well.)

What
to Drink
in 1972

A Dissertation on What to Drink in 1972

Well, what do we drink? The white wines are no problem at all, for preferably, you drink white wine while it is young and fresh. The great advantage about it is that there is no need to invest a lot of money in laying it down for the future, because with the exception of Montrachet and that ilk, within reason you can buy and drink it almost from hand to mouth.

Let us begin with the most northern wine district of all, Germany. The Rhine and Moselle are not blessed with so many good vintages as, say, Burgundy. The 1969 German wines, although not as great as 1953, 1959, and 1964, will be very good for drinking over the next few years. In this case the Moselles are slightly better than the hocks; 1970 again is a year which must not be dismissed, for some of the 1970's are rather good, and since it is a vintage for early drinking, it should also be useful in 1972.

The Côte d'Or, however, is really the star performer in this context; indeed, during the past decade there has been quite a succession of good years. It is interesting to note that often the white wines succeed there when the reds fail. Quite recently, then, for white Burgundy we have two good years, 1966 and 1967, and even 1968, a year where most other wines failed, was not at all bad. Since then there have been 1969 and 1970, both highly successful. In order to show their true worth, the 1970's, especially the aristocrats among them, will need a chance to develop their bouquet, but in 1972 at least the 1966's and the 1967's and the 1969's should all be drinking well.

The fans of the Loire are fortunate, too, because both 1969 and 1970 were first-class vintages for Pouilly Fumé, Sancerre, and Muscadet, not to mention some of the lesser whites and rosés from Anjou and Touraine. Insofar as white wine is concerned, therefore, we have some *bonnes bouches* ahead of us.

While we are discussing wines for easy and quick consumption, Beaujolais looms large upon the horizon; 1969 was an excellent vintage for this district, and provided you deal with an able wine merchant, so too was 1970. In 1970 there was a certain amount of overproduction in the Beaujolais (as well as among the reds of the Côte d'Or), and very careful selection was therefore required, hence the need of a knowledgeable merchant. All the same, some of the successful 1970's are better, if anything, than the 1969's. Beaujolais is a wine, a joyous wine, which should be drunk while it is young and fresh, and if 1971 turns out well, I would recommend you to drink this vintage in 1972—the 1971, that is—when it becomes available, say, from about April or May onwards. The 1970's will still be good, but by then some of the 1969's may have acquired a few whiskers.

Farther north, on the Côte d'Or, the style of the red wine has been changing, if imperceptibly, since the war, although how well I remember the shock I received when I first tasted the 1947's, or was it the 1949's? At first I thought it was the fault of the negociant who had submitted that particular range of samples! Thanks to modern fertilizers and other factors, the Pinot Noir grapes have a larger proportion of juice in relation to the skin than in pre-war days. There is little doubt that present-day Burgundy is lighter in colour, develops earlier, and does not keep as it used to in the old days. So long as we face this fact, all is well. The 1966's, for example, are about ready to enjoy now, and no longer does one put red Burgundy aside for drinking in ten or fifteen years' time.

In my small way, over the past few years I have come across countless people who have laid down the 1966/67 clarets for the future and are now blissfully occupied with the 1970's, but I have yet to meet anyone who has done the same with red Burgundy, except, of course, for the 1969's, but they are so scarce and so splendid, they have to be snapped up quickly while the going is good. If you have been wise enough to have bought some already, please, I beg of you, keep your hands off it for a year or so; it is far too good to waste!

In some ways this modern trend may be a good thing; red Burgundy is becoming more commercial, you do not have to lock up your money for years, there are fewer storage problems, and you do not have to wait decades for your wine to be ready for the table. There is sadness, of course, among the older generation; that is life—"things are not the same as they were when we were young," etc.—but those who bought some of the finer wines of the Dr. Barolet collection will know what I mean!

Now we come to Bordeaux, and what claret do we drink in 1972? This is a bit of a vexed question, because in France they seem to like their red Bordeaux younger than we do in England

and, I believe, in America. As in Burgundy, they have been drinking
the 1966's during the past year, but it would seem to me that the
1966 clarets are nothing like so forward as are the 1966 Burgundies. They seem still to have—is it a kind of band of immaturity
running through them?—and to my way of thinking, they will be
showing themselves off very much better in, say, a couple of years'
time. If you will take my advice, then, you will hang on to your
1966's for a little longer—like the 1969 red Burgundies, they are
too good to waste!

Leaving aside the great growths, among the most successful
Médocs of 1966 were: Montrose, Cos d'Estournel, the two Pichons,
Léoville-Las Cases, Gruaud-Larose, Palmer, Brane-Cantenac, Can-
temerle, Lynch-Bages, Batailley, Grand-Puy-Lacoste, and Lafon-
Rochet.

The better *crus bourgeois* include: Gloria, De Pez, Lanessan,
Liversan, and Cissac.

From the Graves district: La-Mission-Haut-Brion, Haut-Bailly,
and Pape-Clément.

Being a good all-rounder, 1966 produced some excellent Saint-
Emilions and Pomerols: La Gaffelière, for instance, L'Evangile, and
La Conseillante.

To begin with—that is to say, just after the birth of the 1967's
—the two vintages 1966 and 1967 appeared to be rather similar in
style, although the 1966's have always had more depth. Of the two
vintages, it may well be then that the 1967's will be more ready to
drink in 1972. Nineteen-sixty-seven is not quite such a good all-
round vintage as 1966, although it is another good year for Saint-
Emilion and Pomerol and the districts on the east bank of the river
Dordogne. The Médocs were slightly irregular, especially among
the *crus bourgeois,* where some of the wines, but certainly not all,
have a trace of greenness, the reason being that some of the Cabernet Sauvignon grapes were not quite so ripe at the time of the harvest as they might have been.

In 1967, the pattern was roughly the same as in 1966, the best
Médocs being: Brane-Cantenac, Ducru-Beaucaillou, Léoville-Las
Cases, Beychevelle, Montrose, Palmer, Malescot, the two Pichons,
Lascombes, Lynch-Bages, Grand-Puy-Lacoste, and Lafon-Rochet.

As mentioned above, the lesser wines need careful selection,
but among those I recommend are: Gloria, De Pez, Lanessan, and
Cissac.

When it is a question of young vintages, the lesser wines,
such as the *crus bourgeois,* are usually ready to drink before the

grands crus. It may well be then that some of the ones mentioned here will be enjoyable in 1972.

So much for the more recent vintages, but what about the 1964's for drinking now? As we all know by now, the Médocs have a somewhat chequered history; the "baddies" (I dare not mention their names here) can be very bad, and the "goodies" like Ducru-Beaucaillou, Malescot, and Montrose very good. In fact, you are fairly safe with most of the 1964's from the commune of Saint-Julien.

Although they will undoubtedly improve still further, you should be able to enjoy some of the 1964 Médocs in 1972, for, after all, that gives them a good six years in bottle. This applies especially to the Saint-Emilions and Pomerols, because they usually develop a little earlier than the Médocs. In fact, 1964 is a wonderful year for these two districts. At home, I am drinking the 1964 Cap-de-Mourlin, little known it seems, but a *grand cru* nevertheless; the colour is as dark as dark, the bouquet is rich, and being so rich and powerful, is a proper mouthful! If this particular wine could not convert a Burgundy lover to the wiles of Bordeaux, I do not know what will!

The highlight for present drinking, is, of course, 1962, that once rather frowned upon vintage. The 1962 Médocs have been a delight for some time past, and I see no reason why they should be not equally good in 1972. The Médocs are the ones to go for in this case, because, with perhaps a few exceptions, the Saint-Emilions and Pomerols were much weaker brethren.

It is fitting, perhaps, that we should end with the 1961's, that noble vintage, but it has really little relation to present drinking, because apart from the lesser fry such as the 1961 Fronsadais (which, incidentally, I am also enjoying at home), having resisted temptation for so long, it would be a pity not to do so for just a few more years. So good are they that in spite of the greatly increased price, I am still buying them; it is fatal to be born a collector!

I think all that remains for me now at this writing is to wish all readers *bonne santé, bon appétit et surtout, bonne degustation!*

Index

All châteaux are found at "Château," indexed by the next principal word, using "Ch." as an abbreviation. Discussions of particular vintages will be found at "Vintages, Beaujolais," etc.

Aaron, Sam, 155
Adamson, Dr. and Mrs. Robert, 32, 41, 42, 122, 152
Algiers, 113
Alicia, 154
Almadén
    Blanc de Blanc Champagne, 56
    Gewürtztraminer, 117
    Mountain Red Burgundy, 52
    Mountain Red Claret, 52, 115
    Zinfandel, 115
Amis du Vin, Les, 5, 114
    Atlanta, 106
    Buffalo, 103–04
    San Francisco, 146–47
    Washington, D.C., 13–20, 97–101
Apellation Contrôlée, 135, 184, 193, 203
L'Auberge Clochemerle, 201
Avery, Ronald, 41, 209, 210
Avery (port), 209, 210

Bacchus on the Wing, 156
Bamford, Martin, 32
Barolet collection, xv, 104, 105, 215
Barsac, 81, 154
Bassin d'Arcachon, 89
Bâtard-Montrachet, 35, 36, 118, 120
Beauclair Johannisberg Riesling, 23

Beaufort Pinot Chardonnay, 23, 27
Beaujolais, 198, 199, 201–06, 214
    French restaurants serving 1970 vintage, 207–08
    region, 201
    regional cooking and restaurants, 206
Beaujolais Blanc, 106, 203
Beaujolais-Villages, 203, 205
Beaulieu Vineyard, 6, 21–27 (tasting), 31
    Private Reserve, 23, 24, 27, 31, 106
    Red wines, 26, 30
    White wines, 26
Beaumont Pinot Noir, 23
Beaune. *See* Côte de Beaune, Hospices de Beaune, Clos des Mouches, Toussaints
Beaune Grèves, 126
Beauregard, 62
Beaurepaire, 62
Beaurosé, 23
Beerenauslese, 126
Bennion, Mr. and Mrs. David R., 132, 146
Berg, Dr. Harold, 21
Beringer
    Napa Valley Burgundy (Private Stock), 53
    Winery, 109

Berkeley Wine and Food Society (California), 35
Berkmann, Joseph, 169
Berry, Charles Walter, 167
Berry, Francis, 167
Birnhaum, Leonard and Bonny, 155
Blayais, 98, 185. See also Côtes de Blaye
Blaye. See Côtes de Blaye
Bollinger, 43, 169
Bonnes-Mares, 36, 67, 127
Boodles (London club), 159, 161, 163, 164
Bordeaux, Bordelais, passim, see Table of Contents
Bordeaux, Marché de, 88–93
Bosche, 108, 111, 129
Bouchard Père et Fils, 119
Bourg. See Côtes de Bourg
Bourgeais, 98, 185. See also Côtes de Bourg
Brackenbury, John, 169
Branded table wines (England), 113
Bristol Cream, ix, 4
Broadbent, Michael, x, 41, 105, 168, 169
Brooks's (London club), 159, 161, 163
Brouilly, 203
Buena Vista Sonoma Burgundy, 53
Burgundy (France), passim, see Table of Contents
vigor, "truculence," 184
Burgundy (generic California), 53, 54, 114, 115
Burton, Mr. and Mrs. Stanley, 146
B. V. See Beaulieu Vineyard

Cabernet Franc, 16, 82
Cabernet Sauvignon (Bordeaux), 16, 75, 82, 92, 93, 111, 173, 174, 185, 216
Cabernet Sauvignon (California), 6, 21, 23, 27, 29, 30–31 (tasting), 33–34, 107, 108, 109, 110, 111, 112, 128, 129, 131, 132, 133, 134, 135, 136, 142, 144, 145, 149, 152, 153, 154
Cadaujac, 81, 84

Cairol, Philippe, 169
California, University of, at Davis, 21, 140
Department of Enology, 21
Vineyard, 152, 153
California wines, 4, 5–6, 21–27, 29–31, 32–34, 107–12, 113–17, 155. See also Table of Contents
day-to-day, 113–17
generic, 48–56
varietal, 107, 110
Calvert Wine and Spirits Shop, 13, 33
Campbell, Ian, 167
Cannon, Poppy, 156
Cantenac-Margaux (commune), 18
Carneros (California), 24, 27
Carpy, Mr. and Mrs. Charles, 128, 129
Carraudes de Lafite, Les, 8, 193
Carriuolo, Chris, 25
Cassis, 14
Cent Chevaliers du Vin, Les, 7, 8
Cercle de l'Union (San Francisco), 43
Cerons, 81
Chablis (California), 55, 56, 116
Chagny, 198
Chalone Vineyard, 121
Pinot Blanc, 121
Pinot Chardonnay, 121
Chambertin, 101, 133, 204
Chambertin-Clos de Bèze, 67
Chambolle Musigny, 68, 105
Chambolle Musigny Charmes, 105
Chambolle Musigny les Amoureses, 105
Champagne
California, 29, 56
France, 36, 43, 126
New York, 29
Chapin, Dan, 146
Chappelet, Don, 144
Chappelet Vineyard, 144–45
Chappelet & Cuvaison, 109
Chardonnay. See Pinot Chardonnay
Charmes. See Meursault and Chambolle Musigny
Charmes-Chambertin, 67

Chassagne-Montrachet, 35, 61, 62, 118

Ch. d'Angludet, (1967) 7, 18

Ch. Ausone, 15, 70, 71, 72, 73, 76, 77, 122, 124, 177, 179, 181

Ch. Bahans, 83

Ch. Batailley, 15, 17, 18, 216

Ch. Beauregard, 177

Ch. Beau-Site-Haut-Vignoble, 79

Ch. Belair, 176, 179

Ch. Bel Air, 42

Ch. Bel-Air-Coubet, 99

Ch. Bel-Air Marquis d'Aligre, 78

Ch. Bellevue, 176

Ch. Beychevelle, 19, 76, 170, 216

Ch. Bourdieu-la-Vallade, 99

Ch. Bouscaut, 84, 86, 87

Ch. Brane-Cantenac, 76, 77, 80, 179, 180, 216

Ch.-de-Brem, 99

Ch. du Broustéras, 78

Ch. Calon-Ségur, 19, 75, 156, 161

Ch. Canon, 186

Ch. Canon-de-Brem, 100, 184, 186, 187

Ch. Cantemerle, 216

Ch. Cap-de-Mourlin, 217

Ch. Carbonnieux, 84, 86, 100, 101

Ch. de Carles, 99, 184

Ch. La Chapelle, 184

Ch. La Chapelle-Lariveaux, 186, 187

Ch. Chasse-Spleen, 40, 79

Ch. Cheval Blanc, 15, 17, 70, 71, 72–73, 76, 77, 80, 122, 123, 124, 177, 178, 180

Ch. Cissac, 169, 196–98, 216

Ch. Clerc-Milon, 189

Ch. Climens, 123

Ch. La Clotte, 70, 175

Ch. La Conseillante, 72, 177, 180, 216

Ch. Cos d'Estournel, 15, 17, 19, 75, 215

Ch. La Croix-de-Gay, 178

Ch. de la Croix Millorit, 188

Ch. Curé-Bon-La-Madeleine, 70

Ch. La Dauphine, 184, 186, 187

Ch. Ducru-Beaucaillu, 15, 17, 19, 76, 77, 98, 216, 217

Ch. L'Evangile, 72, 177, 216

Ch. Falfas, 188

Ch. Feytit-Clinet, 177

Ch. Fieuzal, 84, 86

Ch. Figeac, 15, 71, 73, 176

Ch. La Fleur-Pétrus, 71

Ch. Fonplégade, 101

Ch. Fonroque, 40, 176

Ch. Fourcas-Hostein, 79

Ch. Gaby, 184

Ch. La Gaffelière, 70, 103, 176, 216

Ch. Gallais-Bellevue, 77

Ch. Le Gay, 176

Ch. Giscours, 40, 100

Ch. du Glana, 79

Ch. Gloria, 17, 79, 80, 98, 195, 216

Ch. Grand-Puy-Lacoste, 15, 17, 92, 216

Ch. Grand-Renouil, 184

Ch. Gressier-Grand-Poujeaux, 79

Ch. Gruaud-Larose, 15, 17, 19, 216

Ch. Guiraud, 123

Ch. Haut-Bailly, 17, 84, 85, 86, 87, 216

Ch. Haut-Brion, 15, 16, 17, 75, 81, 82, 83, 84, 85, 86, 124, 138, 180

Ch. d'Issan, 18

Ch. la Joncarde, 99, 188

Ch. Labégorce-Zédé, 78

Ch. Lafite (or Lafite-Rothschild), 15, 18, 23, 76, 77, 124, 152, 171, 196

  magnums, 167, 168

  triple magnum, 41, 104

  Les Carraudes de Lafite, 8, 193

Ch. Lafleur, 71, 100

Ch. La Fleur-Pétrus, 71, 177

Ch. Lafon-Rochet, 8, 15, 17, 19, 100, 103, 152, 215

Ch. Lagrange, 71, 177

Ch. Lannessan, 79, 80, 196, 216

Ch. Lariveau, 186

Ch. Lascombes, 102, 216

Ch. Lassale, 78

Ch. Lastère, 184, 185, 186

Ch. Latour, *see also* Forts de Latour: 7–12 (various vintages), 15, 17, 18, 23 (1874), 41 (1865), 41, 76, 80, 92, 100, 102, 103, 104, 106, 123, 124, 126, 146, 147–48 (tasting),

Ch. Latour—*Cont.*
    152, 156, 161, 168, 171, 179,
    180, 189, 193, 194
    stainless steel tanks at, 112
Ch. Latour-Martillac, 84
Ch. Latour-Pomerol, 15, 17, 71, 177
Ch. Léoville-Barton, 15, 19, 40, 170,
    171
Ch. Léoville-Las-Cases, 15, 17, 18,
    19, 103, 170, 215
Ch. Léoville-Poyferré, 19, 76, 98,
    161
Ch. Liversan, 79, 80, 188, 216
Ch. Loudenne, 32
Ch. Lynch-Bages, 15, 17, 75, 216
Ch. Magdelaine, 15, 71, 73, 176
Ch. Malakoff, 99
Ch. Malartic-Lagravière, 84, 86
Ch. Malescot-Saint-Exupéry, 92,
    165–66 (tasting), 216, 217
Ch. Margaux, 7, 75, 80, 124, 146,
    171, 179, 180
Ch. Mayne Vieil, 184
Ch. de Meursault, 35
Ch. La Mission-Haut-Brion, 15, 16,
    17, 40, 75, 76, 81, 82, 83, 84,
    85, 86, 92, 104, 138, 152, 180,
    216
Ch. Montrose, 15, 17, 19, 77, 92,
    216, 217
Ch. Moulin-du-Cadet, 175
Ch. Moulinet, 40, 78
Ch. Mouton-d'Armailhac, 126
Ch. Mouton-Baron-Philippe, 101,
    189–92
Ch. Mouton-Rothschild, 10, 15, 18,
    75, 77, 122, 124, 126, 170,
    172, 179, 189–92 (tasting)
Ch. Nenin, 36
Ch. Olivier, 84
Ch. Les Ormes-de-Pez, 80
Ch. Les Ormes Sorbet, 78
Ch. Palmer, 15, 17, 171, 216
Ch. Pape-Clément, 15, 17, 82, 83,
    84, 85, 86, 87, 97, 216
Ch. Patache d'Aux, 78
Ch. Pavie, 70, 176
Ch. Pétrus, 15, 17, 70, 72, 76, 77, 80,
    122, 123, 124, 178, 180
Ch. de Pez, 79, 98, 170, 196, 216
Ch. Phélan-Ségur, 79

Ch. Pichon-Longueville-Baron, 15,
    76, 80, 102, 179, 215
Ch. Pichon-Longueville-Lalande,
    15, 17, 75, 103, 180, 216
Ch. Plainpoint, 184
Ch. Pontac Monplaisir, 122
Ch. Pontet-Canet, 15, 161, 171
Ch. Potensac, 78
Ch. Poujeaux, 79
Ch. Rausan-Ségla, 76, 161
Ch. Reychotey, 185, 186
Ch. Rieussec, 127
Ch. Rouet, 99, 184, 185, 186
Ch. Rouget, 133
Ch. Rousset, 188
Ch. Saint-Bonnet, 78
Ch. Saint-Pierre Sevaistre, 170
Ch. de Sales, 176
Ch. la Salle de Pez, 77
Ch. Smith-Haut-Lafitte, 84, 86
Ch. Suduiraut, 150
Ch. Tasta, 184, 186
Ch. Terrey-Gros-Caillou, 79
Ch. Tertre-Daugay, 20
Ch. La Tour Blanche, 133
Ch. La Tour de By, 77
Ch. La-Tour-Haut-Brion, 84, 86
Ch. La Tour-Martillac, 86
Ch. La Tour-de-Mons, 78
Ch. Trotanoy, 15, 17, 72, 177
Ch. Trottevieille, 15, 19
Ch. Vieux-Château-Certan, 71, 98,
    177
Ch. Vrai Canon-Badet-Latour, 184,
    186, 187
Châteauneuf du Pape (white), 104
Chénas, 203
Chenin Blanc (*also called* White
    Pinot), 135, 142, 144, 145
Chevalier-Montrachet, 118, 120
Chiroubles, 202
Christian Brothers
    Burgundy, 52
    Pineau de la Loire, 116
    Pinot Saint George, 115
    Select California Burgundy, 54
Christie's, x, 41, 105, 167, 168
Clair, Louis, 63
Claret, xiii, xiv, 5, 43, 59, 97, 160,
    163, 196
    château-bottled, 49

definition, xiii *fn.*
Clochemerle, 201
Clos des Avaux (Hospices de Beaune), 47, 68
Clos de Bèze. *See* Chambertin
Clos de la Boutière (Côte de Beaune-Villages) 64, 65
Clos la Forest, 78
Clos Fourtet, 70, 170, 175, 180
Clos des Mouches (Hospices de Beaune), 47
Clos des Mouches (Santenay), 64
Clos Rousseau, 62
Clos de Tavannes, 62, 63, 64
Clos de Vougeot, 97, 98
Cockburn (port), 160, 172, 209
Cocoa Tree (London club), 159
Coffee Houses (London), 159
Comme, La, 62, 63, 64
Commerce Club of Atlanta, 106
Cornell University, 140
Corti, Darrell, 39, 118
Corti, Frank, 39
Corton, 8, 47, 97
Corton-Charlemagne, 106
Corton Clos du Roi, 47
Corton, Dr. Peste, 47
Côte de Beaune, 61, 62, 66, 121, 199
Côte de Brouilly, 203
Côte Chalonaise, 199
Côte d'Or, 108, 114, 144, 172, 199, 201, 215
Côte Rotie, 156
Côtes de Blaye, 5, 13, 16, 80, 93, 98
Côtes de Bourg, 5, 13, 16, 80, 93, 98, 99, 188 *185*
Côtes-Canon-Fronsac, 98, 99, *passim* 184–87
Côtes-de-Fronsac, 5, 16, 80, 93, 98, 99, *passim* 184–87
Cottin, Philippe, 189
Cottis, John, 101
Crane, Mr. and Mrs. H., 132
Croft (port), 150
Croix Sorine, 64
Cru, *see following; see also* Grand Crus, Premier Crus, Premier Grand Cru
Crus artisans, 77
Crus bourgeois, 5, 15, 74, 77–80, 98, 184, 185, 196, 216

Cruse, Edouard, 178
Cussac, 80

D'Agostini
California Burgundy, 53
Reserve California Burgundy, 53, 54
Danglade, Patrick, 179, 180
Danglade, Roger, 184, 185
Darney, Mr. and Mrs. William, 151
Davies, Mr. and Mrs. Jack, 128
Davis (California), 21, 140
decanting, xiv–xvi, 42–43
Delbeck (N.V.), 102
Delmas, Jean, 83, 87
Deutz, (1961) 122
Dickerson, Dr. and Mrs. William, 46, 123
Domaine de Chevalier, 12, 20, 84, 85, 86
Domaine de la Romanée-Conti, 4, 37–38, 39, 119, 120
Dordogne, 16, 69, 182, 185, 216
Dorsen, Margaret, 156
Dow (port), 209
Draper, Paul, 132, 146
Drescher, Harry, 122
Duboeuf, Georges, 204, 205
his wines at London restaurants, 206

Echezeaux, Les, 38
Embers (Washington, D.C.), 8
Esquin Imports, 37, 128
Evannow, Angelo, 101

Feurty, M., 68
Fisher, John Henry, 134
Fleurie, 202
Flora, 149
Fonseca (port), 161
Forster Freundstück beerenauslese, 126
Forts de Latour, 192–94
Foster, Mr. and Mrs. Richard, 132
Fourchaume (Chablis), 146
Four Seasons (restaurant, New York), 156
France, maps of wines, 58, 158
Frank, Dr. Konstantin, 155
Franzia California Chablis, 116

Freemark Abbey, 108, 109, 128–30
French oak casks, 121
Fronsac (see Côtes-de; Fronsa-
     dais), 182–87
   communes, 183
   history of the region, 182–83
Fronsadais, x, 98, 99, 168, 182–87,
     217

Gallo
     Chablis, 55
     Chablis Blanc, 116
     Chianti, 51
     Hearty Burgundy, 51, 114–15
     Paisano, 51
     Winery, 140
Gamay Beaujolais (California), 23,
     27
Gamay Noir (France), 201
Gamay Precoce (grape), 27
Gannaway, Derek, 208
Gardère, Jean-Paul, 189
Garrick Club (London), 162–63
Gevrey-Chambertin, 67
Gewurtztraminer (California), 117,
     142
Gewurtztraminer (Germany), 149
Givry, 198
Goldman, Sidney, 8
Gonet (Champagne), 126
Graham (port), 161, 210
Grand Cru Club, 122, 123
Grands crus
     Beaujolais, 203, 217
     Bordeaux, 70, 71
Grands Echézeaux, 38, 68, 105
Graves, red, 15, 16, 20, 40, 80–87,
     104, 180, 216
Graves, white, 101, 102, 122
Gravières, Les, 62, 63, 65
Green Hungarian, 149
Greenwald, Harry, 7, 8
Guards Club (London), 160, 161
Guild
     Tavola Red, 114
     Tavola White, 115
     Vino da Tavola, 51

Haeni, S., 66
Hanzell Vineyard, 22

Haraszthy, Colonel Agoston, 21, 24
Harmonie Club (New York), 155
Harveys, ix, 3, 161, 169, 178
Harveys of Bristol, 41
Healey, Maurice, 167
Hearthstone Manor, 102
Heitz, Joseph A., 22, 32, 151
Heitz Wine Cellars, 22, 32–34, 108,
     121, 144
Heriot, Raymond, 68
Heublein, Inc., 3, 22, 25
Hickey, Mr. and Mrs. William, 146
Hill, Jack, 169
Hodge Liquors (Buffalo), 103
Hospices de Beaune, 47, 61, 68
Hostellerie du Vieux Moulin (near
     Savigny), 7, 68
Hôtel les Maritonnes, 206

Ichinose, Ben, 42
Inglenook Vineyards, 31
     1966 North Coast Counties
        Vintage Burgundy, 53, 54
International Wine and Food So-
     ciety, 165
Italian Chamber of Commerce,
     tasting in Beaune, 66
Italian Swiss Colony
     Burgundy, 51, 114, 115
     Chablis, 55
     Claret, 51
     Napa Sonoma Mendocino Pre-
        mium Burgundy, 51
     Napa Sonoma Mendocino
        White, 55
     Premium Chablis, 116
     Zinfandel, 51

Jackson's of Piccadilly, 209, 210
Jaeger, Mr. and Mrs. William, 128
Jalle de Blanquefort, 81
Jocky Club (Paris), 162
Johannisberg Riesling (California),
     23, 128, 129, 142, 144, 145
Johannisberg Riesling (New York),
     155
Jug Wines (California), 48–56, 113–
     15
Juliènas, 203

Kew, Ken, 128

Kiedricher Nussbrunnen Riesling, 39
King, James T. and Martha, 104, 105
Knickerbocker Club (New York), 164
Korbel, 56
Krause, Ray, 141
Krug, Charles, 30, 133

Labrusca (*Vitis labrusca*), 55
Lafon, Comte, 169
Lameloise (restaurant), 199
Latour, Georges de, 22–23, 25
Latour, Louis, 23
Léognan, 81, 84
Libourne, 183
Lichine, Alexis, 22
Limousin oak casks, 48, 142, 145
Lindcrest Vineyard, 152
Linton, Dr. George, 24, 26, 28, 29
Live Oaks Premium California Burgundy, 53, 54
Lockets (restaurant), 169, 206
Lorenzo's (restaurant), 143
Louis, Victor (architect), 184
Louis Roederer Cristal, 36, 98
Luper, Mr. and Mrs. Jerry, 128

Mâcon, 198, 199, 202, 205
Madrigal (restaurant, New York), 156
Maison de Truffes, La, 205
Maladière, La, 62
Malbec (vine), 15
Malescot, Simon, 165
Mandelstam, Charles, 156
Maps, wines of France, 58, 158
Margaux (commune), 15, 18, 19, 40, 166, 171, 179
Martha's Vineyard, 34, 108, 129, 152, 153, 154
Martillac (commune), 84
Martin, Henri, 189
Martini, Louis M., 24, 31, 108, 126
  Chablis, 56
  Mountain Folle Blanche, 126
  Mountain Red Light Burgundy, 52
Masson, Paul
  Burgundy, 52, 114

  Chablis, 56, 116
  Emerald Dry, 117
  Pure California Burgundy, 54
  Rubion Baroque, 115
May, Tom and Martha, 154
Mayacamas Winery, 109, 134–37
McCall, Russell, 104, 105, 106
McCrea, Fred, 22
McNally, Alexander, 22
Médoc, 5, 8, 10, 11, 14, 17, 69–70, 74–80, 81, 82, 92, 93, 98, 99, 101, 122, 133, 165, 170, 174, 183, 184, 185, 188, 189, 195, 216, 217
Meighan, Howard and Marie-Elaine, 156
Meldon, T., 101
Memorial Art Center (Atlanta), 104
Mercurey, 198
Merlot (California), 111, 129, 130, 145, 152
Merlot (France), 16, 75, 82, 93, 173, 174, 175, 185
Meursault, 35
Meursault-Charmes, 98
Meursault Perrières (Comte Lafon), 169
Mirassou, Dan, 141
Mirassou, E. A., 139
Mirrassou, Pierre, 138
Mirrassou Vineyards, 111, 138–43
Moët & Chandon, 43
Mondavi, C. K.
  Chablis, 55
  Chianti, 51
  Claret, 51
  Zinfandel, 51
Monot, André, 63
Montagny, 198
Monterey County, 111, 142
Montrachet, 38, 43, 118–20 (tasting), 136, 137, 169, 214
Moreau, Jean, 63, 65
Morgon, 202
Moriconi, Alfio, 8, 13, 36, 97, 146
Moueix, Jean-François, 179
Moueix, Pierre (of Libourne), 70
Moulin à Vent, 202, 203, 204
Mountain Folle Blanche, 126
Mount Veeder Vineyards, 134
Mouton Cadet, 191

Muscadet, 213
Musigny Vielles Vignes, 146
Muzard, Lucien, 63

Napa Valley, 22, 48, 107–12, 118,
    134, 144, 151, 152
Nevers oak casks, 48, 145
Nouveau Cercle (restaurant, Paris),
    162
Nuits-Saint-Georges, 60

Occidental Vineyard, 109
Olympia oysters, 28, 151
Oxidation, 111–12, 139, 140, 141

Paillard, Robert, 63
Parducci (Mendocino), 108
Park, Mr. and Mrs. Garry, 125
Passetemps, Le, 62
Pauillac (commune), 15, 18, 40, 75,
    76, 83, 102, 103, 171, 179,
    180, 189
Pellier, Louis, 138
Penning-Rowsell, Edward, 178
Pepe, Albert, 101
Pepe, Pat, 101
Pernand-Vergelesses, 8
Perrières. *See* Meursault Perrières
Pessac, 83, 84
Peterson, Dr. Richard, 25, 136
Peterson, Walter and Frances, 49,
    128, 133
Petit Sirah, 142
Petri Burgundy, 51
Petrowsky, Karl, 122, 125
Phylloxera (insect), 41, 139
Pick of the Bunch, The, 134
Pinot Blanc (White Pinot), 121,
    135, 152
Pinot Chardonnay (California), 6,
    23, 24, 26 (tasting), 32–33,
    107, 108, 109, 112, 121, 128,
    129, 134, 135, 136, 137, 142,
    144, 153, 154
Pinot Chardonnay (France), 108,
    198
Pinot Noir (California), 23, 24, 26,
    29, 30, 107, 108, 109, 128,
    129
Pinot Noir (France), 198, 215

Place des Grands Hommes (Bor-
    deaux), 88
Pomerol, 10, 11, 14, 16, 17, 21, 69–
    73, 74, 75, 81, 92, 93, 101,
    111, 133, 160, 168, *passim*
    173–78, 180, 185, 186, 216
"Pontac" (claret), 82
Port, vintage, 160, 161, 210–12
Pouilly-Fuissé, 199, 200, 202
Pouilly-Fumé, 214
Pouilly-Loché, 200
Pouilly-Vinzelles, 200
Pratt's Club (London), 164
Premier Cru Club, 123
Premier Grand Cru, 70–72
Premiers crus, 62, 68
Provençal, Le (Washington, D.C.),
    7, 13, 98
Puligny-Montrachet, 118
Pupu Pupu Club (San Francisco),
    28

Quinta do Noval, 133

Rapet Père et Fils, 8, 97
Reed's Liquors (Buffalo), 103
Rhodes, Dr. and Mrs. Bernard L.,
    xi, 32, 34, 36, 39, 41, 42, 149,
    152
Richebourg, Les, 38
Richelieu, Cardinal, 183
Ridge Vineyards, 131–32
Ridge Winery, 109, 146
Roederer, Louis, 36, 98
Romanèche-Thorins, 204
Romanée-Conti. *See* Domaine de la
    Romanée-Conti
Romanée-Saint-Vivant, 38
Rosé (California generic), 56
Rosen, Mr. and Mrs. C., 132
Rully, 198
Rutherford (California), 21, 23

Sacramento, 39–40
Saint-Amour, 203
Saint-Émilion, 10, 11, 14, 15, 16, 17,
    19, 20, 40, 42, 69–73, 74, 75,
    81, 92, 101, 103, 111, 160,
    168, 170, *passim* 173–78, 180,
    185, 186, 216

Saint-Estèphe, 8, 15, 19, 75, 77, 79, 102, 103, 170
Saint-Exupéry, Comte Jean-Baptiste de, 165
St. James's Club (London), 163
Saint-Julien, 15, 16, 19, 40, 79, 92, 98, 103, 170, 171, 217
Saintsbury, George, and Saintsbury Club, 16
Salle de Dégustation, 201
Sancerre, 214
Sandeman (port), 127, 161, 162, 209, 211
San Francisco, 28, 37, 43, 122, 125, 131, 134, 146
San Francisco Wine Sampling Club, 49, 50
Santa Clara Valley, 138
Santenay
    damage to 1970 crop, 63
    growers, 63–65
    tasting, 62–65
Sauternes, 81
Savigny-les-Beaune, 66, 68
Schenk, firm of (Geneva), 66
Schramsberg, 56, 128
Scott, Sir Samuel, 41
Sebastiani, August, 154
Sebastiani, Samuele
    Mountain Red Light Burgundy, 52
    Mountain White Dry Chablis, 56
    Premium Quality Bin 210 California Burgundy, 53
See, Harry and Theo, 151
Seibel, Mr. and Mrs. Larry, 35, 37
Sémillon (vine), 149
Senard, M., 66–67
Sercial (1870), 43
Sessions, Robert, 135
Sherry-Lehmann, 155
Sichel, Peter, 169
Simon, André, 43, 167
Sionneau, Lucien, 189
Smith, James F., 43
Smoller, Dr. and Mrs. Marion, 118
Soledad (Monterey County), 111, 138, 141
Somerset Club (Boston), 164
Sonoma Valley, 134

Souverain Cellars, 22, 149
    Cabernet Sauvignon, 149
    Flora, 149
    Green Hungarian, 149
    Napa Valley Burgundy, 54
    Pineau, 121
Spring Valley, 151
Stay Me with Flagons, by Maurice Healey, 167
Stewart, Lee, 22, 121, 149
Stirman, Marvin, 7, 8, 33
Stony Hill Vineyard, 22, 152
Sullivan, Mrs. Dagmar, 25
Sutter Club, 39

Tâche, La, 38, 39
Taillevent (restaurant, Paris), 169
Taittinger, 155
Talence, 83, 84
Talleyrand, 82
tastings, *passim; for some blind tastings see* 29, 63, 75, 84–87, 91, 123, 126, 136–37, 169, 179–80, 188, 189
Taylor, Jack and Mary, 134
Taylor Port, 36, 160, 161, 209, 210
Taylor-Restell, Alan, 169
Tchelistcheff, André, 6, 21, 22, 23, 25, 26, 27
Terry, Michael and Liz, 106
Tesseron, Guy, 19
Thruway Liquors (Buffalo), 103
Togni, Phil, 144
Toussaints (Beaune), 47
Trailing Tendrils of the Vine, by Ian Campbell, 167
Traminer, 149
Travers, Robert and Elinor, 134, 135
Tupper, J., 122
21 Club (restaurant, New York), 156

Uvas (Bonesio Winery) California Burgundy, 53, 54

Vaux-en-Beaujolais, 200
Vialard, Louis, 169, 197, 198
Vieux Château-Certan, 71, 98, 177
Villamont, Henri de, 66, 105
Villefranche, 205

Villenave d'Ornan, 81
Vin-de-l'année, 203
Vin ordinaire, 4, 113
"Vineyard Crushing" (mechanical
    grape harvesting), 139–41
Vintages, Beaujolais
    1966, 203 04
    1967, 203–04
    1969, 203–04, 214
    1970, 203–04, 214
Vintages, Bordeaux red
    1920, 160
    1924, 160
    1926, 160
    1928, 160
    1929, 43, 160, 161
    1934, 160
    1945, 167, 170–72
    1953, 161
    1957, 11
    1959, 10
    1960, 14, 18, 174
    1961, 10, 15, 69–71, 167, 174,
        217
    1962, 15, 174, 217
    1963, 18, 174
    1964, 15, 174, 184, 216
    1965, 18, 174
    1966, 5, 18, 40, 174, 216
    1967, 18, 84, 174, 179–81, 216
    1968, 18, 174, 175
    1969, 18, 174
    1970, 173–78, 185
Vintages, Burgundy red
    1923, 160
    1926, 160
    1929, 160
    1959, 47
    1961, 59
    1962, 59
    1964, 59, 63
    1966, 59, 63, 67–68, 215
    1969, 59–60, 63, 67, 215
    1970, 61
Vintages, Burgundy white, 108
    1966, 35, 68, 214
    1967, 59, 214
    1968, 214
    1969, 59, 214
    1970, 214

Vintages, Moselle and Rhine
    1953, 214
    1959, 214
    1964, 214
    1970, 214
Vogüé, Comte Georges de, 146
Volnay Blondeau (Hospices de
    Beaune), 47
Volnay Général Mateau (Hospices
    de Beaune), 68
Vosne-Romanée (commune), 21, 67
Vosne-Romanée Beaux Monts, 133

Wackenheimer Gerumpel Trocken-
    beerenauslese 1947, 36
Washington, D.C., 7, 98
Washington Students' Club (D.C.),
    98
Webb, Mr. and Mrs. Bradford, 128
Weibel California Burgundy, 53
White's (London club), 159, 163
Wile, Julius, 13
Wine
    collecting and buying, xii
    Merchants, xii-xiii, 5
    When drinkable, xiv, 214–17
Wine Advisory Board (California),
    140
Wine and Food Society, 4
    Berkeley, 118
    International, 165
    New York, 155–56
Wine Magazine, ix, x
Woltner, Henri, 83, 152
Wood, Anthony, 146
Wood, Mr. and Mrs. Laurie, 128,
    129
Woodruff, Charles, 45
Wyndham (London club), 159, 160

Yountville (California), 151

Zellerbach, James D., 22
Zinfandel, 24, 108, 109, 131, 132,
    134, 136, 142, 154
Zinfandel Associates, 32–33, 121,
    129, 152, 153
Zinfandel Essence, 132
Zuger, Mr. and Mrs. Paul, 165
Zuger, Roger, 165